AF560845

MARGARET ATWOOD

A Jewel in Canadian Writing

MARGARET ATWOOD

A Jewel in Canadian Writing

Neeru Tandon
Anshul Chandra

Published by
ATLANTIC
PUBLISHERS & DISTRIBUTORS (P) LTD
7/22, Ansari Road, Darya Ganj, New Delhi-110002
Phones : +91-11-40775252, 40775214, 23273880, 23275880
Fax: +91-11-23285873
Web: www.atlanticbooks.com
E-mail: orders@atlanticbooks.com

Printed & bound in India by Atlantic Print Services

Preface

Canadian writing was stimulated by a renaissance of interest in literature and culture, with special focus on women's writing. Margaret Atwood is one of those few modern Canadian novelists in English, who have tried to understand intimately the predicament of their female protagonists.

She pleads for a balanced, harmonious man-woman relationship in which two sexes are viewed as complementary and not as a battle of sexes or a winning or losing game.

Canadian fiction has witnessed a transition from exposition, inventory and catalogue to more varied analytical and interpretative directions. Margaret Atwood's writings belong to the postmodern literary genre of feminist protest. Her novels reveal an intense awareness of the relation between bonding and bondage, i.e. between a woman's need for connection with others and her equally strong need for freedom and independence.

Margaret Atwood is concerned with the treatment of woman as normal human being and feels that she must be allowed her imperfections. She criticizes the social system that assigns roles to the sexes and then categorically labels them as inferior or superior, sinful or chaste. She is intensely preoccupied with women fighting against the female norms of life—sexuality, dichotomy between career and the claims of the family. Most of Atwood's novels grapple with the politics of gender and deal with women's experience in a male-dominated society. She exposes the silent and hidden operations of gender and confronts its politics, thereby recommending the rewriting of women's history. She demands demolition of gender system and hopes for a new world in which men and women are equal at every level of existence.

The Edible Woman in many respects was created during a time of whirlwind change, and Margaret Atwood takes up for exploration in this novel, the theme of women's place in society, particularly in a male-dominated society. She successfully links together ideas of marriage and consumerism as related to the ideas and the perceptions of the self. This novel proves that financial independence is no independence at all. The awareness of being subjugated and victimized has to come from within the self of an individual. The novel describes the reasons for the suppression of women within and without marriage. The title of the novel *The Edible Woman* suggests that the central metaphor is that of woman as food, as object and theme is women's effort to attain humanity, and human identity. The message of the novel is that women are not mere objects of beauty meant for carnal consumption of men.

Surfacing deals with the theme of confronting the submerged layers of the self. This novel evaluates Atwood's receptions of the feminine being. It is the most powerful text expressing the politics of gender and describes man's imposition on woman in matters of profession, marriage and motherhood, which cripples her intellectually, emotionally and morally. *Surfacing* shows how gender politics has relegated women artists to a lower order and how their history is subsumed into the dominant patriarchal discourse. *Surfacing* represents the feminine consciousness and shows a woman's struggle to free herself. Her association with the people and Nature raises her consciousness of victimization of woman. When her feminist consciousness reaches its climax, the protagonist makes ready the ground for revolt against exploitation and oppression. She makes us feel that we have not landed into an era of post-feminism and there still is a need to change the society's attitude towards women. The protagonist becomes a 'metaphor' for all those who are exploited and abused because of their powerlessness. At the end of the novel she emerges triumphant; she has come to realize that it is the binary vision which creates problems and leads to disintegration. Rejecting the dualistic vision, she seems to have discovered, "a new way of being, a third way that transcends polarizations, thus enabling the individual to be free of crippling limitations. She emerges as a brave new woman who is capable of establishing her identity".

Lady Oracle is the portrait of the writer as a woman and a "survivor" in a patriarchal culture. It shows how gender conflict is viewed and presented in society that is petty and ignorant.

It attacks male ego mercilessly without any compromise. It represents a challenge to patriarchal culture. Through *Lady Oracle* Margaret Atwood proclaims that both men and women are equal as they have the same human capabilities and therefore gender-based injustices should be fought against in the society. It also urges men to share the nurturing role. In brief, it is a feminist writer's frontal attack on the dominant pattern of gender relations in contemporary society.

Bodily Harm shows that the condition of women is bleak and they are still where they were a century ago. In this novel, gender politics is contextualized with the frightening world of political intrigues and the novel depicts the process of self-discovery and re-humanization against the backdrop of cruelty. Sexual politics is often disguised, as 'love' is one more form of power politics. It focuses on gender/sexual power politics. It is concerned with all sorts of bodily harm, perpetrated on women as body image, female sexuality, male-female relationship and male brutality in patriarchal society. This novel shows that in society bodily harm is everywhere. There is no limitation of it but a woman should reject her submissive role and be ready to speak out the truth about the exploiter. Rennie's story emerges as a warning against disabling female fantasies of innocence and victimization, which displaces women's recognition of the dangers of real life.

The Handmaid's Tale shows Margaret Atwood in her most radical light as she has revised the categories of 'Canadian' and 'female' through which her own identity is constituted. The novel examines the patriarchal structures of domination and power and the woman's quest for a meaningful identity. It offers a different perspective on the relationship between men and women. Sexuality and power argue how power dominates on sex. The novel also carries patriarchal power to its logical and nightmarish extreme and shows how women live in such a situation and create female space for themselves through various strategies. As a woman's story of resistance, it is far more concerned with gender politics than with nationality. While giving a shocking treatment of the theme of sex, procreation and love, this novel takes on the character of grim, prophetic vision of a future world where male chauvinism would have, once and for all, destroyed the finest chords of wifehood, motherhood and womanhood.

The novel can be interpreted as a metaphor of the condition of women, which has changed minimally over the centuries. Since reading and writing is forbidden in Gilead, Offred challenges these traditional values and refuses to be a silent victim. She develops her feminist consciousness towards the slavery syndrome and triumphs as the author of her own story.

Cat's Eye deals with the interaction between adulthood and childhood, as well as the relationship between art, artists and interpretation. It offers an alternative art history which foregrounds women's achievement as artists. It also shows how art promotes feminism and freedom for women. The importance of the past and past memories and the need to deal with this in order to cope with present reality seems to be the viewpoint presented in this novel.

The title of the novel symbolizes the vision, which can see the victimization of women and turns them over and over in the light of truth through the protagonist's paintings. Her paintings advocate human rights of women and equal healthy relationships between men and women.

A cursory survey of Margaret Atwood's fiction shows that she is new in the dimension of time by being a rebel against the general current of the patriarchal society and in exploring her true potential, all with the struggle to fulfil her urges and needs. Survival is key word for Margaret Atwood and she wants her protagonist to refuse to be a victim and demand equal space as man. Her novels do not intensify the war between male and female but desire for a real, healthy and balanced human relationship. Her feminist vision is neither male-centered nor female-centered but it offers a fresh perspective on women's problems.

The book will be extremely useful to the students and teachers of English literature, and research scholars in this field. Those who are concerned with women's writing shall find it highly informative.

Neeru Tandon
Anshul Chandra

Contents

Introduction

1

> Canada is an unknown territory for the people who live in it, and I'm not talking about the fact that you may not have taken a trip to the Arctic or to Newfoundland, you may not have explored as the travel folders have it—This Great Land of Ours. I'm talking about Canada as a state of mind, as the space you inhabit not just with your body but with your head. It's that kind of space in which we find ourselves lost.
>
> What a lost person needs is a map of the territory, with his own position marked on it so he can see where he is in relation to everything else. Literature is not only a mirror; it is also a map, a geography of the mind. Our literature is one such map, if we can learn to read it as *our* literature, as the product of who and where we have been. We need such a map desperately; we need to know about here, because here is where we live. For the members of a country or culture, shared knowledge of their place, their here, is not a luxury but a necessity. Without that knowledge we will not survive.[1]
>
> Margaret Atwood, *Survival*

As Atwood's statement demonstrates, Canadian literature is concerned with place and displacement, and with the development of an effective identifying relationship between self and environs. Canada is a unique, diverse country and it has two 'home cultures'; French and British. Like other colonial literatures, Canadian literature has encountered a number of obstacles in its growth. Northrop Frye observes that Canadians have an identity crisis with a difference for they are less perplexed by the existential question "Who am I?" than by some such riddle as "Where is here?"[2]

It has had to overcome the oppressive psyche of being dominated by the American and British literary traditions.

Canadian literature has a much longer history than is generally assumed, which includes a long phase of 'invisibility'. It took decades of struggle and persistent efforts to come into 'visibility' in stages. It was first recognized politically as an "area to enquire into the value system of the land or to study the distinctive features of cultural nationalism".

Canada's literature whether written in English or French reflects three main parts of Canadian experience. First, Canadian writers often emphasize the effects of climate and geography on the life and work of their people. Second, frontier's life is part of Canada's experience that appears frequently in its literature. Third, Canada's position in the world profoundly affects many Canadian writers. French Canadians often feel surrounded by their English speaking neighbours. They have made a determined effort to preserve their own institutions and culture. But English Canadians frequently have a similar feeling of being surrounded by the people and culture of the United States. Many novels and poems show how Canadian writers feel about such problems.

In the seventies and the eighties, Canadian writing was stimulated by a renaissance of interest in literature and culture. The quest for definition of a Canadian identity became a national obsession, particularly after the Second World War.

The spirit of cultural nationalism, assisted by federal support and aid, has greatly facilitated Canadian writing and its canonization. A noticeable change can be observed in the Canadian writings during the 1920s and 30s. There is a clear break from the influence of importation. Writers consciously moulded a native tradition in their writing. It was Frederick Philip Grove's *Settlers of the Marsh* (1925) which marked a decisive breaking away from the traditional pull of England and France and the technological challenges of the United States. He wrote about human nature and psyche for the first time. Along with Grove, Gabrielle Roy's and Morley Callaghan's writings also represent the emergence of serious Canadian fiction in the 1920s and 30s.

Gabrielle Roy was born in St. Boniface, Manitoba in 1909. Her father worked at a federal settlement officer but when he lost his job, Roy's mother supported the family by sewing. Roy was educated at Saint Joseph's academy. After training as a teacher at the Winnipeg Normal School, she taught in rural schools in Marchand and Cardinal before accepting a job at the Provencher School in Saint Boniface. In 1937, she moved to Europe to study theatre but was forced to return to Canada in 1939 at the outbreak of World War II and settled in Montreal. She passed away in 1983 from heart failure.

Her first and perhaps best known novel *Bonheur d'occasion* (1945), gave a starkly realistic portrait of the lives of people in Saint Henri; a working class neighbourhood of Montreal and the effects of the war on the society. It was translated in English in 1947 by Hannah Josephson as *The Tin Flute*. It marks a significant shift in French-Canadian literature. Her second novel *La petite poule d'eau* (1950) (English title: Where Nests the Water Hen) features a family living on an isolated farm. Another novel by her brought additional critical acclaim. *Alexandre Chenevert* (1954) (English title: The Cashier) returns to the city and deals with post World War II Montreal. It is a dark and emotional story that is ranked as one of the most significant works of psychological realism in the history of Canadian literature.

Rue Deschambault (1955) (English title: Street of Riches) reflects Roy's life growing up in St. Boniface. The book won a Governor General's Award in 1957. In *La Montagne secrete* (1961) (English title: The Hidden Mountain) she writes about the need for solitude for artistic invention. *La Route d'Altamont* (1966) (English title: The Road Past Altamont) explores the complicated relationship between mother and daughter. *La Riviere sans repos* (1970) (English title: Windflower) is a story of a young Inuit woman. Her other works are *Cet etc qui chantait* (1972) (English title: Enchanted Summer), *Un jardin au bout du monde* (1975) (English title: Garden in the Wind), *Ma Vache Bossie* (1976) (English title: My Cow Bossie), *Ces Enfants de ma vie* (1977) (English title: Children of my Heart), *Fragiles Lumieres de la terre* (1978) (English title: The Fragile Lights of Earth), *Courte-Queue* (1979) (English title: Cliptail).

Her autobiography *La Detresse at l'enchantement* (1984) (English title: Enchantment and Sorrow) was published posthumously in 1984. She is considered as one of the most important Francophone writers in Canadian history and one of the most influential Canadian authors.

Morley Callaghan was heavily influenced by American naturalist literature. Callaghan was born in Toronto in 1903 to Roman Catholic parents. He was educated at the University of Toronto. Although he completed a law degree in 1928, his first love was writing. He worked part time with the *Toronto Star Weekly,* where he met Earnest Hemmingway, who became an early mentor. Callaghan began writing stories that were well received and soon was recognized as one of the best short story writers of the day. He then went to France, where he socialized with Earnest Hemmingway, F. Scott Fitzgerald, Jame Joyce and others.

Callaghan's works are marked by undertones of Roman Catholicism, complex characterization and ambiguous treatment of love. His first novel was *Strange Fugitive* published in 1928. His first short stories collection *A Native Argosy* was published in 1929. He was established as an important figure in North American literary circles. His other novels are *It's Never Over* (1930) and *A Broken Journey* (1932). *Such is My Beloved* (1934) is his most commercially popular book; followed by *They Shall Inherit the Earth* (1935), *Now That April's Here and Other Stories* (1936) and *More Joy in Heaven* (1937).

Callaghan published little between 1937 and 1950—an artistically dry period. However, he involved himself in many aspects of writing including nonfiction and autobiography *That Summer in Paris* (1963). His later works include, among others, *The Many Colored Coat* (1960), *A Passion in Rome* (1961), *A Fine and Private Place* (1985), *A Time For Judas* (1983), *Our Lady of the Snows* (1985). His last novel was *A Wild Old Man Down The Road* (1988). He was awarded Governor General's Award in 1951, the Lorn Pierce Medal in 1960 and the Order of Canada in 1982. Callaghan died after a brief illness in Toronto in 1990.

Hugh MacLennan is another writer who became aware of the real problems facing Canadian and was a firm supporter of

Canadianness in terms of space and thematic concerns. He has been regarded as a representative novelist of the contemporary world.

MacLennan was born in 1907 in Glace Bay, Nova Scotia. He was educated at Dolhousie University. He taught English at McGill University and retired as a professor. He died in 1990. His first novel *Barometer Rising* (1941) gave him national and international recognition as an author and he followed up on the success with *Two Solitudes* (1945), which won the Governor General's Award. The Novel examines the problem of a divided culture that existed in Canada at the time. His novel *The Precipice* (1947) and two non-fiction with the collections of essays *Cross Country* (1949) and *Thirty and Three* (1954) also won GG award. After the death of his wife Dorothy, he published his novel. *The Watch that Ends the Night* (1959) which is consider as his best novel and won his record fifth GG award. His third collection of essays *Scotchman's Return and other Essays* was published in 1960. His last two novels are *Return of the Sphinx* (1967) and *Voices in Time* (1980) in which he has a more negative view of Canadian politics and society.

Hugh MacLennan was a clearly nationalist and articulate Canadian tradition in fictional terms. MacLennan and Callaghan may rightly be considered as the founding fathers of serious Canadian fiction.

Sinclair Ross's *As For Me and My House* (1941) is another landmark in Canadian fiction. Set in the economic Depression of the 1930, it is set in diary form, this work is the portrait of Horizon, a fictional town known for its false architectural facades. The Canadian novel, however, begins to 'take off' in the 1950s with Robertson Davies, Mordecan Richler, Mavis Gallant and Sheila Watson. By the 1960s Canadian fiction came into its own. It not only broke free from the shackles of influence of other literature but it also confidently overcame its preoccupation with cultural and national identity. It was marked by a spirit of self-confidence. The sixties were years of challenges and authors like Robert Kroetsch and Rudy Wiebe broke new ground by adopting a postmodernist stance and expression. It was also the time of an upsurge in Canadian nationalist politics and of the rise of the women's movement. A number of accomplished women writers have emerged since the 1950s and they were dealing with issues ranging from national identity to gender politics. They have pointed to shared themes of powerlessness, victimization and alienation as well as to a certain ambivalence or ambiguity.

In the late sixties and early seventies, the majority of Canadian women worked full time as housewives. Barbara Pressman in her writing deals with how to recognize, improve and treat family violence in good therapeutic context. She made an assessment that, "about ten percent of all Canadian wives were being battered by their husbands",[3] with the result today there is a high proportion of divorces in relation to marriages. They were exploited by men and their contribution to public life has been dismissed as unimportant. It is against these social factors that the 'New woman' rebelled. In Canada she is struggling to break away from the stranglehold tradition. Now she reexamines the depth of marriage and man-woman relationship for a better understanding and sharing of mutual love and respect. Discussing the role of the writer in society Margaret Atwood remarks that the writer, "tends to concentrate more on life, not as it ought to be, but as it is, as the writer feels it, experiences it. Writers are eye witnesses, I—witnesses."[4]

The Canadian novel takes an altogether new turn in the 1960s with the appearance of women novelists who tend to write more as women than as patriots. Though separated by time and gender, the woman and the Canadian find, they have much in common. Women and Canadian writers seem to share a necessary, self-defining challenge to the dominant traditions. Feminist writing may thus appear more conservative but in fact it is just different. Women must define their subjectivity before they can question it; they must first assert the selfhood they have been denied by the dominant culture.

Many of Canadian women writers are, "engaged in a struggle with language and inherited conventions to find more adequate ways of telling about women's experiences, fighting their way out of silence to project more authentic images of how women feel and what they do"[5] through their protagonists. A close study of their novels reveal that their focus is so much on, "the inner world of feeling and sensibility that even the impact of feminist movements has generated more of poetic or lyrical articulation of the inner tensions of women than social documentaries voicing the cause of women."[6]

Margaret Atwood, Alice Munro, Margaret Laurence, Margaret Gibson, Susan Musgrave, Marian Engel, Mavis Gallant and Boverley Simons are some of the outstanding one. While Alice Munro, Margaret Laurence and Margaret Atwood represent the well established veterans, the other are comparatively less known and represent the new voices. Alice Munro, Marian Engel, Mavis Gallant, Margaret Laurence and Margaret Gibson are represented by fiction, Susan Musgrave by poetry, Margaret Atwood by poetry and fiction and Beverley Semons by drama.

The women's movement has provided many of these novelists with the courage and motivation to break out of traditional patriarchal forms to depict how women have been abused, exploited and oppressed. Their novels move towards the discovery of the self and women's encounter with the world. They are concerned with exploration and survival and tend to project the image of a woman who is confident, intelligent and assertive. In their works, Canadian feminists attempt to focus on the 'new woman'—self-aware, independent, seeking to evolve an identity of her own. Thus, the aim of women writing in Canada is to bring about remarkable changes in the lives of Canadian women and society. They want gender equality in Canadian society. They are, "improving women's life-chances and have the sense that women can contribute to the building of a major peaceful caring world."[7]

Mavis Gallant was born in Montreal, Quebec in 1922. Her father died when she was young and her mother remarried. Gallant was educated at 17 different schools. In her twenties she worked as a reporter for the *Montreal Standard* (1944-50). She moved to Europe in 1950 and ultimately settled in Paris, where she has continued to live. Gallant has been forthright about the protectiveness she feels towards her independence and privacy. She is acclaimed for her mastery of the short story. Many of Gallant's stories have debuted in *The New Yorker* magazine, which has continued to be an important vehicle for her short fiction.

The main objective of her writing is development of specific situation and reconstruction of the state of mind or of heart. Gallant's stories focus on expatriate men and women who have come to feel lost or isolated. Janice Kulyk Keefer says, "Gallant is a writer who dazzles us with her command of the language, her innovative use of narrative forms, the acuity of her intelligence, and the incisiveness of her wit. Yet she also disconcerts us with her insistence on the constrictions and limitations that dominate human experience."[8]

Among her story collections are *The Other Paris* (1956), *My Heart is Broken* (1964), *The End of the World and Other Stories* (1964), *In Transit* (1988) and *Across the Bridge* (1993). She has also written two novels *Green Water, Green Sky* (1969) and A *Fairly Good Time* (1970); a play *What is to be Done?* (1984) and a non-fiction work *Paris Journals: Selected Essays and Reviews* (1986).

In 1981, she was honoured by her native country and made an officer of the Order of Canada for her contribution to literature. She also received the Governor General's award for literature for her collection of stories *Home Truths*.

In 1989 Mavis Gallant was made a Foreign Honorary Member of the American Academy of Arts and Letters. In 2000 she won the Matt Cohen Prize and in 2002 she received the Rea award for the short story.

Margaret Laurence has been the most prominent contemporary Canadian women novelist in English. She was born in the small town of Neepawa, Manitoba on July 18, 1926 to a middle class family of Lowland Scots and Iris Descent. Despite the fact that Laurence was raised by a loving aunt, who become her stepmother, her fiction is concerned with themes of disinheritance, dispossession, roots and orphanage testifies to the long-lasting effect her parents' deaths had on her.

She worked as a reporter for the *Winnipeg Citizen*, a labour newspaper after her graduation. In 1950, she moved to British Somali Land with her husband. There she wrote a translation of a Somali book of prose and poetry, *A Tree for Poverty* (1954). A travel book *The Prophet's Camel Bell* (1963) written some years later; describes the Laurence's experience in Somali Land. Then they moved to Accra, Ghana where she began writing fiction seriously. She produced her first novel *This Side Jordon* (1960), which won the Canadian Beta Sigma Phi Award. A collection of short stories, *The Tomorrow Tamer* (1963) was written which is set in West Africa. She returned to Canada but her experiences in Africa left an indelible mark on her writing. Africa was the catalyst for Laurence's creativity. In Canada she approached her work with maturity and with a subtle ambivalence somewhat lacking in her earliest fiction. *The Stone Angle* (1964), her first novel set in Canada, represents a significant contribution to Canadian literature and established Laurence as a major Canadian novelist. In many ways the most technically sophisticated of her works, this novel introduces Manawaka, the imaginative Prairie landscape, which dominates her four works of Canadian fiction. The woman protagonists in Manawaka fiction are humanized and individuated women. It depicts their journey towards survival and inner freedom in the violent world. As Nancy Bailey says in her Manawaka novels Laurence gives us, "unforgettable portraits of women wrestling with their personal demons, striving through self-examination to find meaningful patterns in their lives."[9] Laurence signals a new stage of independence for Canada and for women when she confidently uses different women's perspectives to portray their individual experiences.

The Stone Angle presents the grievances of old women. Ninety-year-old Hager Shipley is the metaphorical stone angle of the novel, whose experiences in the present trigger memories of her past, drawing to a revelation of self-knowledge. *The Stone Angle* delineates the psychic turmoil, fear and anxiety of the protagonist who fails to relate herself to her husband and children.

In *A Jest of God* (1966), the second novel, Margaret Laurence is concerned with showing how a negative self-concept or low self-esteem is not congenial to the maintenance of harmonious human relationships.

Her third Manawaka novel, *The Fire Dwellers* deals with the problems encountered by women in provincial Canada. The protagonist Staceys is undergoing an emotional crisis and finds herself alone, frightened, dependent, deceived and deceiving. The world around her has become a virtual hell where she finds it difficult to survive.

The Diviners (1974) is the story of the novelist Morag Gunn. She has to wage a fierce battle with herself and her husband Brooke, who imposes "a one dimensional persona" on her.

Thus it can be argued that for protagonists in Laurence's fiction, a system of harmonious relationships is a primary condition of human life at every level. They typify the common people particularly Canadian in the contemporary world.

Margaret Laurence does not deny that she is writing about the situations of women; still she advocates a more balanced view of man-woman relationship. She herself admits that she cares a lot about her male characters. In her fiction, therefore, "the quest narrative does not issue from the paradigm of the male/female binary opposition; it issues, instead from the tension generated by her women characters' inability to perceive and accept the true value of their inheritance."[10] She says:

> I'm 90% in agreement with women's Lib. But I think we have to be careful here. For instance I don't think enough attention has been paid to the problems men have and are going to have increasingly because of the changes taking place in women. Men have to be reeducated with minimum damage to them. They are our husbands, our sons, our lovers.... We can't live without them and we can't go to war against them. The change must liberate them as well.[11]

Thus, she believes in "individual freedom" to both men and women.

A fellow writer, Alice Munro is a short-story writer. Her stories create interesting situations and then deliver surprises and make artistic leaps that feel exactly right. In her writing, a recurring theme is the woman's search for self-understanding and personal fulfilment.

Alice Munro was born into a family of farmers on 10 July 1931. She began writing in her teens. Her first collection of stories, *Dance of the Happy Shades* (1960) won Governor General's Award. In this collection, she questions and challenges the dependency of women. This success was followed by *Lives of Girls and Women* (1971), a collection of interlinked stories that was published as a novel. In *Something I've Been Meaning to Tell You* (1974), Munro depicts man-woman relationship from the woman's point of view. It explores the psyche of a woman who has been married twice; it gives a review of her two husbands, Hugo and Gabriel. Her collection *Who Do You Think You Are* (1978) focuses on the woman's experience and the female tradition. The central character Rose, struggles with her lack of self-esteem and the inability to regard herself as a sentient, autonomous person rather than an adjunct of a male. Her other short-story collections are *The Moons of Jupiter* (1982), *The Progress of Love* (1986), *Friend of My Youth* (1990), *Open Secrets* (1994) and *Selected Stories* (1996). In her writing Munro is concerned with human experience and the record of cultural dimensions of female sexuality. The chief characteristics of Munro's art are simplicity and realism though she is perhaps too partials to human beings to satisfy the most stringent taste. The detailed portraits of female constraint distinguished her writing from contemporary writers. She has presented 'the battle of the sexes' in vivid, complex images of women and men as powerful and powerless through her stories. She describes the female side of the human condition, a synthesis of insight gained from their own femininity. She believes that there is a change coming in the lives of girls and women. Thus like Margaret Atwood, she begins with, "the traditional female concerns with personal relationships and the details of daily life and expands these concerns to include a wider and wider swath of human experience".[12]

Marian Engel was born in 1934. Before her death in 1985, she had published seven novels, two collections of short stories and numerous essays and articles. Engel emerged as a writer during that period in Canada when nationalism increased and 'New feminism' dawned. Although she is recognized as a distinguished woman of letters, she has not been widely studied. Engel's writing has not received the critical attention it deserves. A comprehensive study of Engel's body of work, *Lifelines* fills a major gap in Canadian literary criticism.

In *Lifeline: Marian Engel's Writings* Christ Verduyn analyses Engel's work, written from 1940s to her death, from a feminist literary perspective. She is concerned with women's experiences and perception of the world, female identity and the social constraints on its development, female subjectivity and self, the mother-daughter relationship and forces opposing women's artistic self-expression. Verduyn demonstrates the extent to which Engel's work not only deserves to be ranked with the best of Canadian literature but also enriches our understanding of women's experiences and broadens our view of women's worlds. Some of Marian Engel's works are *Bear* (1976), *Monodromos* (1973), *One Way Street* (1974), *The Year of the Child* (1981), *The Honeyman Festival* (1986) and *Sarah Bastard's Notebook*.

Margaret Atwood is the first major novelist of Canada who attempts to focus on the new-woman as self-aware, independent, seeking to evolve an identity of her own. Margaret Atwood in her writing systematically thematizes the personal quest for fulfilment as inextricably involved in a communal quest for cultural identity.

Margaret Eleanor Atwood was born in Ottawa, Canada on November 18, 1939. Her father was a forest etymologist and she spent part of her early years in the bush of northern Quebec, where he undertook research. The childhood experiences gave material, later to Margaret Atwood's metaphorical use of the wilderness and its animals as in *Wilderness Tips* (1991).

She graduated from Leaside High School in 1959 and studied at the University of Toronto. She won a Woodrow Wilson fellowship, and became a graduate student at Radcliffe College, Cambridge Massachusetts, receiving her M.A. in 1962. She has held a variety of academic posts and has been writer-in-residence of numerous Canadian and American Universities.

As a writer Margaret Atwood made her debut with *Double Persephone* (1961), a collection of poem, at the age of nineteen.

Another early collection, *The Circle Game* (1964, rev. in 1960) received the Canadian Governor General's Award for poetry in 1966.

In this poetry collection, she examined the ways by which people 'invent convenient versions' of them, using stereotypes and conventions of the language and "belief" to exclude from their consideration whatever is uncertain, unknown or threatening.

Later poems consider this impulse as an aspect of colonialism—the coloniser's refusal to recognize the virtues in a society different from their own. In *Journals of Susanna Moodie* (1970) she evokes Canadian history. In *Power Politics* (1973) and *You Are Happy* (1974) she considers women's lives as submissive territories colonized by men. *Two Headed Poems* (1978) explores the duplicity of language. In *True Stories* (1981) she portrays women as victims.

Murder in the Dark (1983) is an experimental, postmodern prose poems and short fictions, which excited critical attention in new circles. Margaret Atwood continued to alternate prose with poetry with *Interlunar* (1984) followed by *Selected Poems II* (1986).

In 1995 Margaret Atwood published *Morning in the Burned House*, her first collection of new poems in a decade, which included a sequence of elegiac poems, demonstrating a new emotional range in her work.

Her short stories collection *Dancing Girls* (1977), attracted more positive notice, winning the City of Toronto Book Award, the Canadian Booksellers Association Award and the Periodical Distributors of Canada Short Fiction Award. Her another collection *Bluebeard's Egg* (1983) explores the question of women's marginal position within hegemonic discourse. *Wilderness Tips* (1991) is the collection of stories with Gothic overtones about women facing middle age mixed with narratives about confrontations with the wilderness; followed by *Good Bones* (1992) which is about female body parts and social constraints written with devastating wit.

While working as an editor at the Toronto Publishing House, Anansi in the early 1970, Margaret Atwood published her controversial study *Survival; A Thematic Guide to Canadian Literature* (1972) in which she stated that the key pattern in Canadian writing is that of victimization. It is considered as the most startling book ever written about Canadian literature. It is often described as her "literary history", "the victim survival thesis" and "Layman's guide". Her second work of criticism is *Second Words* (1984) in which she describes Canadian poetry and contemporary women's writing to feminism and international human rights. Her another literary criticism are *Strange Things: The Malevolent North in Canadian Literature* (1995) and *Negotiating with the Dead: A Writer on Writing* (2002).

She has also written Children's books. *Up in the Tree* (1978) introduced Atwood the artist, which is followed by *For the Birds* (1990) and *Princess Prunella and the Purple and Peanut* (1995) exhibiting her delight in word play.

Her literary career as a novelist begins with her maiden novel, *The Edible Woman* (1969). It is a novel in which themes of women's alienation echo those in her poetry. It is an early feminist treatise, a both funny and terrifying story about a young woman, who works for a consumer company.

Surfacing (1972) is Atwood's most remarkable novelistic achievement in which the technology nature conflict is cast in political terms. It serves to illuminate Atwood's strong nationalist as well as feminist ideologies. As in her other novel, the protagonist goes through an archetypal retreat to the irrational the wilderness where she undergoes transformation through contact with native and Quebec cultures before reintegrating into society.

Her third novel *Lady Oracle* (1976) is a gothic romance. Margaret Atwood as a feminist uses parody to deconstruct male discursive form of writing. It won the 1977 City of Toronto Book Award and a Canadian Booksellers Award. *Life Before Man* (1979) is her most domestic novel with its triangular plot. This novel has brought international recognition for Atwood. *Bodily Harm* (1981) focuses on the contrast between affluent thinking and the brutal reality of power and sexual politics.

The Handmaid's Tale (1985) received the Governor General's Award, the Los Angeles Times Prize, and short-listed for the Booker Prize. It is a dystopian novel, a tale of a bleak future portraying a time where women are prized only for their reproductive gift. Although the novel is shocking, there are moments of lyrical comfort and wit. *Cat's Eye* (1988) focuses on the issues of women through art, for the first time in history. It exposes male prejudices against women's creativity and talent and shows how art can be used as a weapon against tyranny in all its manifestations.

The Robber Bride (1993) is a feminist thought provoking novel. It examined Toronto lifestyle and women's friendships. *Alias Grace* (1996) used a genuine 19th century criminal case to weave a fictional exploration of the class, psychological and gender politics surrounding a female alleged murderer. It is also Atwood's most sophisticated articulation of her longstanding philosophical and political concerns with power, culture and identity. The book was nominated for the Booker Prize and short-listed for the Governor General's Award.

The Blind Assassin (2000) earned Atwood the Booker Prize. It is a meta-fictional fairy tale. Her latest novel *Oryx and Crake* published in 2003 is a vision of mankind's uncompromisingly bleak future.

Margaret Atwood is a prominent figure in national and international cultural politics. She is also a founder member of the Writer's Union of Canada and an active member of Amnesty International and P.E.N. She is the recipient of many honorary doctorates, and fellow of the Royal Society of Canada, a companion of order of Canada and an honorary member of the American Academy of Arts and Sciences. All her writing is noted for its careful craftsmanship and precision of language, which give a sense of inevitability and a resonance to her words.

Atwood's recognition as a versatile writer becomes clear when we go through several critical works based on her fiction and non-fiction. *Margaret Atwood: Language, Text and System* (1983) edited by Sherill E. Grace and Lorraine Weir is one of these critical books. In this essay collection the authors examine her 'system' or 'set of codes' from variety of critical perspectives, which, considered together, demonstrate the overall consistence of Margaret Atwood's work.

Margaret Atwood's Fairy-Tale Sexual Politics (1993) authored by Sharon Rose Wilson is a feminist structuralist analysis of Margaret Atwood's texts. Wilson describes the motifs found in Atwood's works. Particularly she catalogues, analyses and interprets the fairly tale parallels in her fiction.

Margaret Atwood, The Shape Shifter (1998) edited by Coomi S. Vevaina and Coral Ann Howells, regards Atwood as a writer. It is a collection of various essays on Atwood's fiction, short stories and poetry. The various articles show that there are hundreds of possibilities for changing shape in Atwood's writing and her fictive world is one of continual metamorphosis.

Judith McCombs's book *Critical Essays on Margaret Atwood* (1988) focuses on themes and patterns of social criticism, feminism and women's literature. The book also describes Gothic and popular genres and folklore in Atwood's fiction.

Sherill E. Grace in her book *Violent Duality* (1980) has not discussed Atwood's work as a specific critical category but she argues that Atwood's work is a 'violent duality'.

Babara Hill Rigney's *Margaret Atwood* (1987) covers Atwood's work from the 1960s and it draws out her recurring themes of Canadian identity and the wilderness, the representation of women and female bodies and history and its narration. Arnold Davidson and Cathy N. Davidson in their book, *The Art of Margaret Atwood* (1981) explore Margaret Atwood as a versatile writer—a poet, a novelist and a critic.

Margaret Atwood: Vision and Forms (1988) edited and published by Kathryn Van Spanckeren and Jan Garden Castro is a study of Atwood's novels, poetry and non-fictional prose. It discusses feminism in Atwood's work including the gothic element and cultural politics.

Margaret Atwood: A Feminist Poetics (1984) authored by Professor Frank Davey seems to be biased and it offers a male perspective. It is a misinterpretation of Margaret Atwood's progressive protagonists. In this study Davey argues that all Atwood's protagonists are against to the reconstruction and unity of the world and they refused doctrine of liberalism and desired to be 'whole'. In this way Davey blames Atwood of exaggerating the problems of women in her fiction. My study shows that Atwood has not overestimating the problems of women but holds a mirror to actual social status of women in patriarchal society through her female characters who are true to life. She has described the portraits of realistic protagonists. As a writer of realistic fiction, Atwood cannot claim for her characters greater autonomy than actual women can reasonably claim.

A study of these critical books on Margaret Atwood shows that many of them reveal similar narrative and feminist concerns. There is no particular full-length study available in which women characters are viewed on the basis of victim positions described by Margaret Atwood in her non-fiction *Survival.* I have discussed the ways in which Atwood uses feminist "consciousness-raising" and her feminist approach with reference to these victim positions. I have critically studied Margaret Atwood's female characters against the background of family and society so that systems, persons causes relating to her claustrophobic existence may be brought to light. Atwood female characters present different concept of feminism and challenge the traditional roles of women and propose image of women not just a "two legged womb" but a dynamic human, different from the male but no less human for that. As Margaret Atwood says:

> Women both as characters and as people must be allowed their imperfections. If I create a female character, I would like her to be able to show her having emotions all human beings have...without having her pronounced as a monster, a slur or a bad example.[13]

Margaret Atwood's feminist ideology, which has been most powerfully expressed through her fiction is explicitly stated in an interview that, "I'm defining my feminism as human equality and freedom of choice."[14] What Atwood is concerned with the treatment of woman as normal human being and therefore she must be allowed her imperfections. She criticizes the social system that assigns roles to the sexes and then categorically labels them as inferior or superior, sinful or chaste. She is intensely preoccupied with women fighting against the female norms of life-sexuality, dichotomy between career and the claims of the family.

Margaret Atwood's fiction is often organized thematically around images of both cultural and individual issues of survival, as she has sought to portray the entrapment of women in patriarchy, and of men and women in suffocating social cultural imprisonment. Her feminist concerns are, "her wider humanitarian concerns with basic human rights and their infringement by institutional oppression."[15] Her fiction provides a comprehensive review of the problems women confront in attaining full recognition and enjoyment of all human rights and fundamental freedom. The basic premise of Margaret Atwood's feminist thought is survival which shows women the ways of struggle and the means of survival in an antagonistic, male chauvinistic, and sexist society. By 'survival' she does not mean continuity of mere physical existence, but a striving for dignity in the battle with society and circumstances. Her fiction is a reflection on the violation of women's rights and it includes:

> Any act, omission or conduct by means of which physical, sexual or mental suffering is inflicted, directly or indirectly, though deceit, seduction, threat [harassment], coercion, or any other means, on any women with the purpose or effect of intimidating, punishing or humiliating her or of maintaining her in sex-stereotyped roles, or of denying her human dignity, sexual self-determination, physical, mental and moral integrity or of undermining the security of her person, her self-respect, or her personality or of diminishing her physical or mental capabilities.[16]

In her work Margaret Atwood problematize the alignment of woman with nature and silence, as well as the complete adherence of the female subject to the symbolic order of communication. She shows a preoccupation with examining the question of the women's place in society *vis-à-vis* the patriarchal structures of dominion and power and since she sees a relation between the feminine search for a distinctive identity and Canada's similar quest for a national identity, the narratives of her women characters become also, by implication and extension, the narratives of the nation. As Linda Hutcheon says, "the two issues are not, wholly distinct for Atwood."[17] As a Canadian woman writer, Margaret Atwood deals with the issues of victimization and survival as conditions of both, "the Canadian experience and female experience."[18] She says, "I have always seen Canadian nationalism and the concern for women's right as part of a larger, non exclusive picture."[19]

Most of her novels grapple with the politics of gender and deal with women's experiences in a male dominated society. She explains in *Second Words*, "By 'political' I mean having to do with power: who's got it, who wants it, how it operates; in a word who's allowed to do what to whom, who gets what from whom, who gets away with it and how."[20]

In her fiction she challenges traditional image of women presented by patriarchy. She believes that the silencing of woman, the thematic of victimization functions not only through women's conscious or unconscious complexity in the matter. In her novel she exposes the silent and hidden operations of gender and confront its politics there by recommending for rewriting of women's history. She demands demolition of gender system and hopes for a new world in which men and women are equal at every level of existence. In the process of struggle for change the protagonists in her fiction are sought to be organized into a powerful force and invested with a streak of rebellion. As Christine Gomez says:

> At the thematic level, Atwood's novel examines themes related to the politics of gender such as the enforced alienation of women under patriarchy, the delimiting definition of woman as a function, the patriarchal attempt to annihilate the selfhood of women, the gradual carving out of female space by woman through various strategies and woman's quest for identity, self-definition and autonomy...not only at the thematic and structural levels, but also in the organization of women characters, Atwood's novels are based on the politics of gender.[21]

Margaret Atwood's novels deal with women's experience in a male dominated culture. They present women caught in oppressive stereotypes from which some women struggle to create a female space for themselves. This may be done through autonomy of thought, through self-definition and self-reconstruction of one's own history, through creative composition, oral or written, through bonding among women and through a refusal to the role of subjugation.

In *Survival*, Margaret Atwood describes the four basic victim positions to categorize her female protagonists. It serves as the theoretical model or organizing framework for the characterization of women in her novels:

(1) Denial of the fact that one is victim,

(2) Acknowledgement of the fact of being a victim but the acceptance of it as something inevitable "an act of fate, the will of God, the dictates of Biology",

(3) Acknowledgement of the fact of being a victim but a repudiation of the victim role, and

(4) Becoming a creative non-victim.

Margaret Atwood firmly believes that one fixed notion in Canadian writing is the sense of victimization which she classifies by defining basic victim position. These positions can be applicable to women in general and to fictional women characters in particular. As Atwood herself says, "the positions are the same whether you are a victimized country, a victimized minority group or a victimized individual".[22]

The first kind of basic victim position denies one's victimhood because they, "are a little better off than the others in the group and so are afraid to recognize that they are victims for fear of losing the privileges they possess".[23] It implies a suppression of anger in this denial and bestows a sense of superiority on its adherents for having risen above victimhood.

The second position is to acknowledge oneself as the inevitable victim of Fate, God, Biology, History, Economics or the Unconscious. Such victims do not want to change their position and suppress anger against self and others by displacing or transferring their sense of oppression to unreal sources. They accept their position as if it is given by a greater power. As R.W. Connel says, "men…enjoy patriarchal power but accept it as if it were given to them by an external force, by nature or convention or even by women themselves, rather than by an active social subordination of women going on here and now".[24]

The third basic victim position implies awareness of the cause of oppression and the ability to mobilize into constructive action. It is dynamic and rebellion. It is very difficult to maintain this position. In an interview, Atwood herself says, "It is all very well to say I refuse to be a victim, but then you have to look at the context in which one is or isn't a victim. You can't simply refuse. You can refuse to define yourself that way, but it's not quite so simple as that."[25]

The fourth position is to be a creative non-victim so that one can avoid the anger of victim one, the injustice of victim two, and the forced remedial action of victim three. By becoming a creative non-victim, one can set oneself free from the dialectic of the gender-power struggle. The creative, non-victim accepts individual experience for what it is and does not seek to distort it like the other victims.

These four victim positions are not strait jackets, which imprison the characters. The same character may occupy more than one position at different times. It works as a helpful method of approaching woman's grievances and it is also useful to explore victim-victimizer syndrome in Margaret Atwood's fiction.

Particularly this is the parameter I had adopted to categorize the female characters of Margaret Atwood and place them in the particular category they belong to, in the following chapters.

REFERENCES

1. Atwood, Margaret. *Survival: A Thematic Guide to Canadian Literature*. Toronto: Anansi, 1972.
2. Frye, Northrop. "Conclusion to a Literary History of Canada", *The Bush Garden: Essays on the Canadian Imagination.* Toronto: House of Anansi, 1971, 220.
3. Pressman, Barbara M. *Family Violence, Origins and Treatment.* Guelph: Children's and Society of Guelph, 1984.

4. Atwood, Margaret. "On Being a Women Writer", *Second Words: Selected Critical Prose*. Toronto: Anansi, 1982, 203.
5. Howells, Coral Ann. *Private and Fictional World, Margaret Atwood.* London: Macmillan Ltd., 1996, 5.
6. Ramamurti, K.S. "The Canadian Women Novelists in a Multicultural Context", *Commonwealth Literature: Theme and Techniques*, ed. R.K. Rajan et al. Delhi: Ajanta, 1993, 182-83.
7. Burt, Sandra. "The Second Wave of Canadian Women's Movement", *Canadian Politics: An Introduction to the Discipline*, ed. Alain G. Gagnon and James P. Bickerton. Ontario: Broadview Press, 1990, 548-49.
8. Keefer, Janice Kulyk, Reading Mavis Gallant, Quoted from http://en.wikipedia.org/wiki/Mavis Gallant.
9. Bailey, Nancy. "Margaret Laurence, Cart Jung and the Manawaka Women", *Studies in Canadian Literature*, Vol. II, No. 2, Summer 1977, 306-21.
10. Salat, M.F. "Canadian Nationalism and Feminist Ideology: Margaret Atwood", *The Canadian Novel: A Search for Identity*. New Delhi: B.R. Publishing, 60.
11. Atwood, Margaret. "Face to Face", *A Place to Stand On: Essays by and About Margaret Laurence*, ed. George Woodcock. Edmonton: Newest Press, 1983, 23.
12. Snitow, "The Front Line: Notes on Sex in Novels by Women", *Women, Sex and Sexuality*, eds. Catherine R. Stimpson and Ethel Spector Peison. Chicago: University of Chicago, 1980, 174.
13. Atwood, Margaret. *Second Words*. Toronto: Anansi Press, 227.
14. Atwood, Margaret. Conversations, Earl G. Ingersoll. London: Virago, 1992, 142.
15. Howells, 7.
16. "Report on the results of the Meeting of Experts to consider the Viability of an Inter-American Convention on Women and Violence, Caracas, 5-9 August 1991" *Inter American Commission on Women*, CIM/Doc. 1/91, Doc. OEA/Ser./II 7.4.
17. Hutcheon, Linda. *The Canadian Postmodern: A Study of Contemporary English-Canadian Fiction*. Don Mills: Oxford University Press, 1988, 138.
18. Rubenstein, Roberta. "Nature and Nurture in Dystopia: The Handmaid's Tale", *Margaret Atwood: Vision and Forms*, ed. Kathryn Vanspankeren and Jan Garden Castro. Carbondale and Edwardsville: Southern Illinois University Press, 1988, 101.

19. Cited by Linda Hutcheon, DLB 53, 33.
20. Atwood, Margaret. *Second Words: Selected Critical Prose.* Toronto: House of Anansi Press, 1982, 353.
21. Gomez, Christine. "From Being an unaware victim to Becoming a Creative Non-victim: A Study of Two Novels of Margaret Atwood", *Perspectives on Canadian Fiction*, ed. Sudhakar Pandey. New Delhi: Prestige Books, 1991, 74.
22. Atwood, Margaret. *Survival: A Thematic Guide to Canadian Literature.* Toronto: House of Anansi Press, 1972, 36.
23. *Ibid.*, 36.
24. Connell, R.W. *Gender and Power.* California: Stanford University Press, 1987, 125.
25. Castro, Jan Garden. "An Interview with Margaret Atwood—20 April 1983", *Margaret Atwood, Vision and Forms*, 219.

The Edible Woman

2

> *The Edible Woman* is "an imaginative transformation of a social problem into comic satire as one young woman rebels against her feminine destiny" as the edible woman.[1]
>
> Coral Ann Howells

The Edible Woman is Margaret Atwood's maiden attempt at fiction writing. As the novel predates the women's liberation movement, Margaret Atwood rightly describes *The Edible Woman* as "protofeminist"[2] novel. It shows the influence of Betty Friedan's *The Feminine Mystique* and Simone de Beauvoir's *The Second Sex*. It exposes how even an economically independent woman takes a long time to be conscious of her marginalization as the 'second sex'. *The Edible Woman* is the first Canadian novel by Margaret Atwood that anticipates the trends of feminism found in the later women novelists such as Doris Lessing, Margaret Drabble and Tony Morrison. It is a very highly complex piece of realistic fiction.

According to Alan Dawe, "*The Edible Woman* is a novel about choices."[3] *The Edible Woman* lays bare the ruthless and hypocritical postures of patriarchy through the dramatization of identity crisis in the soul of Marian. J. Brooks Bouson says, "Atwood deploys her female protagonist, Marian MacAlpin, to expose and subvert the ideological constructs that have long defined and confined women."[4]

The Edible Woman pleads for radical changes in the gender relations in the society and indirectly indicates "a way out of the gender power-struggle". As such, it serves as a feminist guide in the context of male domination in respect of sexual status, role and temperament. It forcefully drives home the message that women are not mere objects of beauty meant for carnal consumption of men.

Margaret Atwood's conflict in her fiction, however, is not only to expose woman's complicity in the processes that lead to her victimization. She wants to explore the possible tics of combating patriarchal structures to power and domination that refuses female's equal claims as an individual in society. In *The Edible Woman* for instance, she de-constructs Marian's fictional journey from an adopted posture of self-negation and self-effacement towards one of self-certitude and self-assertion. According to Alan Dawe, Marian can either be the "scheming super female" like Ainsley or she can be like Clara, "the earth mother" and like the "office virgins", but these alternatives are however not acceptable to Marian.

The Edible Woman embodies several voices arising out of her belonging to a distinct geographical terrain, her association and involvement with a specific cultural situation, and because of being a woman, these voices are simultaneous and condition each other. The novel is structured like a journey in which through her association with several male and female acquaintances and friends, Marian sees and assesses different ways of understanding what it means to be a woman and this gives the book the quality of the novel of ideas. The various alternatives before Marian are comprehensively dramatized in a series of scenes, which are well integrated to constitute the main action of the novel.

Margaret Atwood's claim that *The Edible Woman* is an "anti-comedy"[5] only goes to show in a brittle way that in a consumer society where people are ready to gobble up each other, there cannot be a reaffirmation of the social order, a traditional comedy. All that we know is that Marian has saved her, how long she can continue to do, is a different question. *The Edible Woman* gives hope that woman like Marian would eventually succeed in life-knowing how to deal with men around irrespective of family or social castigation.

The Edible Woman is largely realistic and even the more, "self-indulgent grotesqueries...derive...from the society by which (Atwood) found herself surrounded".[6] Interestingly, the attitudes and choices presented in the novel have by and large remained the same over the years. Margaret Atwood says that, "the tone of the book seems more contemporary now than it did in, say, 1971, when it was believed that society could change itself a good deal faster than presently appears likely".[7]

To add to it all, the novel is an ironic rendering of popular romances of the Harlequin type in which marriage equals everlasting happiness. In *The Edible Woman* Peter, Len, Emmy, Lucy, Millie, Clara, Joe and the older ladies are shown to be both victims and predators swamped their social system in varying degrees. Most of the characters in the novel, including Marian, reveal passionate desire to appear normal and well adjusted. Little do they realize that their frustrations and anxieties stem from the fact that their society is itself sick.

As far as the theme of the novel is concerned, it deals with the relation of sexes in a consumer society; it is a society where men view women as commodities to enhance their social status. Atwood is indeed a writer with diverse interests. She is both a satirist and a prophet; she holds a mirror up to our time. She tends to project the image of a woman who is intelligent, confident and assertive.

Marian McAlpin, the heroine of *The Edible Woman* is a sensitive, self-reflective and finely articulate female. She uses quite an artful language, to voice forth the changes that take place in her attitudes and feelings, as she journeys through her various associations with different characters and realizes strategies of exploitation of a woman in male dominated society. The whole novel is divided into three unequal parts, each of which signals a particular stage in Marian's fictional journey towards self-actualization.

In Part I, Marian narrates her tale in the first person indicating there by a subjective and hence a limited perspective. Marian tells about herself in her own voice. Coming from a small town, Marian prefers to move in the set direction or standard of life.

She is a normal office going girl working for a market research company. She shares an apartment with Ainsley, lives in a symbiotic adjustments but Marian is different from Ainsley. Marian is sedate, subdued accommodative and pliable while Ainsley is modish, short tempered, excitable and forward looking.

Marian experiences identity crisis in her company Seymour Surveys because all top positions over there are occupied by men. The company where Marian works for, has highly stratified, three-tiered hierarchic structure. The top floor is occupied by men and is not accessible to her. The bottom is managed mostly by old housewives and she does not wish to go there. Marian does not want to continue her job in the middle point for whole of her life. This disturbing awareness is the direct result of a technologically advanced society (a culture specific phenomenon) which by its very advancement forces individuals into fabricated roles, and is therefore of a general nature.

Emmy, Lucy and Millie, who are known as office virgins avoid sexual relations with men for different reasons, but all of them agree that the best thing available to a woman is to get married. In the elaborate scene of the married life of Marian's friend Clara and Joe, she knows about a different facet altogether of love and marriage. Their marriage is a fairly good one with three children.

Margaret Atwood takes pleasure in decrying motherhood by showing Clara's pregnant body bulgingly obvious, looking like "a boa-constrictor that has swallowed a watermelon" (36). Marian thinks about Clara that:

> Clara simply had no practicality, she wasn't able to control the more mundane aspects of life, like money on getting to lectures on as time...her own body seemed somehow beyond her going in its own way without reference to any direction of hers. (35-36)

When Peter proposes Marian, she imagines her marriage to be different from that of Clara. Despite her dreams as to their future, she also has her own doubts towards sex and general behaviour, she feels at times, that "he was treating her as a stage prop; silent but solid, a two-dimensional outline" (71) but she is able to forgot all her doubts and misgivings in his arms.

Marian in fact lets Peter take the reins of her life into his hands completely, but as the marriage nears Marian begins to wonder whether she is doing the right thing by being meek, by allowing Peter to dominate. Sometimes Marian thinks that Peter tries to manipulate her. Once he had driven her to make love on the bedroom floor, at another time in a scratchy blanket in a field, and in a bathtub. These incidents disturb her a great deal, almost precipitating another identity crisis. The realization shocks Marian, but she does nothing about it. In one of the parties, she is annoyed with his excessive drinking and his disgusting attitude, but these moments of unease and outrage, which could have forced her to reconsider her relationship with Peter, pass off, when he touches her softly, just after she has expressed her anger with him, she melts like the heroine of sentimental novels. When Peter proposes her, she accepts, because in the late sixties a woman had no other option except marriage. Peter is trying to fit Marian into a, "conventionalized, even stereotyped image of a woman, passive and dependent". She thinks that marrying him would be a release from the anonymous existence at her company named Seymour Surveys. Sometimes Marian feels uneasy at the acceptance of his proposal, tries to defend her choice, "I'd always assumed through high school and college that I was going to marry someone eventually and have children, everyone does.... I've never been silly about marriage the way Ainsley is.... She's against it on principle, and life isn't by principle but by adjustments" (102).

Marian meets Duncan when the period of romancing is over; she accepted the proposal of Peter. She had met Duncan while she was doing a survey for Moose Beer. However, probably for the first time, Marian realizes that her entire future is at stake if she continues to avoid responsibility and allows others to make decisions for her. She meets Duncan again at the Laundromat and not only is she involuntarily drawn towards him but allows herself to be even kissed by him, a real total stranger. The Duncan-Marian chance encounter is as mystifying as it is irrational.

The second part of the novel shows deep, penetrative probe into Marian's psyche, because now she begins to realize that by agreeing to marry Peter, she had ceased to be herself. Now Marian is assailed by serious doubts as to whether she made the right choice. Her relationship with Peter seems to have undergone a sea change and Marian realizes that she had let herself be sold as some kind of a desirable commodity. That is why going through a series of fast moving situations; we see her losing control over her mind and body. Now Marian feels that Peter wanted to monitor her, transform her according to his needs and happiness. She fails to identify the real Peter underneath all that sophistication and doubts her understanding of his true self.

For a clearer perspective on her relationship with Peter, she deliberately starts cultivating Duncan. She began to see that with both of them she was being used.

Marian stops eating by Peter's hunting activities, soon she finds it difficult to eat anything at all. The more uncertain her relationship with Peter, the more disturbed she becomes and her mental strain weans her away from food and she feels more reluctant to eat nothing. She experiences psychic changes as well. The gradual loosening of control over her makes her increasingly conscious of her unreality. She thinks that she is not normal and that she ought to see a psychiatrist. Robert Lecker suggest, "Marian, stops eating for two reasons (a) her job with an advertising research provided by an artificial society and (b) she equates the consumption of food with her feeling that she has been assimilated and exploited as female object".[8]

In her engagement party, she feels uneasy because she thinks that Peter manipulated her cleverly and made her a puppet in his hands. She recognized her loss of identity and her edibility to Peter. Her sense of victimization becomes acute after she talks with Joe. He says:

> She gets the idea she has a mind, her professors pay attention to what she has to say, they treat her like a thinking human being; when she gets married, her core get invaded...her core.... The center of her personality, the thing she's built up, her image of herself.... Her feminine role and her core are really in opposition. Her feminine role demands passivity from her. (235)

She assumes her role after marriage as a meek and docile woman; dependent on her husband, allowing him to destroy her slowly. She leaves the party and after trying to find some way of overcoming her anxiety in the company of Duncan, she goes back to her place. Marian believes that Duncan is another alternative but when she knows that Duncan wants to seduce and sexually exploit her, it turns out that he is not the alternative. After she returns to her place, Marian bakes a cake in the shape of a woman. When Peter comes to see her she offers it as a woman-substitute to Peter to eat.

The novel, however, continues in the brief final part III. Marian herself dismisses the need to give any great weightage to the symbolic cake. Peter leaves without eating it and Duncan finishes off the cake. Marian eats the cake and she begins to enjoy taking food. After realization that her decision to marry Peter was a denial of her womanhood, Marian is restored to her normal physical and mental health.

At the end of the novel, the final chapter of the book is once again in her voice because now she has begun to talk of herself in the first person singular, a new and confident voice of a distinct being. The reversion to first person narration signifies the return to position zero. Marian comes back full circle to where she was at the beginning. Now Marian is looking for another job. Margaret Atwood does not offer any alternative; she must keep on searching for one. As Margaret Atwood said to Linda Sandler, "*The Edible Woman* is a 'circle', the heroine ends where she began".[9]

The Edible Woman nicely introduces us to many of the themes, thoughts and ideas that Margaret Atwood explores across many of her novels. The novel is structured beautifully, and in it Margaret Atwood creates a world; centered on that of a young woman, Marian McAlpin, who is thrust into the role of fiancée and the traditional societal expectations inherent in that symbolic position. Margaret Atwood is critical of the feminist facile optimism of the post liberation era, concerning the state of women's emancipation. The question according to her is much more complex than what the feminists make it out to be. Margaret Atwood raises certain questions concerning the biological realities and the gender psychology issuing out of centuries of male domination. Women continue to be looked down upon as sex objects. They are physically weaker than men and are bullied into submission.

The title of the novel *The Edible Woman* suggests that the central metaphor is that of woman as food, as object and the theme is woman's effort to attain humanity and a human identity. All the characters in the novel are trapped in their respective ego-cages and are involved in power games. As a result of it none of them are capable of love in the truest sense of the term.

The protagonist, Marian McAlpin, a fairly sensible intelligent young woman shares an apartment with Ainsley Tewce and the relationship between them is purely non-obligatory. Ainsley works as a tester of defective electric toothbrushes in a company. She is a self-proclaimed feminist who is fond of paper-back books on psychology and anthropology. She describes in the novel as 'scheming female' and plans to be an unwed mother because she thinks, "the thing that ruins families these days is the husbands" (40).

Ainsley, though against marriage, does not deny motherhood. She has strong views about the male-dominated 'consumer' society. She thinks that motherhood satisfies one's "deepest femininity". She wants child by her choice and hunts for a strong handsome, intelligent man as 'biological father' for her child. She finds Len as a perfect man who can fulfil her dreams of getting pregnant. Marian, repulsed by Ainsley's cold-blooded attitude to men and marriage and thinks it is all wrong.

Later, A psychologist's lecture on the importance of a strong father image for the normal healthy upbringing of a child radically changes Ainsley's view of marriage. She is now determined to get a husband, just to provide the father image to her child. She marries Fischer to provide a father to her child she is carrying. She ultimately accepts the traditional role of a wife and mother. Ainsley occupies victim position number three that is acknowledgement of the fact of being victim, but a repudiation of the victim role assigned to woman and her rejection of marriage as an exploitative relationship probably stems from this.

Clara, Marian's former classmate a natural blonde, had been "everyone's ideal of translucent-perfume advertisement femininity" (36), during her school days. She had fallen in love with Joe in her college time and had been swept into matrimony and motherhood. She is not practical and sensible enough to manage and run a well-organized marriage. Clara, has become a victim of biology. She is a mother of three and is far from happiness. Marian feels sorry for her and says:

> The babies had been unplanned, Clara greeted her first pregnancy with astonishment that such a thing could happen to her, and her second with dismay; now during her third, she had subsided into a grim but inert fatalism. (36)

During her pregnancies and even after the children are born, Clara does not feel inclined to do any work. Ainsley is furious about Clara's passivity:

> She just lies there and that man does all the work! She lets herself be treated like a thing.... She should do something; if only a token gesture.... Lots of pregnant woman finish their degrees. (38)

Ainsley wants Clara to atleast finish her degree. When Joe suggests that she should go to night school, she just gives him a 'funny look' as if that is impossible. She probably considers her position to be unchangeable because she believes to be inevitable that is victim position number two—acknowledgement of the fact of being a victim but the acceptance of it as something inevitable "an act of fate, the will of God, the dictates of Biology".

Joe, Clara's husband is considered as a very good husband. Joe thinks that getting married attacks a woman's personality and spoils the image of her. Once a woman gets married:

> Her feminine role and her core are really in opposition; her feminine role demands passivity from her...so she allows her core to get taken over by the husband. And when the kids come, she wakes up one morning and discovers she doesn't have anything left inside, she's hollow, she doesn't know who she is any more; her core has been destroyed. (235-36)

Joe's attitude to women is gentle and patronizing. He tends "to think of all unmarried girls as easily victimized and needing protection" (35). He sees opposition between woman's self-image and her feminine role as a wife and mother:

> It's harder for any woman who's been to university. ...I can see it happening with my own female students. But it would be futile to warn them (236). He concludes, may be women shouldn't be allowed to go to university at all; they wouldn't always be feeling later on that they've missed out on the life of the mind. (236)

He means that women should only enjoy a life of the body. Joe is a considerate and kind husband but he supports the victim position of women as something inevitable.

Marian's spinster colleagues Lucy, Emmy, Millie, whom Ainsley collectively calls "the office virgins" actively hunt for husbands. Lucy has a kind of public relation job, and is platinum and elegantly coiffure. Emmy is the typist with whisk tinted and straggly and Millie, Mrs. Bogue's Australian assistant, brassy from the sun and cropped. Lucy from social quailing, Emmy is the office hypochondriac and Millie from a solid girl guide practically.

The office virgins are artificial blondes because blonde hair is one of the regulation charms of women, as required by the society. They all want to travel extensively before they get married and settle down. None of them even dreams of becoming a career girl. They hope that their prince charming will give them the identity they lack and rescue them from Seymour Surveys, the market research company in which they work with Marian. Like Lucy, Emmy and Millie, every young middle class white American woman was made to dream of being a happy suburban housewife and find "true feminine fulfilment"[10] in her career as a wife and mother. Lucy is clever and cunning dressed elegantly and systematically visited all the expensive restaurants in town during lunch break in the hope of catching a prospective husband while Emmy and Millie are family dumb and hunt occasionally. When Marian tells about her engagement to Peter, Lucy's first question is "How on earth did you even catch him?" (113).

Lucy, Emmy and Millie accept society's definition of woman as a role, occupant to fulfil the function of a wife. They all occupy the first position that is 'Denial of the fact that one is victim'. They all are unaware of being victim in patriarchal society. Their sole aim in life seem to be getting a husband.

In *The Edible Woman* Marian turns paranoid at a crucial juncture in the novel when she gets engaged to be married to Peter. Peter, "the symbolically named rock of this consuming society"[11] is the most tragically self character in the novel. He lives in an apartment, which is still under construction, his apartment is largely finished and is used as a model for buyers, like his apartment Peter struggles to be a model of modern successful man. Though he is only an amateur photographer and hunter he keeps his camera and his collection of weapons, which comprise two rifles, a pistol and several wicked-looking knives, a pegboard in his bedroom.

Peter, the steady boy friend dominant and assertive, decides to get married because that is what his other friends have done, "marriage itself would be a kind of respectability...the clients like to know you've got a wife; people get suspicious of a single man after a certain age, they start thinking you're a queer or something" (89).

Most importantly it is time for him to settle down and Marian would be the ever obedient bride. Peter the vain and meticulous lawyer, takes all the major decisions concerning Marian and himself. He likes Marian, as she never demands anything from him. Peter proposes to her and explains the reason for wanting to marry her. He says:

> I can always depend on you. Most women are pretty scatter brained but you're such a sensible girl. You may not have known this but I've always thought that's the first thing to look for when it comes to choosing a wife. (89)

Marian soon realizes that Peter is using her for his own benefit and there is no thought of Marian in his life. Marian is always be there for him, silent and solid but always boosting his ego. She identifies Peter with an anonymous caller who has introduced himself to ladies as a surveyor on underwears.

Marian's curse is her own meekness and when she realizes this, the fear of disintegration makes her speculate about her own place in Peter's life. She thinks that Peter is monopolizing her both physically and psychologically and she decides to do something about it.

With Peter she is unsure of his motive, the real Peter was eluding her and that makes her conscious of the vague, slippery status of herself. When Marian knows that Peter enjoys shooting and killing of rabbits and other animals mercilessly as a matter of pleasure and pride and he is very fond of non-vegetarian food. She becomes disillusioned. Like Peter, Marian's college friend Leonard Slunk also lacks a core and is as much of a victim and predator as he is. Len is a "self consciously lecherous skirt chaser" (87). He is a kind of inverted moralist. Instead of thinking that love is a beautiful relationship, he only regards love as a game to be won. When a pure and unobtainable girl attracts to Len he spoils and throws her away. For the thematic intent of the novel he is portrayed as a beast enjoying and discarding its prey. When Ainsley tries to rope him into marriage he reveals himself as an emotionally insecure person and shouts, "all you clawed scaly bloody predatory whoring fucking bitches can go straight to hell" (215). It is an antifeminist comment in a feminist fiction.

At a crucial stage in her life, Marian meets Duncan, but it is like jumping into fire from the pan. Duncan takes her into his bed saying that he is a "virgin", who needs to be introduced to sex. Duncan says that sexual relationship with her, "was fine, just as good as usual" (264). Critics like George Woodcock[12] and T.D. MacLulich[13] look at him as a parasite and narcissistic cannibal. In the novel, Duncan serves as Marian's Double. The character's place in the novel is almost like the character's own description, small, thin, unattractive but at the same time, important and revelatory. When Marian puts on Duncan's dressing gown, he comments that she looks exactly like him. Acting as a link between Marian's fantasy world and her real one, he appears mysteriously in illogical places where Marian least expects him. Duncan is full of self-pity. He and Marian, in fact exploit each other shamelessly in the matter of comprising pain to see who suffers more and thus deserves the greater sympathy. His personality is androgynous. He is not only sexless but ageless as well. His roommates are surrogates parents who feed him:

> I've been running away from understudy mother ever since I can remember. Duncan tells Marian, ...that's what you get for being an orphan. (140)

During Duncan and Marian's visit to the museum he tells her, he is writing a paper called, "mono syllabus in Milton" which was to be as intense stylistic analysis done from a radical angle. However for ever two and a half weeks he confesses being stuck on the opening sentence, "It is indeed highly significant that...." It is evident that Duncan, Fish, Trevor do not derive any intellectual or emotional gratification from their work as a result of which they often feel the need to escape from it. Duncan is the archetypal trickster figure as it evident from his desire to be shapeless and flexible like an amoeba. Being wily by nature, he enjoys manipulating the emotions of all those around him as it gives him a feeling of power over them.

Duncan's roommates Trevor and Fish appear to be victims of the graduate culture but they are also predators like everyone else. Three of them act as if they are family—Trevor, a latent homosexual, assuming the role of a mother, Fish, that of a father and Duncan of the only child. Duncan's role in the novel is ambiguous, as he seems to be more of symbolic than a real character.

Marian in *The Edible Woman* is described as a young woman of growing manipulativeness and cynicism for her rebellion, whether in the form of cake creation or her refusal to eat. However it should be understood that Marian's reaction itself is a form of protest. She has to be manipulative to save herself. Marian is decently liberal in her views and somewhat defensive about her own individuality and her responsibility to others. The women shaped cake reveals Marian's complete control over her and a confidence that she cannot be manipulated by any man. Part of a "consumer society" Marian is faced with a choice of being 'edible' to her fiancé and remaining single as an individual and asserting herself. She chooses the latter and thus refuses to be an edible woman, but the choices available to her are limited. She has to confront several issues crucial to her. What does it mean to be a woman, what is her situation, and what constitutes femininity. In *The Edible Woman* Marian is presented as 'a perfect foil' to her friends, owing to her coming into contact with them she learns immensely of women's problem.

The Edible Woman is a quest for self-identity by Marian, the main character of the novel. Facing an identity crisis she is confronted with various alternatives. Firstly, Marian has to face and overcome at her work place. In her company 'Seymour Surveys' all responsible and respectable positions are occupied by men and is not accessible to her. Marian soon realizes that she is literally and figuratively trapped. She remarks that her company is layered like an ice-cream sandwich with three floors; the upper crust, the lower crust and her department the gooey layer in the middle. Marian says:

> The prospect of getting grooved into the fixed middle point of the office structure for the whole of her life with a pension at the end of her tenure of job, makes her feel that in front of her "a self was waiting, performed, a self who had worked during innumerable years for Seymour Surveys and was now receiving her reward. (21)

Marian's crisis, however, acquires a feminine colouration when she looks for alternatives to her present situation. These alternatives are represented in her office colleagues; Emmy, Lucy, Millie, her friend Clara and her husband Joe, Peter and Ainsley, her roommate. Choices and alternatives presented by her friends apart Marian also feels outraged by the attitudes adopted by Seymour Surveys towards its woman employees. The manager Mrs. Bogue regards the very act of marriage and pregnancy as offensive and disloyal to the company. Marian does not want live life without her identity. She seeks something different from life. She wants to live meaningfully but she does not wish to change her society. She hopes that she would be able to lead a better life with Peter. She thinks that Peter is an ideal choice. He is attractive and bound to be successful. He seems to be a godsend to relieve her from her monotonous life at her company Marian says, “I was seeing him in a new light...a rescuer from chaos, a provider of stability” (189).

Marian believes that marriage is necessary in life and also that it is maintained by adjustments, but gradually she realizes that only wives have to adjust. In *The Edible Woman*, Marian struggles with her self-identity and seems losing her mind begins to ‘find’ herself. Soon she knows that Peter is a manipulator and gets insight into the truth of her relationship with him. She feels:

> My mind was at first as empty as though someone had scooped out the inside of my skull like a cantaloupe and left me only the rind to think with. (83)

Marian realizes that her identity and interests can never be safe in the event of her marriage with Peter. She thinks that Peter is a destroyer of her individuality and identity. The image of Peter as a hunter upsets Marian emotionally. As the marriage approaches Marian suffers from apprehensions. Her escape to Duncan, a new person, makes her aware that she doesn’t know Peter well at all. Duncan exploits her and says:

> I don’t want you to think that all this means anything. It never sort of does, for me you’re just another substitute for the Laundromat. (145)

Marian is not angry with Duncan’s behaviour instead she is faintly relieved because she knows her relationship with him but with Peter she is confused about his personality and his motives. She wants to know that where does she stand in relation to him?

Marian’s mind gets crazed as she grasps Peter’s way of observing things. Marian being his latest target he becomes an acute analyst of her. This makes Marian feel that she is on a doctor’s examination table. Marian’s visualization of herself in Peter’s hands gets stronger when she watches Peter eating:

> ...The capable hands holding the knife and fork, slicing precisely with an exact adjustment of pressure. How skilfully he did it; no tearing no ragged edges. And it was a violent action. (150)

Now Marian thinks that Peter was treating her in as civilized a way as he was handing the steak on his plate, devouring it with relish and style. It is this fear, which makes her a total vegetarian finally making her give up food.

When Peter arranges the cocktail party on the occasion of their engagement, Marian wears new red dress, heavy make up and gold earring. She does all because Peter tells her to do this. She looks her image in the mirror, which seems to mock at her:

> She held both of her naked arms out towards the mirror. They were the only portions of her flesh that was without a cloth or nylon on leather or varnish covering, but in the glass even they looked fake, like soft pinkish-white rubber or plastic, boneless, flexible.... (229)

Marian feels that a woman's primary market value in the marriage depends upon her charming image. In party when Peter aiming his camera right at Marian, the image of Peter as the hunter becomes stronger in her mind. She imagines Peter as the dark intent marksman with his aiming eye has been there all the time hidden by the other layers. He is waiting for her at the dead center, like a homicidal maniac with lethal weapon in his hands.

Now Marian thinks that Peter has ability to devour her in a civilized way and he has a strong motive to negate her individuality. He is expecting her to assume the roles of a traditional wife and mother. J. Brooks Bouson says:

> As a realistic novel *The Edible Woman* shows how female passivity and submersion in the traditional wife and mother roles can pose a serious threat to the very survival of the self.[14]

Marian does not want to be trapped in a decorative life where her identity and individuality are likely to be crushed. Marian realizes that her destiny is to be another soap woman after marrying Peter. Her future image is clear to her and she recognizes her own self, a tiny two-dimensional small figure in a red dress, posed like a paper woman in a mail order catalogue, turning and smiling, fluttering in the white empty space.

She needs fresh air, the freedom to grow and develop her personality. She refuses to be Peter's 'edible woman'. She refuses to marry him and runs away from the party, it shows her feminine valour and her potential for wholeness.

When Marian goes to Duncan's place with this hope that she find some kind of safety and shelter but Duncan takes advantage of Marian's innocent nature and she becomes the victim of Duncan's lust Marian is pained to realize she is not the first and "[T]he starched nurse like image of herself she had tried to preserve as a last resort crumpled like wet newsprint" (264).

Duncan tells Marian "You might do something destructive: hunger is more basic than love. Florence Nightingale was a cannibal, you know" (100). By hunger he means the desire to feed on the emotions of others. After seducing Marian, Duncan remarks:

> It's no use. I must be incorruptible.... I don't exactly know what's wrong. Party I don't like not being able to see your face.... (253)

This remark makes Marian stunned and she decides to stop eating. According to Robert Lecker Marian has been from the beginning a, "packaged product of a male dominated corporate society and rejection of food is synonymous with her rejection of a culture which tends to exploit women and treat them as edible objects".[15] Emma Parker says, "her no eating is physical expression of her powerlessness and at the same time, a protest against that powerlessness".[16]

Now Marian thinks that she is a destitute girl and feels dejected about future. She recognizes both Peter and Duncan in their true colours and understands how she has allowed both the men in her life to use and consume her, thus actually helping the process of victimization. This new awareness provides her a renewed strength and purpose in life. She rejects her passivity and refuses to be a victim. After she returns to her place, Marian bakes a cake that resembles her, "as a traditional woman's skill, the baking of the cake is her mute and 'feminine' act of protest which also bears the seeds of potential liberation: She will hence forth, refuse to be consumed",[17] says Patriacia Waugh. It shows the role of women as servers and women as consumables. Although she speaks only through the marginal art of culinary decoration, rather than through the culturally approved channels of 'high art' and although her protest is ambiguous (Peter and

Ainsley interpret the act in different ways), she has registered a voluntary and intentional protest which releases her body from its involuntary rejection of food. For although Marian has felt herself to be an independent agent in the world, college-educated and economically self-providing, psychologically she manifests all the dependency traits of the 'classic' image of femininity what contradictoriness is finally voiced, involuntarily, through her female body. Marian offers baked cake as a woman substitute to Peter and says:

> You've been trying to assimilate me. But I've made a substitute, something you'll like much better. This is what you wanted all along, isn't it ? (271)

At this behaviour of Marian, Margaret Atwood says that, "by doing so Marian is trying to depict: an action, a preposterous one in a way, as all the pieces of symbolism in a realistic context are, but what she is obviously making is a substitute of herself".[18]

Peter leaves the place with embarrassment, now Marian feels hungry. She offers the cake woman to Ainsley. She says:

> Marian.... You're rejecting your femininity. (272)
>
> Marian looked back at platter. The Woman laid there, still smiling glassily, her legs gone. "Nonsense", she said. It's only a cake. She plunged her fork into the carcass, neatly severing the body from the head. (273)

Marian can eat the cake because she no longer identified with the spurious "wholeness" which has been offered to her as "essential femininity" in a culture where women are in fact continuously anatomized for consumption.

The cake, which Marian bakes and eat, shows the development of her vision and her refusal to be a victim. Marian claims that she cannot be manipulated by the people like Peter and Duncan. Marian is also able to destroy the society's synthetic stereotype of femininity through the ingenuous mirroring device of the cake and free herself to realize her own true identity. At the end of the novel she proclaims that a cake is edible but a woman is not. The cake-woman represents woman as an object for male consumption. It is said to be gesture of defiance a way of saying no to a system that defines woman as commodity and devours them. It also seems a reflection a way of seeing herself in a mirror and it expresses a truth not before perceived. Further it signifies her recognition and rejection of the former compliant self, culminating in her new ability to respond to the own inner feelings. Sharon Rose Wilson says, "by baking, decorating, serving and consuming the cake-woman image.... Marian announces, to herself and others, that she is not food."[19] With reference to the four victim positions, described by Margaret Atwood in Survival, Marian, the protagonist of *The Edible Woman* moves through at least three of the four victim positions.

At the beginning of the novel, there is uncertain acceptance of the victim role that is position number two—acknowledgement of the fact of being a victim but the acceptance of it as something inevitable. Marian says:

> Ainsley says I choose clothes as though they're a camouflage or a protective coloration, though I can't see anything wrong with that. (13-14)

Marian's reaction at the prospect of pension plan of her company shows subconscious acceptance that women's ultimate destiny is marriage and wifely role. Her relationship with Peter, their odd love making, her adjustments to Peter's mood conforms of his expectations from her. When Peter proposes her, the prospect of marriage makes her accept the role of subservient wife, "[a] tremendous electric blue flash, very near illuminated the inside of the car. As we stared at each other in that brief light I could see myself, small and oval, mirrored in his eyes" (83).

Maria's loss of individuality is indicated by the silencing of the inner self and her rejection of food is caused by her subconscious rejection of the victim role, that is position number three: acknowledgement of the fact of being a victim, but a repudiation of the victim role, of being consumed and assimilated by Peter. It is Duncan who relates her inability to eat to an inner rebellion, "You're probably representative of modern youth, rebelling against the system" (192). This repudiation of the victim role remains at the night of her engagement party. There she runs away from Peter's party and escapes being hunted down by the Peter (photographer/hunter) with his camera/

flashgun. Now Marian tries to create a new image of her. Duncan insists on her making her own decisions Marian finds that, "her image was taking shape" (267). This refers to her new self, as a creative non-victim that is position number four. Baking a woman shaped cake as an image of her former self as a victim—the edible woman for man's consumption. She drives out all the former victim elements from within her and projects them on to her artistic creation that is cake-woman. The immobility imposed by the victim role has slowly drained her. The process of cake making is joyful as she recognizes her own complicity in her former victimization. Marian says, "You look delicious".... Very appetizing, and that's what will happen to you; that's what you get for being food" (270). By saying this Marian actually addresses her that if a woman makes herself edible, she will be consumed. As a woman Marian has definitely changed from the meek, docile, traditional woman to the bold conscious and rebellious feminist. Now she is a representative of modern youth rebelling against the system of gender and its oppression. Marian wants to become neither a man nor a machine:

> I couldn't become one of the men upstairs: I couldn't become a machine person or one of the questionnaire making ladies as that would be a step down. (20)

She wants to become a woman who quest for a meaningful human identity. This is Margaret Atwood's feminist perspective as found in *The Edible Woman* M. Prabhakar says, "Atwood has presented a comedy of resistance to social myths of femininity through the discriminating eyes of Marian, the champion of feminism."[20]

Thus, we can say that Margaret Atwood's *The Edible Woman* is about women and their relationships to men, to society and to food and eating. It is through food and eating that Margaret Atwood discusses a young woman's rebellion against a modern, male dominated world. The female protagonist, Marian McAlpin, struggles between the role that society has imposed upon her and her personal definition of self and food becomes the symbol of that struggle and her eventual rebellion. It seems that Marian has problems not only with food, but with her social relations and with her love life too. It is possible to discern a development by three steps of Marian's life throughout the story. They are all connected with food. The whole story is divided into three part. The first part begins with Marian's hunger and seems often to be hampered, "I had to skip the egg and wash down a glass of milk and a bowl of cold cereal which I knew would leave me hungry long before lunch time" (2).

In the second part, the narration changes over from the first person to the third. Marian stops eating. This is a proper example of self-starvation or "anorexia". At last act of baking a cake-woman symbolizes her having attained the necessary self-knowledge. The final part of the novel describes how the appetite returns and at the same time Marian comes back to herself. George Woodcock calls it an "emotional cannibalism".[21] Marian is finally able to defy Peter's desire to colonize her and refuses to be a mindless body.

Margaret Atwood in the introduction of the novel explains, "...I'd been speculating for some time about symbolic cannibalism. Wedding cakes with sugar brides and grooms were at that time of particular interest to me".[22] So, the eating as well as the refusal of food described in this novel has a symbolic meaning. *The Edible Woman* was written in the late 1960s when the word 'anorexia', was not yet known. However, the phenomenon was present in the society. If we combine the feminist and the anorectic aspects of the story, it seems that the unconscious of the young woman protests against the conventional female role that Marian is expected to enter by marrying Peter. When the relation with the lawyer becomes more serious and he proposes to her, Marian's reaction is pictured is "I could see myself, small and oval mirrored in his eyes". Here small and oval symbolizes an egg. The bride's refusal to eat means that she looks upon herself as an egg that is going to be consumed. As a matter of fact, Marian willingly gives up her position as free and independent individual. She becomes symbolically an egg inside her shell and totally dependent on her future husband.

Like most of the Margaret Atwood's heroines, Marian also lives a double life. Marian resembles Alice, the heroine of Lewis

Caroll's 'Alice in wonderland' in many ways. Like Alice, Marian is smug and self-righteous. Both experience an identity crisis when they start their inner journey. Alice's body is subject to sudden metamorphoses while Marian transforms according to her mental status that is psychologically.

The other characters in the novel also resemble in Alice's tale. Peter resembles domineering caterpillar that make Alice conscious of her identity crisis. Mrs. Bogue resembles the horrible Queen. The office virgins particularly Lucy, looks like the cake with "EAT ME" written on it as if she wants men to gobble her up. Clara and her family resemble the Duchess with her pig of a baby and her mad cook. Duncan seems to look like the Cheshire cat and combination of Rabbit guide and mock-turtle.

Margaret Atwood has attempted to convey the theme of woman as an edible commodity for man through her image sequences. Emotional and psychological states are described throughout the novel in the imagery of food—The company for which Marian works is, "layered like an ice-cream sandwich," Marian's dream makes her feel "like melting jelly". Lucy has "confectionary eyes" and "delicious dresses", "unripe ear of corn" she observes woman's bodies in a continuous flux of taking in and giving out, "chewing, words, potato-chips, burps, grease, hair babies, milk, excrement, cookies, vomit, coffee, tomato-juice, blood tea, cheat, liquor, tears and garbage..." (167).

The zoological images used as the thematic nexus of the novel "a pitcher-plant in swamp waiting for some insect to be attracted drowned and digested" (75), Marian's empty mind is "as though someone had scooped out the inside of my skull like a cantaloupe..." (83).

Animal images used as she drinks tomato-juice "blood thirstily" (83). She sits like "escaping from a giant squid" (84). Clara's remark for her baby "you little leech. I sometimes think she's all covered with suckers, like an octopus" (31). Ainsley's baby is not going to be a "chicken" but a lovely nice baby (160). Marian is frightened as a "sea anemone" to look at the yolk of an egg.

Atmospheric images are used according to the situation, "enclosed in a layer of moist dough" (31). "This day...was windless and oppressive...the air hung heavily like invisible steam, so that the colours and outlines of objects were blurred" (44).

Some pre-figurative images used to indicate the coming situation "In the distance the thunder was beginning" (79), "corresponds with a tremendous electric flash.... It reflects the one for the other.... I could see myself, small and oval, mirrored in his eyes" (83). This image specially used for relationship of Marian and Peter.

Claustrophobic images used for expressing one's mental status, when Marian visits Clara in the maternity ward, and she wants only to escape this "sweet organic scent" and to place "a fixed barrier between herself and that liquid amorphous other" (161).

Marian regards with horrified fascination her friend Clara's fertility and engendering of babies. The image of the pregnant woman is the image of the monstrosity of the female, for Marian. When Clara has given birth, Marian "was thinking that now Clara was deflating towards her normal size again she would be able to take with her more freely" (115).

The Edible Woman offers little hope for radical social change, but it does suggest that the possibility of change for women must lie, in part, in their need to recognize the relationship between the female body and the construction of femininity. In the novel men and women portrayed are not antagonistic, but the women protagonist as indicated by Suresh Chandra, "consciously views these male and female at the two ends of the axis, perceiving reality differently under the shaping influence of conventions and belief. Each one of them has a hemisphere and its center is formed by the concept of a child".[23]

In the transformed circumstances and with a sense of awareness the women in the novel display the much-needed self-realization and in its wake they reject the prevalent notions of femininity. In matters concerning female sensibility and identity they stand together with the aim of achieving wholeness and fulfilment. Women are reduced to the position of victims through their own complicity in the process is also acknowledged. Women may either sink into unawareness and thus deny the fact of being victims, or accept it passively or repudiate the victim role and try to reverse the victor-victim roles or come out of the gender struggle situation by becoming creative non-victims. However, it is difficult to agree with Catherine Mclay in "The Dark Voyage: *The Edible Woman* as Romance" when she asserts that, "Marian seems to alter very little from beginning to end".[24] Marian is probably where she was socially but as a woman she definitely has change from the meek traditional woman to the bold, conscious woman. The 'self-discovery' goes as far as rejecting her passivity, refusing to be a victim.

Margaret Atwood has quite deliberately depicted what seems to be an archetypal quest structure. The novel portrays a woman's apparently successful search for self-assertion. All the trappings of a quest narrative are there, the three parts quite mathematically appear to show Marian's evolution from romantic/subjective impressionism to objective assessment to finally regeneration and reformation.

The novel merely deconstructs the processes of hegemony enhancing and exploitative power structure. *The Edible Woman* is a work of a writer who is not only in full command of her material but is, at the same time, a versatile tactician. In essay "Reconstructing Margaret Atwood's Protagonists" Patricia Goldblatt states that, "Atwood creates situations in which women, burdened by the rules and inequalities of their societies, discover that they must reconstruct braver, self-reliant person in order to survive."[25] At the end Marian partially reconstructs that new persona or concept of self through a renewed relationship to food.

Margaret Atwood in *The Edible Woman* does not adopt an extremist stance as a feminist and hold men alone responsible for the subjugation and inferiorization of women. Matrimony and motherhood as they exist in a patriarchal society are shown to be delimiting and exploitative as far as women are concerned. Women like Marian, allowing them to be colonized and exploited, are equally responsible for perpetuating gender related inequity.

Linda Hutcheon remarks, "As both a Canadian and a woman, she protests and tendency towards easy passivity and naïvety; she refuses to allow either Canadians or women to deny their complicity in the power structures that may subject them."[26]

The Edible Woman is viewed often as contemporary comedy of manner—as a satire on modern society, which in the final analysis offers a depressing vision of life—depicting men as propagators and victims of corruption, vice and lust. Man getting cough in this was deludes himself into believing that his own debased or immoral view does participate in a comedy of manner which comments on a world where men and women are mere faceless non entities and where men and women search for true identity only leads to a "sinking feeling".[27]

Margaret Atwood is successful in portraying Marian's character as a meek docile and non-descript woman to a strong individualistic and active feminist.

REFERENCES

1. Howells, Coral Ann. *Private and Fictional World: Margaret Atwood.* London: Macmillan P. Ltd., 1996, 39.
2. Atwood, Margaret. "An Introduction to The Edible Woman", *Second Words: Selected Critical Prose.* Toronto: Anansi, 1982, 370.
3. Dawe, Allan. Introduction, *The Edible Woman.* Toronto: McClelland and Stewart, 1973, 2.
4. Bouson, J. Brooks. "The Anxiety of Being Influenced: Reading and Responding to Character in Margaret Atwood's The Edible Woman", *Style,* 24.2, Summer 1990, 230.
5. Gibson, Graeme. "Margaret Atwood", Interview in his *Eleven Canadian Novelists.* Toronto: House of Anansi, 1973, 21.
6. Atwood, Margaret. "Introduction", 1979 to the Virgo edition of *The Edible Woman, op. cit.*
7. *Ibid.*
8. Lecker, Robert. "Janus through the Looking Glass, Atwood's First Three Novels", *The Art of Margaret Atwood: Essays in Criticism.* eds. Arnold E. Davidson and Cathy N. Davidson. Toronto: Anansi, 1981, 178.
9. Sandler, Linda. "Interview with Margaret Atwood", *The Malahat Review,* 41, Jan. 1977, 14.
10. Friedan, Betty. *The Feminine Mystique,* 1963; rpt. Middlesex: Penguin Books, 1983, 16.

11. Hutcheon, Linda. "Atwood and Laurence. Poet and Novelists", *Studies in Canadian Literature*, 3, No. 2, Summer 1978, 259.
12. Woodcock, George. "Margaret Atwood", *The Literary Half Yearly*, 13.2. July 1972, 237.
13. Maclulich, T.D. "Atwood's Adult Fairy Tale: Levi Straus Bettelcheim and The Edible Woman", *Essays on Canadian Writing*, 1978, 111-29.
14. Bouson, 231.
15. Lecker, 179.
16. Parker, Emma. "You are What You Eat: The Politics of Eating in the Novels of Margaret Atwood", *Twentieth Century Literature,* 41.3, Fall 1995, 350.
17. Waugh, Patricia. "Margaret Atwood", *Feminine Fictions, Revisiting the Post Modern*, London: Routledge, 1989, 181.
18. Gibson, 25.
19. Wilson, Sharon Rose. "Margaret Atwood's Fairy-Tale", *Sexual Politics*. Jackson: University of Mississippi, 1993, 96.
20. Prabhakar, M. "The Edible Woman: Guide to Feminism", *Feminism/ Postmodernism, Margaret Atwood's Fiction*. New Delhi: Prestige Books, 1994, 47.
21. Woodcock, George. "Margaret Atwood: Poet as Novelist", *The World of Canadian Writing: Critiques and Reflections*. Vancouver: Douglas and Intyre: Seattle: University of Washington Press, 1980, 153.
22. Atwood, Margaret. Introduction, *The Edible Woman*. Virago Press, 1980.
23. Chandra, Suresh. "Women's Liberation in the Fiction of Margaret Atwood and Shashi Deshpande", in *Meerut Journal of Comparative Literature and Language,* ed. Rajiv Sharma. Meerut: Sushila Printers, 1993.
24. Mclay, Catherine. "The Dark Voyage: The Edible Woman as Romance", *The Art of Margaret Atwood: Essay in Criticism*, ed. Arnold and Cathy Davidson. Toronto: Anansi, 1981, 123.
25. Goldblatt, Patricia. "Reconstructing Margaret Atwood's Protagonist", *World Literature Today*. Spring 1999, 275.
26. Hutcheon, Linda. *The Canadian Post Modern: A Study of Contemporary English Canadian Fiction*. Don Mills University Press, 1980, 12.
27. Devi, N. Rama. "Edibility and Ambiguity in Margaret Atwood's The Edible Woman", *Canadian Literature Today*, ed. R.K. Dhawan. New Delhi: Prestige Books, 1995, 117.

Surfacing

3

> *Surfacing*, more than any other of Margaret Atwood's novels is also 'border country', halfway between poem and novel, theological treatise and political manifesto, myth and realism.... *Surfacing* is, quite possibly, the best of all her work.[1]
>
> Barbara Hill Rigney

Surfacing by Margaret Atwood deals with the theme of confronting the submerged layers of the self. It is an archetypal search of a nameless narrator to find out the creative sources of life. Through this novel Atwood explores the feminist perspective both as a concept and a reality. This novel evaluates Atwood's perception of the feminine being.

Surfacing was first published in 1972, at a time when second wave feminism was affecting the lives of women at grass-root level. It clearly answered the emotional, intellectual and social needs of a generation of women who were grappling with a series of issues about women's role in society. With the writing of *Surfacing* Margaret Atwood turns from, "the life of buried, smothered women to examine the other side of the coin",[2] the woman who have fought their way to freedom as artists. With the publication of this novel Margaret Atwood was regarded as a woman novelist who speaks especially for and to women. In it Atwood shows how gender politics has relegated women artists to a lower order and how their history is subsumed into the dominant patriarchal discourse.

Surfacing has received mixed responses from various critics all over the world. Margaret Atwood's teacher and the well-known Canadian critic, Northrop Frye calls it an "extraordinary novel, which perfectly represents her own critical review of Canadian themes".[3] Sherill Grace says, it is "not a treatise on feminism or nationalism, it is a highly moral book".[4] Isobel Mckenna thinks, "*Surfacing* is no novel of escape, but a parable to demonstrate not only the necessity of making some kind of choice, but even greater importance of facing the truth, first and foremost."[5] The nameless protagonist rebels against woman's reduction to the status of an object. Women's convention defines "the term 'discrimination against women' as any distinction, exclusion or restriction made on the basis of sex which has the effect or purpose of impairing or nullifying the recognition, enjoyment or exercise by women, irrespective of their marital status, on a basis of equality of men and women, of human rights, and fundamental freedoms in the political, economic, social, cultural, civil or any other field".[6]

In *Surfacing* Margaret Atwood shows a serious concern with women's destiny in a male dominated world. It is an attempt to expose male prejudices against women's creativity and talent. The novel is a novel about search for identity and self-discovery and it intends to highlight the imbalance of power between sexes. Wimsatt has pointed out, "The beauty of the book is that it saves everything. All the themes Margaret Atwood has been brooding over for years (successfully, in five volumes of verse and a less-noticed novel) are here tied together and made into a whole that is much more than the sum of its parts. The title is better than accurate, it is a well developed metaphor."[7] Annis Pratt looks at *Surfacing* in terms of "a quest for rebirth and transformation".[8] It deals with what Margaret Atwood refers to in *Survival* as "the Canada-as-collective Victim" theme because she is seriously concerned with "the country's predicament as a political victim",[9] and voices Margaret Atwood's sensitiveness to the impact of Canada's border relationship with the United States of Canadian consciousness—the threat of Americanism to Canada's national identity.

Surfacing, thus tells many stories and the stories it tells are inexorably linked to Margaret Atwood's strongly expressed socio-political vision a feminist and a nationalist and as 'a social vehicle'. She makes us feel through her novel that we have not yet landed into an era of post-feminism and there still is a need to change the society's attitude to women.

Josie P. Campbell claims that *Surfacing* goes "quite beyond the borders of Canada, except in details of place, despite her polemics in *Survival*...that consciousness is the central task of humankind everywhere".[10] Thus it is a great novel, in which the female protagonist returns to the natural world in search of mystical vision. Her quest can equally be interpreted as a search for a feminine discourse: her escapes from and challenge to the patriarchal social order.

Carol Christ traces the protagonist's journey from innocence and assumed powerlessness through the recognition of her complicity in evil to self-knowledge and the sense of power. Christ argues:

> Her association of power with evil and her dissociation of herself from both reflect a typical, female delusion of innocence, which hides her complicity in evil and feeds her false belief that she can do nothing but witness her victimization. In order to regain her power the protagonist must realize that she does not live in a world where only others have power to do evil.[11]

Margaret Atwood pays enormous attention throughout her work to myths and religious philosophies. These concerns lead Margaret Atwood to experiment with a range of genres including the Gothic, poetry, utopian or dystopian fiction as well as the mythical quest narrative of *Surfacing*. These genres are not static in her work since she interplays a variety of rhetorical styles and devices drawn from women's magazine as much as high culture. In her novel Margaret Atwood deals with the domestic scene and analyses the roles that women play as daughters, wives, mothers, etc. The protagonist of the novel seeks new definitions of the self and finally moves in different ways to achieve a changed social order. Margaret Atwood's new woman is concerned with arguing that she is a normal human being struggling with her imperfections to establish her identity.

The narrator in *Surfacing* learns to possess myth and identify her parents with Native American totems in her visions because she has a concern for ecological survival. Margaret Atwood's women often gain a self-identity by returning to their ancestors and the wilderness. In the words of Joseph Campbell, this return to her birth place is "a penetration to some source of power, and a life enhancing return".[12]

In *Surfacing*, Margaret Atwood is writing about a search for unity and wholeness in a "divided" person. The novel is divided into three parts. Part one describes the physical background and introduces the characters. The protagonist's father's disappearance and her search for him is described in this part. This section ends on a note of suspense and the narrator's decision to stay at Northern Quebec Island. In part one, narrator's false marriage and divorce and existence of her child, her abortion as a 'sin' shows her nature. The protagonist rejects her sin by constructing a network of deception and lies.

Part two continues to develop the rising action as the search for her missing father goes on. She discovers the truth of her father's missing and some shocking truth about herself. She accepts the truth of her sin that is her aborted baby. In this section the narrator recalls her past events that happened to her in her childhood, vision of her child, her mother, father, etc. that is why this part is in past tense. In the third and final section the narrator has gone from rejecting her sin to admit it. She gets pregnant and thinks that her lost baby is surfacing within her, forgiving her. At the end of this section the narrator emerges as a total human being, complete with feelings.

The unnamed narrator comes back from Toronto to Northern Quebec where she lived as a child. She is anxious and excited:

> I can't believe I'm on this road again, twisting along past the lake where the white birches are dying, the disease is spreading up from the south, and I notice they now have seaplanes for hire. (1)

This sentence foregrounds the dialectical opposition between Canada and America. The narrator finds that Canada is now a victim of Americanism. She remembers all features of the city at the time of her childhood. When she crossed the border into "home ground" the narrator states it foreign territory because she has not kept in touch with it; things have changed. She remembers her childhood, parents and feeling of total safety. She thinks that she did have a happy childhood. There she recalls her parents and her mother's painful death and her visit in the hospital.

The protagonist seems to have come back to her native place after nine years. The reason for this long, separation was that she was exploited by a man whom she loved. She could not face her parents after this disastrous incident and hence she decided not to return. She sent them a postcard regarding her wedding. She had a child but she had lost him to the husband whom she divorced.

While sitting with her friends, she thinks about her unsuccessful marriage and hopes that Anna and David's marriage is successful because they have some special things, knowledge which she missed out on. Now she thinks about her relationship with Joe which is cool and emotionless. Her decision to live with him was "more like buying a goldfish or a potted cactus plant" (36). Although she is fond of him, he doesn't mean very much to her. She says of her separation form her husband, "a divorce is like an amputation, you survive, but there's less of you" (36). The narrator's problem of a 'divided self' is also explained. Her separation from her child is described as "a section of my own life, sliced off from me like a Siamese twin, my own flesh cancelled". The narrator continues to look for clue to her father's disappearance. The search for her father becomes difficult and she thinks that she has done all she can to find him.

As her memories of the past intrude with increasing frequency, so does the occurrence of lies and deception. She tells many lies to her friends, even about herself. She recalls her memories and afraid that she will start inventing memories.

Now she is becoming increasingly concerned with her past and recognizes that something is wrong with her. She remembers her past with emotions but now acting as emotionless. She remembers the painful memories of her previous experience and when Anna tells the truth of her relationship with David, the protagonist believes marriages cannot be successful. Anna tells:

> He always does stuff like that to other women in front of me, he'd screw them with me in the room if he could. Instead he screws them somewhere else and tell me about it afterwards. (92)

The narrator thinks that David is just like her, "we are the ones that don't know how to love, there is something missing in us" (130). When she asks David about this, he tells her that Anna is unfaithful. The narrator realizes that Anna and David's marriage is not based on mutual love and respect. She thinks that there is lack of communication between David and his wife.

She remembers, that her so-called husband is actually her boy friend who is married; he wasn't able to marry her. She has been deprived of the joys and thrills of motherhood. She says:

> That was wrong. I never saw it. They scraped it into a bucket and threw it wherever they throw them, it was traveling through the sewers by the time I woke, back to the sea, I stretched my hand up to it and it vanished. (137)

She calls it a murder and feels that she is responsible for it, "I could have said no but I didn't; that made me one of them too a killer" (165).

This is the turning point in the story, now the narrator accepts her past. She has been lying to others about her marriage and child because she wanted to escape the moral responsibility for the death of her child. Now she presents herself as the victim of a broken marriage because that would not have been totally her fault. Her father's drowning body realizes the truth of her past. She feels her father's gift was knowledge, it teaches her how to see the truth and her mother's gift will teach her how to act:

> My mother's gift was there for me...the gift itself was a loose page, the edge torn, the figures drawn in crayon. On the left was a woman with a round moon stomach: the baby was sitting up inside her gazing out.... The picture was mine, I had made it. (152)

She receives it as a message from her mother to assume her maternal heritage by bearing a child. In Rigney's succinct words, "now she must become the mother".[13]

When her friends tell about her father's body she doesn't believe them. She was convinced that "nothing has died, everything is alive, everything is waiting to become alive" (153).

The final section of the novel is certainly to be understood from a psychological perspective, an experience in madness. The protagonist retreats into a primitive animal like state governed by a number of mysterious injunctions. Now she understands and follows her mother's message by performing sexual act with Joe and suspects she is pregnant. She immediately feels the benefits of sex is something more significant than pleasure:

> Pleasure is redundant, the animals don't have pleasure.... He trembles and then I can feel my lost child surfacing within me, forgiving me, rising from the lake where it has been prisoned for so long.... (155)

She feels full of power and begins to sense the presence of her parents. She is looking for the truth about herself. She is crying, show her grief and rage inspired by the death of her parents:

> I'm crying finally, it's the first time, ... But I'm not mourning, I'm accusing them, why did you? They chose it, they had control over their death, they decided it was time to leave and they left, they set up this barrier. They didn't consider how I would feel, who would take care of me. I'm furious because they let it happen. (166)

She re-experiences primitive emotion and childish thinking. Like a child who mistakes with for reality she endows her parents with godlike control over life and death. She removes her clothes, letting them float away. She purifies herself in the water, as water has long been used as a symbolic means of removing impurities:

> When I am clean I come up out of the lake, leaving my false body floated on the surface, a cloth on the surface, a cloth decoy; it jiggles in the waves I make, nudes gently against the dock. (172)

She survives on mushrooms, plants and berries. She merges with the forest, descending even further along the phylogenetic scale to the level of plants. She loses all sense of a personal identity and reaches a point of total oneness with nature, "I am a tree leaning". She thinks that if she wants to make contact with her parents, she must be in the condition they are in, she suddenly sees her mother:

> ...in front of the cabin, her hand stretched out, she is wearing her gray leather jacket, her hair is long, down to her shoulders in the style of thirty years ago, before I was born, she is turned half away from me. (176)

Next day Joe arrives with some men. She suddenly sees her father's vision and he has been transformed into a fish.

A fish jumped, carved wooden fish with dots painted on the sides, no, antlered fish thing drawn in red on cliff stone, protecting spirit. It hangs in the air suspended, fish turned to icon; he has changed again, returned to the water. How many shapes can he take (181).

Now the narrator realizes that her parents have gone, "They have gone finally, back into the earth, the air, the water, wherever they were when I summoned them" (219).

As Rigney points out, "the protagonist's return to sanity and to human existence is marked by her recognition that she must have food and shelter to survive, that she is neither animal nor primitive god and is therefore incapable of living alone in the wilderness. To live, she decides, is a responsibility to her parents, to society, to herself".[14]

She wants her baby to be "the first true human; it must be born, allow" (185). She refuses to be a victim and stop thinking that she is powerless:

> This above all, to refuse to be a victim. Unless I can do that I can do nothing. I have to recant, give up the old belief that I am powerless.... (222)

She recognizes her past problems with Joe and wants to solve it by avoiding each other and begin to talk she is no longer inclined to have imperfect relationship and predictable failures. It is on this note that the novel ends. It is full of hope.

In her novels, Margaret Atwood creates situations in which women, burdened by the rules and inequalities of their society, discover that they must reconstruct braver, self-reliant person in order to survive. These women faced hostile environment, struggle to overcome and to change systems that block and inhibit their security. *Surfacing* deals with the transformation of female characters from ingénues to insightful women. The narrator remains nameless in the book. She is a young commercial artist. In the process of discovering the circumstances surrounding her father's death, she regains touch with her past and her hidden emotional life. The narrator's father is a pacifist and rationalist. A botanist and tree scientist by profession, he retires to the family cabin where he begins studying Indian rock paintings. He wants to preserve the myth of pristine wilderness but failed to protect the island against devastation. He cannot see truth but with his maps, drawings and pictograph he can show the way to the place of the gods. His father is incapable of true vision because for him logic has never failed. He has always tried to reason away evil. For him even Hitler "many tentacles, ancient, and indestructible as the Devil" (148) is not, "the triumph of evil but the failure of reason" (65). It was to protect his family from evil and the irrationalities of civilization that he had secluded them in the Canadian wilderness where he thought that world war II would be just a subject for the game of children. He does not wish to reason away evil alone but religion too. He thinks that one has to struggle in order to survive. The protagonist learns from her father in her childhood the strategies of "staying alive" of hanging on in spite of all the obstacles one had to fight against. It was Paul who has written to the protagonist that her father has mysteriously vanished. Paul is her father's best friend. Although he is French Canadian, he speaks English. For her father, Paul represents the simple life and like her mother, he is closely linked with nature and growing things.

The narrator's relationship to her mother appears to have been more ambivalent than her relationship to her father. The protagonist's mother is presented as a nature figure in close harmony with her husband's ecological views and with the birds and flowers of their island sanctuary. Mother is remembered by

Paul's wife as a "good woman" and by the protagonist as the coauthor of his own "good childhood". Her mother is a distant and mysterious figure; the protagonist experiences her silent union with nature, her inwardness, and her flights into self as emotional absence. The narrator remembers her as a lonely woman, mild mannered and fond of birds and garden. Her mother died of cancer. The memory of visiting her mother in the hospital right before she died leaves behind a haunting maternal vision. The narrator thinks that the place of father and brother can be filled but the place of mother cannot be filled. The protagonist says, "Impossible to be like my mother; it would need a time warp; she was either ten thousand years behind the rest or fifty years ahead of them" (58). The place of mother has always remained unfulfilled for the protagonist. The narrator remembers her brother who "came home everyday beaten to a pulp" (81). Her brother was a realist, relished it early that one could be either a victim or an exploiter. As a baby her brother once came close to drowning. The narrator seems fascinated by this event. His brother is just opposite to his sister. In his early age he was attracted to science and violence and complements her attraction to fantasy and passivity. He works as a mineral rights explorer in Australia and out of touch with his family.

The protagonist returns to her home with three friends David, Anna and Joe. Anna is narrator's best friend, although they have known each other for only two months. Anna is a failed wife and is always compelled to present an artificially pleasant face in full make-up. She says if "I forgot my makeup he will kill me" (140). A woman has to wear the mask of artificiality as part of her victimization in married life. As Nancy A. Walker says, "reversals of the processes of civilization in *Surfacing* call into question the values of contemporary society, especially of those value impose upon women masks of artificiality".[15]

Anna is not satisfied with her marriage; she is a pathetic woman dependent upon a sadistic husband. Anna is harassed and assaulted as a matter of sexual humiliation masquerading as liberty, revolution, an escape from bourgeois morality. Her marriage is notable for its worst qualities—male sadism, female victimization, mutual deceit and treachery. The narrator realizes that the, "two feed off each other in an emotionally cannibalistic way, exchanging pain instead of love, victimizing and making object of each other. The emotional commitment and love that they have made to each other is rooted in mutual hatred. Anna fights him because she know that if she over surrendered the balance of power would be broken and he would go elsewhere to continue the war" (153-54).

Though Anna repeatedly mouths anti-male sentiments; she slaps layers of make up on her face for David's benefit and invariably sides with the men during moments of tension. This shows her insecurity and emotional weakness in her marriage. The narrator thinks that her friend is pseudo-feminist, a "folded imitation of a magazine picture that is itself an imitation of woman who is also an imitation, the original nowhere" (165). Anna is married but David does not want to get her pregnant, she takes pills for birth control because David compels her for taking these pills so that he can enjoy sex without risk. Anna is a willing victim and often victimized by David. She occupies position number three explained by Atwood in *Survival*. Anna typifies the woman who is inferiorized and idealized by the male will to power and implicitly becomes a metaphoric analogue for woman motif in her relation to David.

David teaches "communications" and is the most talkative of the groups. He is an ex-radio announcer and also once a theology student who sold bibles door to door. David never really seems to communicate with anyone especially his wife Anna. His conversation generally consists of insults, imitations of cartoon characters and political commentary. One cannot easily know what he really feels. He is a fake husband and tries to pose himself as one committed to the equality of women. David appeared in the beginning as charming and humorous but later revealed as vicious weapon used to hurt another person or to establish a position of power. David, like any other man, is possessive and oppressive. He tortures Anna and expects that she should follow those rules in their relationship, which are set by him. He himself is jealous, when he finds Joe and Anna missing, David tries to persuade the protagonist to let him enjoy sex with her not because he loves her but because he wants to revenge. "Tit for tat" is his policy. Men do not want a world that is different from the one they are used to enjoying because they perceive their roles as being under threat in a world that is different from any in the past.

The protagonist thinks that David cannot love anyone because he has not feelings for other. He thinks Anna as a slave and his private property; he can use her according to his needs. As Simone de Beauvoir says, "the male world is harsh, sharp edged, its voices are too resounding, the lights too crowds, the contracts rough".[16] David is a living fraud. Besides being a fake husband, he is also a fake nationalist. Though he voices anti-American slogans, he is as spiritually arid and as much of a killer and a little bug as the "Americans" in the novel.

Joe, the narrator's lover is a failed potter who wants to marry the protagonist. He makes large, difficult pots with a great deal of skill; he then distorts their shapes by bending them. His character in the novel is like a moody and silent person who links himself with nature. Joe is in one sense a better artist than any of the others. His squashed ceramic pots, unsold and unusable, litter their apartment in the city, he too is a failure, but at least he does not compromise, does not tell lies with art or reduces it to artifice.

The protagonist shares the flat with Joe but there is no sexual bond between them because the narrator thinks that he is not much different from other men. When Joe proposes her, she refuses his proposal because she doesn't love him. The protagonist distrusts love and marriage as savage bonds even though she is fond of Joe and wants to attach with him. Her relationship with Joe is characterized by refusal to feel or to commit herself in any real sense. When the protagonist is determined to conceive, she looks for a male companion. She chooses Joe as an option and performed the sexual act with Joe. She thinks she has been redeemed by recovering her lost child: There is no emotional involvement, she has actually used Joe.

The protagonist's journey to the family cabin, touches her with past and hidden emotional life. The protagonist is alienated from himself and from society without identity and name, without the ability to love or feel. She is a divided woman, literally schizophrenic and missing a crucial part of herself. At the beginning, she seems to be in search of a convincing, credible and predictable life. The search for her father leads onto something else—an exploration of her inner self, her nature as a woman and her place in Nature. In her childhood she was awkward and shy with other school children, they tease and torment her. As she grows older she begins to imitate the behaviour of others and does not say what she really feels. She is a psychological suicide, a woman with no name, an artist with no art form and no past or tradition that she can recall correctly. She can neither 'feel' nor 'communicate' effectively. The narrator cannot be trusted because she tells her parents, her friends, her present lover that she is divorced and the mother of a young child who lives with the former husband but actually she was never married. She was involved with her male art teacher. He feels nothing wrong in destroying her creativity as artist. His art teacher thinks that her aspiration to become a real artist is "cute but misguided" (58). The protagonist becomes a paralyzed artist instead of becoming a commercial artist and compelled to survive in a crippling state of utter humiliation. She is manipulated by male chauvinism and prevented from developing into artist.

The 'Art Teacher' insists her to terminate her pregnancy rather than disrupt his life. After her abortion she hates the city life because the city life represents sham relationships and hypocrisy. She comes back to find her missing father. Search for her father is not a literal search but for an integrated self which is the central concern in the novel, "It was no longer his death but my own that concerned me" (123). The protagonist is making a journey into the past history, her origin, in order to explore her own identity. Margaret Atwood believes that, "If you aren't too sure where you are, or if you are sure but you do not like it, there's a tendency both in psycho-therapy and in literature, to retrace your history to see how you got there."[17]

After discovering her father's body in the lake, the protagonist connects it with her aborted foetus. The surfacing body reminds her of her dead child, "I was emptied, amputated...they had planted death in me like a seed." The confused images of father and the aborted foetus jolt the protagonist into "a realization of patriarchal traps, the traps of socialization in which women are largely complicit".[18]

It is this seed of death which turns her cold towards life. She needed to throw out this seed, it is only after this. She needed to throw to realization that her frozen attitude towards life begins to warm into life. The union with Joe gives her a vision of her dead child. She realizes that motherhood would lead her to self-recognition. She thinks that the only way for her of expiating the sin of having killed the previous baby is to conceive again, to produce a baby and to mother it. The baby is necessary not only to her personal psychic salvation, but also to the salvation of the world. The protagonist feels that the past is dead and cannot support life. She struggles to free herself from her sense of victim hood. The power struggle in fact, seems to have come to an end. She feels so confident about her own powers and realizes:

> No gods to help me now they're questionable once more, theoretical as Jesus. (183)

The protagonist has recovered her capacity for love and freedom. She emerges triumphant and finds wholeness and integrity. The protagonist wishes to give birth to a truly human child and a supporter of ideal society.

The other characters in the novel are Mr. Percival the narrator's employer; who is a publisher of children's books. He is a Canadian by nationality but is interested in publishing only that which can sell in the English and American market. The protagonist ironically calls him "a cautious man", avoids any book illustrations that he finds disturbing. He asks narrator to create illustrations, which do not fit her perceptions of a child's taste. The narrator called Quebec Folk Tales as lifeless and commercial. Bill Malmstrom is a member of the Detroit branch of the Wild life Protection Association of America. An executive type who tries to look like an authentic "woodsy" type. He makes an offer to buy the cabin so that his group can use it as a retreat. He appears to be a typical "American" the narrator distrusts him.

Evan is an owner of the Blue Moon cabins. He is an old "bulky Laconic American" who works as a guide. The narrator hires him to take them to and fro the cabin. Claude is son of the owner of the village motel and bar. He is a thin "mottled" young man with an Elvis Presley haircut. In addition to helping his father run the bar, he works as a fishing guide.

The problem of establishing a personal and social identity is a recurrent theme in postcolonial literature: In *Surfacing* Margaret Atwood explores this problem in a manner which parallels that of third world writers in striking ways.

The female quest for identity is one of most important global phenomena today. This chapter presents the female quest for identity with reference to profession, marriage and motherhood. *Surfacing* depicts man's imposition on woman in these matters, which disables her intellectually, emotionally and morally. The novel questions and challenges woman's place in traditional discourse and suggest a rejection of such discourse. It confronts:

> ...convention and ideology, questioning what the masculine tradition has defined as "right" and "acceptable", and work[s] toward opening a space from which a woman can speak her desire—and in her discourse.[19]

The novel seems to interrogate the notion of identity formation, nationality, culture, language, gender, sex, childhood memories, the family relationships, human interaction with nature, etc. The protagonist of the story returns to the undeveloped island that she grew up on to search for her missing father; in the process, she unmasks the dualities and inconsistencies in both her personal life and her patriarchal society. Through the struggle to reclaim her identity and roots, the surfacer begins a psychological journey that leads her directly into the natural world. Like the journey itself, the language, events and characters in Margaret Atwood's novel reflect a world that oppresses and dominates both femininity and nature. Margaret Atwood's *Surfacing* has been interpreted as a feminist novel. This novel can be explained in terms of ecofeminism also.

Colonialism and patriarchy are seen as power structures that exploit. In Canada, colonial exploitation is seen as a kind of exploitation of both Nature and women. Colonial power structures have gone deep into the collective unconsciousness of Canada and have become metaphor for feminine and nature exploitation for women writers in that country. This gives rise to Ecofeminism.

Joyce Nelson says, "Ecofeminism bridges the gap between ecology and feminism: strands of analysis which have existed side by side over past decades without necessarily intertwining. By making explicit the connections between a misogynist society and a society which has exploited 'mother earth' to the point of environmental crisis: Ecofeminism has helped to highlight the deep splits in patriarchal paradigm."[20]

Ecofeminist theory links the oppression of women with the oppression of nature. More specifically, "ecological feminism is the position that there are important connections—historical experiential, symbolic, theoretical—between the domination of women and the domination of nature, an understanding which is crucial to both feminism and environmental ethics".[21]

The protagonist grows up in a masculine world where "it was worse for a girl to ask questions than for a boy". If a boy asked a question the other boys would make derisive sucking noises with their mouths but if a girl asked one the other girls would say "Think you're so great" in the washroom afterwards (112).

Thus growing up in a culture saturated with male bias, women remain reconciled to their own inferiority. Margaret Atwood draws attention to the fact that "the world is masculine on the whole; those who fashioned it ruled it, and still dominate it today, are men".[22]

In *Surfacing* the narrator of the story remains nameless throughout the novel. Commenting on the namelessness of the heroine Nancy A. Walker says that the narrator, "lacks a clearly defined 'self' that can be named".[23] Being nameless the protagonist says to her friend Anna:

> I no longer have a name. I tried for all those years to be civilized but I'm not and I'm through pretending. (162)

It can be said that by depriving her protagonist of a name, Margaret Atwood has been able to suggest that *Surfacing* is not a story of a particular woman but of the millions of women all over the world who may identify themselves with her.

Men resist women's demands for equality. David says outwardly, "I'm all for the equality of women" (132) warns Anna:

> "None of that women's Lib", David said, his eyes lidding, "or you'll be out on the street. I won't have one in the house, they're preaching random castration, they get off on that, they're roving the streets in savage bands armed with garden shears." (104)

David acts as the all powerful and dominating male figure. Because of him, Anna learns to control herself and her appearances. To keep her marriage together she immunes herself to his often brutal use of the language. Anna suffers from a devasting feeling that David wishes for her death, even in her dreams. She is haunted by this feeling. David has his own rules as Anna says, "He's got this little set of rules. If I break one of them I get punished, except that he keeps changing them, I'm never sure. He's crazy, there's something missing in him, you know what I mean? He likes to make me cry because he can't do it himself" (116).

David completely separates himself from all personal emotions and feelings. Anna struggles to get through the mental anguish that he dumps on her. Anna is disgusted with David's exclusive concern with his own needs, with his unconcern for her health. David is a moody man who is not supportive of women's dream. In one horrifying scene, he orders her to strip off her clothes for the movie.

Anna humiliated by the request, nevertheless complies. David succeeds in taking her nude photographs. This makes Anna feel helpless, powerless and expressionless. The protagonist recalls, "The way she was crying, climbing up the sand hill, it was yesterday, since then she has crystallized" (159).

The narrator shows tremendous courage to react against male oppression. She unwinds the camera film and throws into the lake. Thus the protagonist shows her contravention against nude and seminude movies in which women are paid to act in an indecent manner for the sake of stardom, name and fame. She enjoys, watching, "the invisible captured images...swimming away into the lake like tadpoles" (160).

The protagonist discovers that after marriage women's exploitation, oppression and victimization gets sharpened. According to her marriage is nothing but a surrendering of values and distortion of the identity of a woman. Thus the protagonist's journey into the interior provides her, "a means for tapping emotions that would otherwise remain inexpressible, and reveals aspects of her personality hitherto hidden".[24] In an interview Margaret Atwood says, "It seemed to me that getting married would be a kind of death."[25] According to Margaret Atwood, marriage should follow love. A marriage which is not based on mutual love is meaningless. The narrator says she was fool to enter into the bond of marriage. But in reality she never got married. Her lover was a "middle aged", "second hand" and "selfish" man. He has refused to marry her because he is married. The narrator feels shattered when he shows the photographs of his wife and children, "they had names, he said I should be mature" (143).

She is betrayed by selfish lover but says, "for him I could have been anyone but for me he was unique, the first, that's where I learned. I worshipped him...I kept scraps of his handwriting like saints' relics..." (142).

She refuses Joe's marriage proposal, "The finality; and he'd got the order wrong, he'd never asked whether I loved him, that was supposed to come first. I would have been prepared for that" (80).

Joe does not realize the need for it because men except women to be absolutely passive and also because they think marriage is a woman's destiny. The relationship between the protagonist and Joe, offers an interesting insight into male/female dichotomy. The protagonist's acceptance of the partnership is almost fatalistic. She realizes that for Joe sexual need is primary and he wants to dominate and control her. She perceives a killer and victimizer in him.

We can notice the split between the narrator's feminine self that is peace and harmony in married life and her feminist self which suggests Anna to walk out of marriage instead of suffering. Her imaginary divorce caused her tremendous pain and suffering. Remembering her parent's reaction on her divorce she says:

> They never forgave me, they didn't understand and divorce, I don't think they even understood the marriage, which wasn't surprising since I didn't understand it myself. What upset them was the way I did it, so suddenly, and then running off and leaving my husband and child, my attractive full-colour magazine illustrations, suitable for framing. (23)

The narrator cannot forget the misery abortion has caused her. She says: "I couldn't accept it, that mutilation, ruin I'd made" (137).

The narrator loves her art teacher who uses all his skill to seduce her. He gave a wedding ring and almost succeeds in creating the image of himself as her husband. When she is pregnant, he uses all tricks to abort the child. For him it is "simple like getting a wart removed" (138).

The unnatural act of her abortion and the continual struggle for her to feel comfortable with words and language illustrate the extent to which society or man oppressed and consumed the surface. Both empowering and dominating nature of her ex lover shows:

> The unborn child was my husband's, he imposed it on me, all the time it was growing in me I felt like an incubator. He measured everything he would let me eat, he was feeding it on me, he wanted a replica of himself. (28)

Margaret Atwood is emphasizing the fact that men exploit the bodies of women for their needs. They have controlled the process of childbirth which nature has assigned only to women. Men want women to remain powerless victim so:

> They shut you into a hospital, they shave the hair off you and tie your hands down and they don't let you see, they

> don't want you to understand, they want you to believe it's their power not yours. They stick needles into you so you won't hear anything, you might as well be a dead pig, your legs are up in a metal frame, they bend over you, technicians, mechanics, butchers, students clumsy or snickering practicing on your body. (74)

Margaret Atwood's "*Surfacing* takes woman as an existential condition, the condition of being powerless and manipulatable".[26] Since power is centralized in the hands of man, they feel nothing wrong in destroying her dignity or creativity. According to them, a woman has no right to have a baby without a husband. When the pregnancy of the protagonist concluded not in childbirth but in abortion the narrator feels emptied, amputated.

Margaret Atwood displays a superb, penetrating awareness of the traumatic experiences of abortion in the life of sensitive woman. Sushila Singh, an exponent of feminism in India thinks that, "the trauma of abortion has never been dealt with such an extraordinary understanding before in fiction".[27] The protagonist undergoes emotional and artistic death at the hands of her teacher. It is a "planted death in her". As Malashri Lal says, "...the pain of aborting life unhinges the minds to a degree that it creates an alternate 'truth' to the event".[28]

The protagonist suffers from a guilt complex and decides to conceive a baby and resolved that, "this time I won't let them" (187).

The narrator wants to prove that the process of childbirth is women's power not men's and a woman can deliver the baby the natural way. She says:

> This time I will do it myself.... The baby will slip out easily as an egg, a kitten and I'll lick it off and bite the cord, the blood retiring to the ground where it belongs; the moon will be full, pulling. In the morning I will be able to see it: it will be covered with shining fur, a God. (156)

After her abortion, the protagonist comes to develop deep sympathy for the flora and fauna of the Quebec Island. She finds that the beauty of Nature is being destroyed by the Americans. The relationship between nature and Americans is relationship of exploitation and the entire landscape has been mutilated, raped:

> Further in the trees they didn't cut before, the flood are marooned, broken and gray white tipped on their sides, their giant contorted roots bleached and skinless; on the sodden trunks are colonies of plants, feeding on disintegration; laurel, sundew the insect eater, its toe nail-sized leaves sticky with red hairs. Out of the leaf nests the flowers rise, pure white, flesh of gnats and midges petals now, metamorphosis. (161)

Within *Surfacing*, power and domination directly oppress, both the feminine world and the natural world. From the human driven need to control the dam to the destruction of older trees.

Ecofeminists argue that two very defined, contradictory, and dualistic worlds exist in the patriarchal society the feminine and the masculine; on the one hand, the feminine principle represents Mother Nature, the body, irrationality, emotion, invitation and mysticism. On the other hand, the masculine principle represents rationality logic, separation from nature, the head, intellectualism, language and concrete reality. The Surfacer tries to re-unite these two dualities:

> The trouble is all in the knob at the top of our bodies. I'm not against the head or the body either: only the neck, that creates the illusion that they are separate.... If the head extended directly into the shoulders like a worm's or a frog's without that constriction, that lie, they wouldn't be able to look down at their bodies and move them around as if they were robots or puppets; they would have to realize that if the head is detached from the body both of them will die. (75)

The surfacer struggles with the notion that the head (a masculine element) should be remotely separated from the body (a feminine element). In order for each to prosper to the fullest extent, they must work together. The narrator, in the last few pages, sees the natural world as her equal, refuses to fall into the same patriarchal trap that initially destroyed her, and reclaims her ability to trust. Though she does not return to society, she does so as a changed person. She realizes, "that human beings are not radically separate from nature: that the fulfilment of our humanity is profoundly linked with learning to appreciate the nature within us and without" (43) standing there, with, "the trees [surrounding her]...asking and giving nothing", she has embraced the ecofeminist ideal.

Narrator's journey ends off discovering about herself. She discovers about herself and her relation with the world. She explores the power-politics in interpersonal relationship and relates the women's crisis of identity not only to the patriarchal structures of power and domination but also to the women's passivity and complicity in the power structures that subject and subjugate them.

Despite her fear of the consequences, her search for her missing father and her search for self increasingly offers her the power to resist the oppression inherent in their relationship and to reassess her own need. Margaret Atwood seems to be questioning the existing power politics, the traditional notions of male superiority, the mutilation of women by men. She is trying to assert that women can refuse victimization and can gain transcendence from the male defined world and can hope to breathe freely in a world defined by them. Emma Parker says:

> Her rejection of, and return to [nature] society is reflected by what she eats. When she rejects culture and retreats into the wilderness to become a "natural" woman, she gives up eating processed food. Such food is contaminated in the same way that society is contaminated by patriarchal ideology. Both are unnatural constructed man made and both threaten to poison her. Instead, the narrator eats only the raw food that nature provides.[29]

In her search for her identity, the narrator achieves her enlightenment. She rejects the male domination, the odious elements of civilization, its value, its clothing and its canned food. She thinks, "everything from history must be eliminated", (205) because history situates woman as an object. She rejects the world that has victimized her, and refuses to be a victim and creates her own reality. Thus, she fulfils the third and fourth victim positions described by Margaret Atwood in *Survival.* Third position is acknowledgement of the fact of being a victim but a repudiation of the victim role and fourth is becoming a creative non victim. She, "gives up the old belief that I am powerless and because of it nothing I can do will over hurt anyone. A lie which was always more disastrous than the truth would have been" (185). The power struggle seems to have come to an end. She feels so confident about her own power. This is a great feminist awakening. The discovery of her selfhood is emphatically feminist as it is located in the experiences of the body and the mind, and in understanding a woman's relation to institutions and social processes.[30] Now, the protagonist comes to know about her own powers that she can achieve something. She can understand herself as a victim and attains the feminist consciousness i.e. women's power and potential.

Surfacing represents the feminine consciousness and shows a woman's struggle to free herself. Her association with the people and Nature raises her consciousness of victimization of woman. When her feminist consciousness reaches its climax, the protagonist makes ready the ground for revolt against exploitation oppression. As Carol Christ says, narrator awakens, "from a male-defined world, to the greater terror and risk, and also the great potential healing and joy, of a world defined by the heroine's own feeling and judgement".[31]

In order to attain her identity she feels, she must avoid every association with the "metal" killer society and go back into the remotest forest. In course of this impassioned, desperate search she takes her plunge literally in the ancient lake, mentally in the memory of her parents and mystically in the vision of their continued existence in Nature. She also tries to attain some unknown but ancient wisdom, which might have been behind the rock paintings. At the end she reverses the mirror in order "not to see myself but to see", and alone resumes her journey which finally brings her through extreme hardship to the symbolic plunge and to resurface—this time with the defiance never to be a victim any more. The protagonist moves from struggling with the oppression and domination of the male world to associating with various feminine principles and motifs to eventually embracing and returning to the natural world as an equal, unassuming member. This unnatural act of her abortion and the continual struggle for her to feel comfortable with words and language illustrate the extent to which society oppressed and consumed the narrator. The abortion itself illustrates the feminist thought. The abortion rather effectively illustrates the side effect of a patriarchal rational and oppressing world. The negative impact of the abortion takes its toll on the narrator. In her healing process, she begins identifying with highly symbolic character, the dead heron. The horrifying and unnecessary murder of the heron presents a direct parallel to the experiences of the narrator. She feels the deep disgust towards the killing of the bird. She compares it with oppression and harassment of women. Margaret Atwood shows men's misuse and women's use of nature in *Surfacing*. Women's association with fertility and men's with environment abuse specifically as a metaphor of the violation of women by men. Men leave detritus of used beer cans, which spoils the fruit, and vegetable bounty of nature. The protagonist discovers the truth that woman is not a denomination of sex but a symbol stands for all those beings who are powerless, vulnerable such as all the weak people, trees, and animals. There is rejection of patriarchy by the symbolic destruction of the male figures of authority and mother child bonding emerges as the centre of the new feminist world in one protagonist to give birth to herself through her child and in another the very idea of its not having taken root. Margaret Atwood literally pours her feminine and feminist soul into being through her female protagonist. The novel revolves around the relationship between the man and woman. There are two types of relationship, one is between the married husband and wife and other is without marriage relationship. In both cases the female is engaged with a middle-aged man. The females are with loss of identity, the muteness and uncommunicative, but at last they understand the power of women. The protagonist chooses the path of isolation and back to the city to face life, Emerging as a New woman, the protagonist is not only aware of her colonized status but is also challenging traditional notions detesting the idea of being treated as a decorative piece or a commodity. Margaret Atwood's 'New

Woman' is concerned with arguing that she is a normal human being struggling with her imperfections to establish her identity. The protagonist of the novel desires to organize all the weak victims to protest against the oppression of strong victimizers. Thus, she becomes a leader for all exploited person by turning a feminist theme into a universal one in which the battle is not only between two sexes but also between the strong and weak. She ends up as an activist. She says:

> They'll mistake me for a human being, a naked woman wrapped in a blanket: possibly that's what they've come here for, it's running around loose, ownerless, why not take it. They won't be able to tell what I really am. But if they guess my true form, identity, they will shoot me or bludgeon in my skill and hang me up by the feet from a tree. (177)

A natural woman, for a male dominated society is one who is powerless and hence exploitable, consumable.

Margaret Atwood's *Surfacing* is set in Canada; her concerns are not with the questions of multi-culturalism, which are bound up with Canadian life and letters, but with the psychic tensions of a woman striving for a discovery of real self. *Surfacing* depicts against the society, against the backdrop of the female subjugation through enticement or force and the subsequent panic and emptiness shows a woman groping for some assurance through past and nature.

According to Joseph Campbell we live in accordance with our myths but Margaret Atwood strongly disapproves of unnatural boundaries. She, "identifies human failure as acquiescence in those western dichotomies which postulate the inescapable, static divisions of the world into hostile opposites: culture/nature, male/female, straight line/curved space, head/body, reason/instinct, victor/victim".[32] Besides rejecting moral boundaries, Margaret Atwood also rejects literary boundaries as is evident from the manner in which she structures *Surfacing*.

This novel defines teleological linearity and denies all predictability of plot. The plot is the story, which the novelist uses as narrative which in the course of its progress is remembered, dreamed, invented, contradicted, rediscovered, dissolved or distorted.

The heroine of *Surfacing* employs a different discourse, which challenges the readers to see if English language can compel the tale to a more meaningful communication. She ceaselessly contradicts the babble of sound inherent in the social chatter of the Western society of America. Her voice seeks to drawn the so-called civilization noises and rise above the debased media noise, machine noise and mouth noise. It subversively employs the enemy's (man's) language to build a system of lies and disguises, to arrive at a new perspective. Her point of view becomes a theme, which refers to the new meanings within words. Her fiction is more concerned with the narrative than with images. She has greater concern for tangible feeling, which the individuals can orally transmit. The nameless narrator tries to make us aware of man's suicidal violence against nature and tries a strong note of protest. She clarifies:

> It wasn't the men I hated, it was the Americans, the human beings, men and women both. They'd had their chances but they turned against the gods. (151)

Margaret Atwood also becomes a social critic in her use of anti-Americanism in the book. When the protagonist discovers that the men responsible for the senseless killing of the heron are Canadians, she says that it doesn't matter what country they're from, they're still Americans. The narrator finds that nature is being contaminated and spoiled by business and modern technology. American comes to represent anyone who is alienated from nature. In fact:

> Americanism is an ideology and it infiltrates the minds and life-styles of the people of the less powerful, less affluent, submissive countries and then the diseased ideology does not have to derive a direct inspiration from America, for it turns self begetting, self proliferating. Ideological imperialism is the most important international phenomenon, and millions or billions of dollars are spent daily to keep this disease growing, spreading. There is a valid economic and political rationale for so much expenditure. If people of the poor countries turn American in their thoughts, dreams, aspirations, ideas, then real hard business automatically follows.[33]

Americans kill the nature just for fun, for recreation and establishing their power. They senselessly kill the heron, the protagonist sees her own predicament in the death of the heron. The image of the dead heron also presages the dead body of the drowned father. She feels that Americans wish to exploit and victimize Canadians and their country both geographically and psychologically. She hates Americans and so sick of them that she wishes them dead. The narrator thinks that to be an American is unable to understand that we must treat the universe with care because nature is sacred. The anti-Americanism in the novel is not against the United States but against those people who are destroying the planet, nature.

In *Surfacing*, the protagonist thinks in terms of images. The novel replaces the images of division and death with image of unity, wholeness and life. The images are indicative of Margaret Atwood's sensory experiences. According to Woodcock no wonder "If among modern Canadian poets there is in spirit a true descendant of the imagist, it is Margaret Atwood."[34] Margaret Atwood portrays almost life like pictures in her book. She has drawn the pictures so minutely that it shows visual image to the reader. This visual quality of her prose makes it a painter's novel. She has used words somewhat as an artist uses paints, to blend with or to offset one another.[35] In *Surfacing* the auditory powers of the protagonist is so strong that she can hear the sound of love in the north, a kiss, a slap. Her strong hearing sense enable her to hear even "a tiny insect voice". She can hear every voice and says, "Bird's song wakes me.... I listen, my ears are rusty, and there's nothing but a jumble of sound." The protagonist dislikes loud voices. Her sense of smell is also strong, she is capable not only of recalling her past but "I could recall the exact smells". She describes "the smell of lemon polish" while recalling the place where she was taken for abortion. Margaret Atwood also describes the protagonist's food habits as gustatory images. There is the contrast in her food habits in the beginning and the end of the novel. In the beginning she takes tinned food, fish and all kind of foods but in the end she rely on uncooked food. *Surfacing* is fulfil with the images that appeal to the sense of touch, in spite of the fact that the protagonist compares her state to that of the babies who are born "without a sense of touch".

Margaret Atwood uses thermal images for example the lake "is blue and cool". Anna tells the protagonist that she is "cold blooded". The sun is "hot and bright" the protagonist is "cold with fear". The images which are closely connected with narrator's vision of life and integral part of the her perception. The image of nature and Canada is a victim. David is a victim of Americanism and enjoys victimizing other's Anna is also a victim, as a woman and of civilization. Females are victimized by males. The protagonist herself is a biological victim of a man who exploits her. Her unborn baby was killed for no fault. She feels guilty that she could not save her baby. The victim image is sustained till the end of the narrative when the narrator comes to feel that she is strong enough. The animals and human beings are interlinked in narrator's vision. She recalls her unborn and aborted child as an imprisoned frog. The narrator thinks, "an unborn baby has its eyes open and can look out through the walls of the mother's stomach, like a frog in a jar". The images of human get mixed with the images of animals. She calls Joe "like the buffalo on the U.S. nickel". The protagonist recalls her mother as a "bird". David often refers to Americans as "pigs". David wants Anna to look "like a young chick". The protagonist refers to the baby to be born as "shape of a goldfish now in my belly". Margaret Atwood uses images of animal in the context of human beings. She wants to say that animals are not different from human beings, though they have a tendency to victimize animals. She thinks that in many ways animals are better than human beings.

The protagonist of *Surfacing*, in her childhood, wanted to be an artist but due to her art teacher she gave up the dream of becoming a real artist She uses image of colours in her language as colour adjectives. She uses colour for certain patterns with a specific purpose as she visualizes her mother holding the tree, white birch" (159), she uses white colour with nature black in a sharp contrast to white. The dead body of her father is seen as "dark oval trailing limbs" (162).

Red colour is associated with feelings, emotions and passions. The protagonist in *Surfacing* is emotionless so red seems to be missing from her life. "I can't use red" (60). She regrets Green is associated with nature. The green is cool and comfortable and also associated with the protagonist's parents. Brown shows animals that are nearer to nature than are human. Gray is associated with the protagonist's past. She recalls her mother with "a gray leather jacket". Orange denotes artificiality and seduction. Pink and purple is associated with city, power and evil. The narrator dislikes both pink colour and city life, but Anna loves an artificial life. The protagonist journey in the novel is from colourlessness to colours.

The image of death and disease is associated with the death of her father, her aborted unborn child, her mother, animals and nature. She says that ever since her abortion, she had "carried the death inside me", and "Do you realize...that this country is founded on the bodies of dead animals? Dead fish, dead seals, and historically dead beavers" (43-44). The protagonist sees Americanism as a disease. Most of the time she is disturbed by the images of traps. The baby she got aborted "was in a bottle curled up staring out at me like a cat picked—I couldn't let it out, it was dead already" (163). The mirror shows the divisions of self and it differentiates us from our real selves. As Grace says, "The narrator perceives Anna's soul as trapped in her compact mirror just as her body is trapped by the celluloid image in the camera."[36]

The protagonist is a divided self, so she cannot respond as a whole. She describes herself just "a head" or as "a severed thumb". She describes the different parts of Joe's body and looks fascinated by different parts of the body, "arms without hands", "the cut off pieces of early martyrs", etc.

The island shows alienation as it is cut off from the city. City life symbolizes false life and pretences. Image of water related with death as well as life. The death of her unborn baby and her father's drowning dead body is associated with water.

The symbolic journey of the protagonist realizes her to accept her capacity for evil as well as her complicity in the evil-engendering process. She also realizes that she must give up her passivity that has destroyed her wholeness. The symbolic conception towards the end, indicates the re-birth of her aborted child. Margaret Atwood says "the heroine of *Surfacing* does not end where she began".[37] The narrator returns to society, there is a tremendous transformation in her personality for the better. She returns to struggle and survive with dignity.

The setting of *Surfacing* is more than physical background. It helps highlight several of the ideas Margaret Atwood has set out to explore. The idea of dualism, two different things opposing one another, occurs throughout the novel, most noticeably in the apparent separation between the narrator's mind and her body or emotions. It is also connected with the character's journey. The story opens with an ordinary journey and ends with the journey of self-realization.

Margaret Atwood's experience as a poet can be seen in *Surfacing*. The language she uses in this book reveals things about the protagonist because she presents it as if it is the protagonist's choice of words. The language is cool, impersonal and precise. It effectively conveys the narrator's cool approach to life and her inability to feel. Margaret Atwood's protagonist argues that the common definition of sanity is, "To have someone to speak to and words that can be understood" (220).

She knows that language helps maintain mutual interdependence of self and world. She asserts, "a language is everything you do" (148). Margaret Atwood also thinks that any language, which does not contain sufficient words for subtle feelings to like love, is "wrong" because it cannot convey the exact meaning of the word.

In *Surfacing*, the protagonist herself uses language to falsify reality. She keeps misleading everyone with the help of language. As the narrator begins her strange visionary experience towards the end of the book, however, the language begins to change. The drastic change in the language reflects the changes in the narrator. The language becomes less complicated and more direct, less intellectual and more emotional, just as the narrator does.

Margaret Atwood has exploited juxtaposition of opposites in *Surfacing*. It is one of the features, which give clarity and intensity to her prose. Few examples are, the protagonist recalls "a wooden house with two doors and a man and a woman who lived inside" (26). She feels that "pleasure and pain are side by side" (128).

Frequent use of similes and metaphors is indicative of Margaret Atwood's poetic, imaginative mind. She uses it from the most common everyday elements and as a way of experiencing the facts.

The symbols in *Surfacing* work to support the themes. Images of separation and dualism are common in the book. One symbol comes to represent the idea of unity or wholeness: the fish, water and air, work together to provide powerful symbols. They highlight the protagonist's psychological quest into herself. The images, similes and metaphors that the narrator chooses to describe other people reveal a great deal about the character of narrator and other. Images of fragmentation come frequently in the novel. They reinforce the idea of the narrator's separation of her head from her body, one of the central ideas of the book. Image of death and decay can be linked to the rediscovery of her child's death and discovery of her father's death. They also highlight the emotional "death" that has taken place with the surfacer. Image of mirrors and cameras reinforce the idea of the stealing of identity or soul. In *Surfacing*, the choice of motherhood represents a fusion of the personal and mythic, but it is not to be seen as a categorical imperative. In Margaret Atwood's utopian vision woman leads the way, but she does not do it alone, the male too is necessary, if only as progenitor. Having coupled with Joe, the protagonist says, "I'm grateful to him, he's given me the part of himself I needed" (191).

Certain major themes lead up to and converge in the novel's cataclysmic ending. Those which command our attention are: the search for parents, the relationship of female to male, the confrontation with the existential reality of non-being, and the opposition between death and life as symbolized in the experiences of abortion and childbirth. All of these concerns are embedded within a central topes, which is the search for self or rather, the destruction of a fabricated self in order to allow a more authentic self to "Surface".

The images and symbols that have been discussed here show how through these images one feel as if he is participating in all that is happening. The images, in fact, provide a life like quality to Margaret Atwood's prose. She creates the exact desired significance with the help of these images, symbols, etc. *Surfacing* shows a new hope that a woman can emerge as a New woman with a new courage to lead an authentic life. In Rigney's words, "possibility of self-actualization for woman despite the psychologically divesting effects of the male supremacist societies in which they live".[38] Thus, *Surfacing* raises the consciousness among women that even though the male world tends to allow woman no other place except that of an object. It is not impossible for women to deconstruct the myth of 'femininity', to refuse a secondary place in the world.

Margaret Atwood wishes men to understand that death of woman is the death of mankind, that "if I die it dies, if I starve it starves with me...it must be born, allowed" (185). Hence, the need of the hour is to keep women alive, physically as well as psychologically. In fact, two sexes are complementary and neither is complete without the other. It justifies Margaret Atwood's effort to present her idea of feminism before the world through her fiction. The protagonist's return to human existence at the end of the novel is, Rigney says, "To Live, she decides, is a responsibility to her parents, to society, to herself."[39]

In *Surfacing*, the choice of motherhood represents a fusion of the personal and mythic, but it is not to be seen as a categorical imperative. Margaret Atwood believes that all Canadian artists are schizophrenics of one kind or another. She writes:

> We speak to isolated people as being "cut off", but in fact something is cut of, from them; as artists, deprived of audience and cultural tradition, they are mutilated. If your arm or leg has been cut off you are a cripple, if your tongue has been cut off your are a mute, if part of your brain has been removed you are an idiot or an amnesiac, if your balls have been cut off you are a eunuch or a castrate.... Artists have

suffered emotional and artistic death at the hands of an indifferent or hostile audience.[40]

But the protagonist of *Surfacing* emerges triumphant. The narrator has come to realize that it is the binary vision, which creates problems and leads to disintegration. Rejecting the dualistic vision, she seems to have discovered:

> A new way of being, a third way that transcends polarizations, thus enabling the individual to be free of crippling limitations.[41]

At the end 'the winning and losing games are finished' for Margaret Atwood's protagonist. Now she realizes that she cannot turn away from society but can be cautious. She has been recovering the part of herself she had lost. Her journey has been a journey from death to life, from withdrawal to reintegration with society.

Surfacing leaves us with a vision of madness that is meaningful for the individual and symbolic for the species. As a narrative about psychic disintegration and reintegration, it is a noteworthy example of the modern psychiatric novel.[42]

The protagonist seems prepared to return to the city with new courage and is prepared for challenges of life. She emerges as a brave new woman who is capable of establishing her identity.

REFERENCES

1. Rigney, Barbara Hill. *Margaret Atwood, Women Writer Series*. London: Macmillan Education, 1987.
2. White, Roberta. "Margaret Atwood: Reflections in a convex mirror", *Canadian Women: Writing Fiction*. ed. Mic Pearlman Jackson. University Press of Mississippi, 1993, 61.
3. Frye, Northrop. "Conclusion", *Literary History of Canada: Canadian Literature in English*, 2nd ed. Carl F. Klinck, III. Toronto: University of Toronto Press, 1976, 321.
4. Grace, Sherill. *Violent Duality: A Study of Margaret Atwood,* ed. Ken Norris. Montreal: Vehicle Press, 1980, 108.
5. Mckenna, Isobel. *The Town and Country*. Dec. 13, 1972.
6. Women's Convention on the Elimination of All Forms of Discrimination Against Women, 1979.

7. Wimsatt, Margaret. "Surfacing", *Commonwealth,* 7 Sept. 1973, 483.
8. Pratt, Annis. "Surfacing and the Rebirth Journey", *The Art of Margaret Atwood: Essays in Criticism*, eds. Cathy N. and Arnold E. Davidson. Toronto: Anansi Press, 1981, 139.
9. Atwood, Margaret. *Survival: A Thematic Guide to Canadian Literature.* Toronto: Anansi, 1972, 242.
10. Campbell, Jossie P. "The Woman as Hero in Margaret Atwood Surfacing". *Mosaic,* No. 3, Spring 1978, 18.
11. Christ, Carol. "Margaret Atwood: The Surfacing of Women's Spiritual Quest and Vision", in *Signs*, Winter 1976, 320.
12. Campbell, Joseph P. *The Hero with a Thousand Faces.* 1949, rpt. Glasgow: Paladin Grafton Books, 1988, 35.
13. Rigney, Barbara Hill. *Madness and Sexual Politics in the Feminist Novel.* Madison: University of Wisconsin Press, 1978, 110.
14. Rigney, Barbara Hill. *Lilith's Daughters: Women and Religion in Contemporary Fiction.* Madison: University of Wisconsin Press, 1982, 89.
15. Walker, Nancy A. *Feminist Alternatives: Irony and Fantasy in the Contemporary Novel by Women.* Jackson: University Press of Mississippi, 1990, 149.
16. Beauvoir, Simone de. *The Second Sex.* Tr. & Edited by H.M. Parshley. Penguin Books, 1949, 557.
17. Atwood, Margaret. *Survival: A Thematic Guide to Canadian Literature.* Toronto: Anansi, 1972, 112.
18. Lal, Malashri. "Canadian Gynocritics: Contexts of meaning in Margaret Atwood's Surfacing", *Perspectives on Women: Canada and India*, ed. Aparna Basu. Delhi: Allied Publishers, 1995, 186.
19. Robinson, Sally. "The Anti-Logos Weapon: Multiplicity in Women's Texts", *Contemporary Literature*, 29.1, Spring 1988, 122.
20. Joyce, Nelson. "Speaking the Unspeakable", *Canadian Forum*, March 1990.
21. Warren. "The Power and the Promise of Ecological Feminism", *Environmental Ethics*, 235.
22. Beauvoir, 298.
23. Walker, Nancy A. *Feminist Alternatives: Irony and Fantasy in the Contemporary Novel by Women.* Jackson: University Press of Mississippi, 1990, 79.

24. Stewart, Grace A. *New Mythos: The Novels of the Artist as Heroine 1877-1977*. Montreal, Canada: Eden Press, Women's Publication, 1981, 156.
25. Valerie, Mine. "Atwood in Metamorphosis: An Authentic Fairy Tale" in Myrna Kastash, et al. *Her Own Woman: Profiles of Ten Canadian Women*. Toronto: MacMillan of Canada, 1975, 16.
26. Jaidev. "Problematizing Feminism", *Feminism and Recent Fiction in English*, ed. Sushila Singh. New Delhi: Prestige Books, 1992, 54.
27. Singh, Sushila. "Joyce Carol Oates and Margaret Atwood: Two Faces of the New World Feminism" in *Punjab University Research Bulletin*, Vol. 18, No. 1, 1987, 90.
28. Lal, 186.
29. Parker, Emma. "You Are What You Eat: The Politics of Eating in the Novels of Margaret Atwood", *Twentieth Century Literature*, 41.3, Fall 1995, 350-51.
30. Lal, 185.
31. Christ, Carol P. "Margaret Atwood: The Surfacing of Women's Spiritual Quest and Vision", *Signs: A Journal of Women in Culture and Society*, 2.2, Winter 1976, 325.
32. Grace, Sherill E. "Articulating the Space Between: Atwood's Untold Stories and Fresh Beginnings" in *Margaret Atwood: Language, Text and System*, *op. cit.*, 5.
33. Jaidev. "A Study of Margaret Atwood's Surfacing", *Lessons for M.Phil. English, Correspondence Courses*. Punjabi University Patiala, 1990, 66.
34. Woodcock, George. *The World of Canadian Writing: Critiques and Recollections*. Seattle: University of Washington Press, 1980, 151.
35. Weaver, Richard M. *A Rhetoric and Handbook*. New York: Holt Rinehert and Winston, 1967, 80.
36. Grace, 105.
37. Sandler, Linda. "Interview with Margaret Atwood", *The Malahat Review*, 4, January 1977, 14.
38. Rigney, 1978, 119.
39. Rigney, 1982, 89.
40. Atwood, 184-85.
41. Grace, 98.
42. Yalom, Marilyn. *Maternity, Mortality and the Literature of Madness*. London: The Pennsylvania State University Press, 1985.

Lady Oracle

4

> *Lady Oracle* re-imagines the Delphic Oracle again under the control of women. This is a figurative way of saying that the novel is attempting to imagine a way in which women can take back their rightful place as poets and writers. We can think of the various modes of writing in *Lady Oracle* as musing upon the place of gender in the politics of literary production....[1]
>
> Marilyn Patton

Lady Oracle published in 1976 is Margaret Atwood's third novel, a comic masterpiece in its parodies of literary forms and subversion of literary expectations. It is one such polymorphous text in which several strands are gathered together to give a pattern. She creates a new genre in the fictional kind. The novel is the portrait of the writer as woman and a "survivor" in a patriarchal culture. According to Sandra M. Gilbert and Susan Gubar, patriarchy has perpetuated a phallocentric myth of creativity in which literary production is a male prerogative throughout history. Hence they argue, "Women...must escape just those male texts which deny them the autonomy to formulate alternative to the authority that has imprisoned them."[2] By projecting woman writer and asserting her greater measure of freedom, Margaret Atwood seems to agree with Helene Cixous who argues that, "woman must write herself: must write about women and bring women to writing from which they have been driven away as violently as from their bodies".[3] As a female writer, the heroine of the novel Joan, "plays the part of a metaphorical sibyl, 'an oracle', for whom writing is a visionary experience".[4] The oracle is "beyond herself". Commenting on the significance of "Oracle" Howells says:

> An oracle is that it is a voice which comes out of a woman's body and is associated with hidden dangerous knowledge.... The voice of the Delphic Oracle was the voice of the god Apollo, or earlier the voice of the Earth Goddess.[5]

Joan Foster unfolds her oracle to reporter about the politics of gender. Virginia Woolf calls as the "Angle of the House" or damnation of woman as a temptress and seductress. Marilyn Patton aptly says, the heroine Joan Delacourt Foster "liberalizes the oral in oracle".[6] *Lady Oracle* is a parody of the gothic and the picaresque genre to make a feminist critique of male-female relationships. According to Susan J. Rosowski Atwood performs "a feminist parody of the gothic".[7] Lucy M. Freibert adds that Atwood performs "a feminist parody of the picaresque"[8] in the novel. Herbert Rosengarten says, the novel is a fascinating "compound of domestic comedy, Jungian psychology and social satire, stirred with wit and flavoured with the occult".[9] According to Sybil Korff Vincent, "Atwood more accurately depicts the psychological condition of the modern woman than does the traditional Gothic novel".[10] Le Anne Schreiber describes it as "a successful motley, a striking work made out of bright patches with all the crooked seams showing".[11] *Lady Oracle* is a delightful mixture of all three genres which Atwood identifies "as typical of Canadian humour; parody, humour and satire".[12]

The protagonist in the novel is a woman writer who in order to survive turns into a picaro—"a protean figure, who assumes many roles and guises, either successively or simultaneously and who eventually becomes an escape artist".[13] Such are the travails of a female writer in a patriarchal society. In western male literary tradition, women are often criticized for the sin of loving their own images. Margaret Atwood in her fiction challenges this traditional image of women. In *Lady Oracle*, "mirrors symbolize not the moral and psychological limitations of the female protagonist but rather the crippling emphasis the society places on the female image as consumer item".[14] The satire in it is directed against stereotypical images associated with women writers. For instance, reviewers tend to devote a lot of attention of the physical appearances of women writers rather than their works. Joan says that every reviewer of her book "had mentioned her red hair in their reviews" and concludes, "hair in the female was regarded as more important than either talent or the lack of it" (14). M. Prabhakar says, "*Lady Oracle* raises its voice against stereotypical gender roles imposed upon women in a paternalist society as these role-models inferiorize women and thereby distort and problematize their self-perception".[15] Atwood shows in this novel, how the socialization process of patriarchy shapes and institutionalizes sex roles and suggests that "the characteristics of maleness and femaleness are biologically determined; rather they are based on cultural definitions"[16] of a male chauvinistic and sexist society. The novel also explores the problems faced by female writer in assuming an equal place with man in the realm of literature. Her work is discriminated against on the basis of sex, which Atwood calls "sexual bias".[17] She says:

> A man's work is reviewed for its style and ideas, but all too often a woman's is reviewed for the supposed personality of the author as based on the jacket photograph. When a man is attacked in print, it's usually for saying what he says; when a woman is attacked in print, it's often for being who she is.[18]

In order to establish herself as a writer Joan changes her look, she dyes her hair, puts on dark glasses and flees to Rome. Her search for a new identify is met with a stiff resistance from the patriarchal order. Commenting on this Roberta Sciff Zamaro observes:

> In *Lady Oracle* Joan's [concealment] clearly symbolizes the feminist writer's imprisonment in canons dictated by society in which art has been the domain of men, and her quest for a new self represents the woman-writer's quest for a new identity as an artist, an identity freed from the traditional stereotypes imposed by a patriarchal culture.[19]

Lady Oracle is mainly about the growth of a girl Joan Foster to maturity. She wishes to transform society through writing. She is an "escape artist". She feels scared of the "costumed man" when she realizes and assesses different male strategies of the exploitation and oppression of women in the mask of costumes. In the novel she depicts the relationship between men and women in society. She unfolds to a harmless reporter the politics of gender such as condemning female writers to kitchen, devaluation of their creative work, prescription of feminine roles, narrow categorization of women as wives and mistresses. Thus *Lady Oracle* raises its voice against the imposition of sexual and gender roles upon women in a paternalist society as those role models inferiorize women and thereby distort and problematize their self-perception. *Lady Oracle* is a feminist writer's frontal attack on "the dominant pattern of gender relations in contemporary society".[20]

Margaret Atwood's *Lady Oracle* analyzes the relationship of popular women's fiction to the actual lives of woman through the quest of the narrator-protagonist, Joan Foster, a writer of Gothic romances. As the novelist told Joyce Carol Oates, "the hypothesis of the book, in so far as there is one: what happens to someone who lives in the 'real' world but does it as though this 'other' world is the real one?"[21] This question regarding the connection between life and art is the fundamental theme, which explores in its examination of the growth and development of the woman-as-artist/artist-as-woman in a society where both these roles are marginalized. The conflict between the person, the artist and the social environment is after all particularly acute for the woman, for whom the quest for selfhood itself is problematic.

The story begins with the narrator's fake suicide, "I planned my death carefully" (1). The heroine, Joan Foster composes popular 'costume Gothic' aimed at female readers and as well, lives out the genre's fantasies of escape and transformation. As a slim, attractive adult, Joan conceals her former life, her unhappy childhood when she was chronically overweight. She also conceals her secret identity as Louisa K. Delacourt—the name under which Joan publishes her books like *Love, My Ransom*.

Joan experiments with automatic writing and composes a best-selling poetry collection, *Lady Oracle*. In her book Joan challenges to patriarchal culture. The success of the book causes her to become prey to a blackmailer who threatens her to her identity. Therefore Joan works out a plan to fly to Rome. Joan takes an accidental drowning and escape to Italy under another false name. There she writes the truth about her book and emerges as a serious writer. Plainly, Joan Foster's life is a catalogue of the gothic conventions she employs in her writing. The transition from fat child to a stunning young woman represents the magical transformation. Joan's early life begins in Toronto. Her father is an irresponsible man and her mother remains a silent victim at his hands.

Part two of the novel is about the continuous conflict between mother and daughter. It also perpetuates Joan's obsession with her obesity. During one of the stage shows she wants to be a butterfly in the 'Butterfly Frolic'. Joan is eager to wear coloured cellophane wings while performing the group dance but she is compelled to be a 'mothball' amidst the colourful butterflies. More than the dance, the greatest loss is not wearing the wings, "can I wear my wings? I asked. I was beginning to seep through to me, the monstrousness of the renunciation she was asking me to more" (49). This incident takes a deep-root in her psyche; "all her later fantasy-making in her own life, and the trashes she creates, can be associated to this psychic nodule".[22] Being fat, Joan is aware that she cannot wear a butterfly dress. When her mother and teacher play wicked witches and transform her into a mothball, Joan is desolate and inconsolable. When Joan is eight years old, she tries to live out the suggestions in the Brownie handbook but fails to make others happy.

Later on Joan comes into contact with Aunt Lou. Joan is practically brought up by her Aunt Lou. She gives Joan all the warmth, affection and attention, which she needs as a child and teenager. Joan learns the oppressive nature of the patriarchal world and the role of woman as a weak person in the contemporary society from the life of Aunt Lou. Once Joan meets Leda Sprott, the spiritualist who helps Joan to develop her "great powers". She claims to see Joan's mother astral body standing behind Joan's chair at the Jorden chapel.

Joan's Aunt Lou is also fat and understands the psychology of obesity. Joan's mother accuses Joan of going to extremes; she will starve to death and tries to frustrate her by baking goodies and leaving them around in the kitchen to tempt her. Joan realizes, "that in a lesser way she had always done this" (123).

Fear of obesity makes Joan gluttonous, fear due to loss of obesity creates a fabricator in her. She begins to tell lies, to protect her self-created fake identity; Louisa Delacourt, her aunt's name. To realize a new self is to reject totally the bitter past, Joan decides to leave Toronto and go to England.

She starts her new life as a writer. As the chapters progress, Joan's different lives become indistinguishable from those of the characters she is inventing for *Stalked by Love*, the working title of the costume gothic she is currently composing. In England she meets Paul and after that Arthur. She meets Arthur by chance while composing *Escape from Love*, which she writes to escape from Paul. In the early stages of their relationship, she continues viewing him through rose-coloured glasses as is evident from her words, "I myself was bliss-filled and limpid-eyed: the right man had come along, complete with a cause I could devote myself to. My life had significance" (171) but soon Joan gets bored and frustrated in her marital life with Arthur as he expects her to be a cook. She publishes her book *Love Defied* but conceals her identity as writer from Arthur. Later Joan realizes that Arthur enjoys her defeats. Joan's failure was a successful performance, he enjoys her every error and mismanagement, for that boosted his ego. Joan's relationship with various male characters compels her to experiment with the supernatural power and automatic writing. It results her to get her book on "male-female relationships". Arthur is shocked by the news of publication and feels embarrassed by the theme of the book. Life becomes difficult for Joan. She wants to have reconciliation with Arthur so she sells her book *Love, My Ransom* and takes Arthur for "honeymoon". But there is no change in his attitude. After Arthur's painful behaviour she gets involved with Chuck, the Royal Porcupine. When this affair begins to threaten her married life, she calls a halt to it and blames Arthur for driving her into another man's trap. She says, "I only wanted to be loved. I only wanted some human consideration, was that so terrible, was that so impossible?" (272).

Chuk Brewer wants to become Joan's husband and tries to manipulate her. Paul also reappears when he comes to know that Joan is not happy with her married life. He says:

> You can trust me. You were a child, you did not know your own mind. Now you are a woman. You will leave this man, you will divorce, we will be happy.... If you tell him it is I you love, he will...but I have friends. If necessary I shall steal you. (280)

Life is not safe for Joan. Paul wants "the adventure of kidnapping her from what he imagined to be a den of fanged and dangerous communists..." (283).

Fraser Buchanan knows the secret of Joan and starts blackmailing her. Joan receives the anonymous phone calls, threatening notes and dead animals on her doorstep. She suspects Arthur, finally Joan knows the true colour of every man with whom she has come across. The problem is that, like all Joan's fantasies, the fabled garden maze of *Stalked by Love* is a trap. Offering rescue is the menacingly handsome Redmond, the ambiguous male protagonist who in turn takes on the appearance of all the men in Joan Foster's life, from her father to her husband.

The familiar plot has unraveled, and Joan realizes that her belief in miraculous rescues and timely escapes in the real danger. Her identity as a writer is distorted. Like all celebrities she visualizes a threat to her life. Therefore Joan plans to her fake suicide and flees to Rome. At last Joan accepts the potential threat of the present moment, and prepares for a man who may actually be following her. She tells him the truth about herself and "the old thing is that I didn't tell any lies" (345). "I suppose I could still have gotten out of it. I could have said I had amnesia or something...or I could have escaped" (344) that she does neither signals the cessation of gothic fantasies is both her life and her work. She will not give up writing, she affirms but "I won't write any more construe Gothic.... I think they were bad for me" (345). By narrating her tale of *Lady Oracle* Joan Foster is released from the stifling cocoon of privacy, freed from the cruel canons dictated by the patriarchal culture and metamorphosed into a creative writer.

Margaret Atwood in her novels exposes one of many contradictions in the western cultural construct of femininity. She challenges the traditional image of women presented by patriarchy. The novel is a perfect example of how gender conflict is viewed and present in society that is petty and ignorant. According to Sherill Grace, *Lady Oracle*, like many other contemporary works, has "the unsettling mixture of humour and sadness, the sense of self-relative satire or self parody, the confusion between life and art or social realities and imaginative plots and a final sense not so much of ambiguity as of in conclusiveness".[23]

It is about a female writer whose bestseller *Lady Oracle* is described by critics as an interrogation of the problems and frustrations of contemporary relationship from a woman's point of view. In her book she writes about politics of gender, prescription of feminine role, narrow categorization of women as wives and mistresses. Joan typifies the character as escape artist, and she represents, from the first pages of her story—a familiar human desire, not so much for origin as for an escape from and a denial of them; in/from the beginning she hopes from "magic transformation".

Joan perceives herself as doomed to a tragic fate: her life, she thinks, is out of her control. On the first page of the novel, she invokes the dual image of the fat lady and the Lady of Shalott as metaphors for her own life, which she says, "had a tendency to spread, to get flabby, to scroll and festoon like the frame of baroque mirror" (3).

The persistent multiples in Joan is so internalized that the demarcation line between the true and false is blurred and the fabricated vision assumes the reality of their own Joan, thus begins to live the Gothic fiction she creates.

Joan's father is an anesthetist at the Toronto General Hospital who is an insensitive and irresponsible man. He goes to war leaving his pregnant wife behind.

"My father had gone off to the war, leaving her pregnant, with nobody to take pictures of her. My father didn't come back until I was five, and before that he was only a name" (68-69).

As a doctor, while working for the French underground, her father began to enjoy killing those who were suspected to be "fakes", but in hospital, he repeatedly fouls up people's suicide attempts by bringing them to life again. Her mother says:

> You don't know what it was like, all alone with her to bring up while you were over there enjoying yourself.... It's not as though I wanted to have her. It's not as though I wanted to marry you.... I had to make the best of a bad job.... (77)

After death of the mother, Joan sees her father as the one who murdered her:

> My suspicions began the next day, when my father said to me at breakfast, looking at me with his new, shy eyes and sounding as if he'd rehearsed it. I began to hunt for motives, another woman, another man, an insurance policy, a single overwhelming grievance. I examined my father's shirt collars for lipstick, I sifted through official looking papers in his bureau drawers, I listened in on the few phone calls he received.... (179)

Joan's mother is a victim of the soul-damaging stereotype created by patriarchy. Instead of accepting Joan's appearance as a fat girl, she tries to transform her. She also transforms self-face by putting on layers of make-up. Joan remarks, "as if she saw behind or within the mirror some fleeting image she was unable to capture or duplicate" (66).

Joan's obesity as a young girl is a matter of much concern to her mother, she devises strategies to make her daughter slim and thin, but Joan fails her mother's plans and secretly enjoys her demonstration:

> ...I had developed the habit of clamping silently but very visibly through rooms in which my mother was sitting; it was a display, I wanted her to see and recognize what little effect her nagging and pleas were having. (71)

By projecting her shadow onto her daughter and viewing her as her negative twin, Joan's mother tries to avoid a confrontation with her own inner darkness. Joan regards her mother as a detached observer of her traumas, this emerges powerfully from the dreams, Joan sees:

> I called out to my mother, who could still have saved me, she could have run across quickly and reached out her hand, she could have pulled me back with her to firm ground. But she didn't do this, she went on with her conversation, she didn't notice that anything unusual was happing. She didn't ever hear me. (65)

This feeling grows so strong over the years that Joan starts viewing her mother as a witch. Joan sees her mother astral body after her marriage. She says, "I carried my mother around my neck like a rotting albatross. I dreamed about her often, my three-headed mother, menacing and cold" (213-14).

Joan's book *Lady Oracle* centers around a dark mysterious lady with unhappy powers who seems to be dark twin of Tennyson's Lady of Shalott. Later she realizes that the strange lady of her poems is in fact her mother and says:

> She'd never really let go of me because I had never let her go. It had been she standing behind me in the mirror, she was the one who was waiting around each turn, her voice whispered the words. She had be the lady in the boat, the death barge, the tragic lady with flowing hair and stricken eyes, the lady in the tower. She couldn't stand the view from the window, life was her curse. How could I renounce her? She needed the freedom also; she had been my reflection too long. (329-30)

Joan's mother feels so oppressed by her life that she commits suicide by throwing herself down the cellar stairs. Her husband and the roles of female in male-dominated society are responsible for her death. As Lucy M. Freibert says, "she was killed by her husband, but chiefly by the romantic conditioning which made beauty, wealth and romance supreme. When the beauty and romance disappeared, the wealth did not satisfy."[24] Joan thinks that she is an "accident", the unwanted daughter of an insecure, unhappy woman.

Joan's Aunt Lou, who is Chief Public Relation Officer in Toronto was perceived as a good mother, loving, permissive and cuddly. Aunt Lou opens the world of fantasy, of stories, of romantic movies like the Red shoes, of carnivals and spiritualist gatherings to Joan. It is she who waves her magic ward originates those fictions, which Joan never outgrows. Joan uses her name in her career as gothic novelist. It is Aunt Lou who gives Joan one thousand dollars in her will. Playing the role of Maiden Aunt, she conceals from Joan for years the fact that she was married at the age of nineteen. Her so-called husband is a gambler, who has no concern and love for his wife but she loves him so much. She says about their relationship:

> Then he'd come back and if he'd tell me how much he loved me, if he'd won he'd complain about being tied down. It was very sad, really. One day he just never came back. May be they shot him for not paying. I wonder if he's still alive: if he is, I suppose I'm still married to him. (84)

After her frustrating experiences with her husband Aunt Lou later on, comes into contact with Robert, her boyfriend who is an accountant. He has a wife and children and comes to her apartment on Sunday evenings for dinner. Joan has pictures Robert as tall, overpowering and a little sinister but instead he is small and dapper, the trimly dressed man. Robert watches Aunt Lou as if she is the most beautiful woman.

In church Joan meets the Reverend Leda Sprott, who is the spiritualist. She is the leader, a stately older woman with blue eyes, blue hair and a Roman nose, dressed in a long white satin gown, with an embroidered purple band, like a bookmark, around her neck. Leda Sprott's messages seem to come from inside her head. She claims to see Joan's mother astral body standing behind her chair at the Jorden Chapel:

> I have an urgent message, she said, "for someone without a number" she was looking straight at me. "There's woman standing behind your chair" she's about thirty, with dark hair, wearing a navy-blue suit with a white collar and a pair of white gloves. (110)

Leda Sprott helps Joan to develop her "great power", "you have great gifts", she said looking into my eyes. "Great Powers. You should develop them. You should try the Automatic writing" (112). After some years Leda Sprott has become the Reverend Eunic P. Revele and performs Joan's marriage ceremony to

Arthur, she is transformed into a kind of sibyl, as in the Aeneas legend. She has one good eye and one bad eye. She is split, multiple and complex. Mr. Stewart, the other spiritualist, is a great skinny gray man who is visiting medium. He does free from messages, pointing to members of the congregation and describing spirits, which are standing behind their chairs; he can actually see dead people.

Joan begins her adult life in England as a versatile writer. She meets Paul in London when she falls off a double-decker bus. Paul is a polish count and forty-one years old. His family background is that before the war he belonged to the upper class "he wasn't a count exactly, but he was something or other, and he showed me a signet ring he wore on his little finger. It was a mythical bird, a griffin or a phoenix" (147). He is married and has a daughter back in Poland well as a mother. In England he obtains a position as a clerk in a bank, working in the foreign exchange department. Later Joan finds that Paul churns out nurse romances under the pseudonym of Mavis Qulip. He is a compulsive and romantic liar. He feels that he has missed his chance of becoming a hero by escaping from Poland in a cowardly manner during the Russian invasion. Paul offers Joan Nurse Novels, which are books with pointless ideas, dealing with illicit relations between doctors and nurses. Paul's attitude towards Joan indicates that he has got the ideas of womanhood directly from fairly tales and romances. He compliments her:

> You have the body of Goddess. (142)

Later Joan realizes that he is a manipulator. He regards women as dependent and naïve; he considers a woman as an "empty vessel" and prescribes her the roles such as childbearing and sewing. Paul categorize women as "mistress". Joan says:

> It's an odd term, "mistress", but that was how he thought of me, these were the categories into which his sexual life was arranged: wives and mistresses. I was not the first mistress. For him there was no such thing as a female lover. (150)

He thinks, "the mystery of man is of the mind,...whereas that of the woman is of the body" (166). Paul's dominating nature does not alter his attitudes over the years. Knowing that Joan is married to communist, he is sure she is very unhappy and is determined to rescue her from "a den of fanged and dangerous communists, armed to the teeth with brain suction devices and slaughterhouse rhetoric" (283). Thus, Paul represents conventional male model.

Joan's Lover Arthur whom she meets while walking through the Hyde Park, she gets involved in a romance within few moments. Her initial reaction is:

> He was wearing a black crew-neck sweater, which I found quite dashing. A melancholy fighter for almost-lost causes, idealistic and doomed, sort of like Lord Byron, whose biography I had just been skimming. We finished collecting the pamphlets; I fell in love.... (165)

Arthur is a Canadian, associated with the ban—the bomb movement, as a leaflet man. His father was the judge, his mother, the religious nut. His is seen as a multi-layered personality as he changes his theories constantly. He shares his flat with two other men, a New Zealander named Slocum who is studying at the London School of Economics. He eats cold ketchup-covered canned baked beans. His second partner is an Indian.

Relationship with Arthur, in the early stages is like Joan's life has significance but after years she gives up "expecting him to be a clocked sinuous and faintly menacing stranger" (216). He proposes Joan because:

> Marriage itself would settle us down, and through it, too, we would become better acquainted. If it didn't work out, well, it would be a learning experience. Most importantly, we could live much more cheaply together than we could separately. (197)

He wants Joan to be a domestic servant to serve him for years. He does not want that Joan wear fashionable dress in public because it may attract the exploiters. He becomes sadistic in the bedroom. Joan wants to have children but "It was Arthur who'd festooned our bedroom with every known form of birth-control device, urged me to take the Pill..." (231).

Joan feels so humiliated that she hides her identity as a writer and her past from Arthur when she gets her book, *Lady Oracle* published. He behaves as though she has committed, "some unpardonable but unmentionable sin". Joan says:

> "Once I'd thought of Arthur as single-minded, single-hearted, single-bodied; I, by contrast, was a sorry assemblage of lies and alibis, each complete in itself but rendering the other worthless. But I soon discovered there was many of Arthur as there were of me. The difference was that I was simultaneous, were as Arthur was a sequence. (211)

Now Arthur involves himself in the work of his magazine *Resurgence.* Marlene is the managing director of *Resurgence* and married with Don. Arthur and Don taught in the same university department and share the same views. Later Marlene becomes Arthur's platonic ideal because she is a tip-top vegetarian cook and has a mind he can respect. Marlene has an illicit affair with Sam, the assistant editor.

It is the indifference of Arthur that Joan gets involved with the Royal porcupine alias Chuck Brewer. Joan meets him after T.V. interview. He appears with, "red hair...an elegant moustache waxed and cured up-ward at the end, the beard pointed. He was wearing a long black cloak and spats, and carrying a gold headed cane, a pair of white gloves, and a top hat embroidered with porcupine quills" (239).

He is a 'non-create" poet. Later on he wants to marry Joan and drags her into sexual immorality. When Joan refuses to marry, he frightens her. He wants to occupy Arthur Place.

Towards the end of their relationship when he suggests a double suicide, Joan sees him as a "homicidal maniac" (272). At last Royal Porcupine strikes as a childish, narcissistic who is incapable of serious emotional involvement. Joan meets Fraser Buchanan after her T.V. interview. He calls himself, the Montreal Poet. He starts a literary magazine; *Reject* that prints only stuff that has been rejected by other literary Magazines. He is a fake researcher and blackmailer too. He has a black notebook, which is a collection of data about those women whom he threatens for sex and money.

Growing up as a female little alone trying to fit into the stereotypical role a woman is expected to fill in a male dominated society can be a trying experience for any woman. Joan, the main character in *Lady Oracle* is no exception from this. Joan is able to provide with a vivid description of the anxieties and ordeals of being female throughout childhood and adolescence. She starts out with the simple desire to love and be loved, to find acceptance. These desires are not gender specific, as both males and females strive to love and be loved and find acceptance. The difference is how women and men actually find these. Due to constant victimization by others a patterns of outsiders becomes Joan's defense and revenge. Joan's early misery and resentment causes her to see life as her adversary because she is made to feel like an object.

The image of a heroine in romantic fiction is that she must be beautiful, slim and tender but the protagonist in the novel is big, fat weighing 245 pounds at the age of 19. Because of her overweight she had to do a teddy bear dance instead of butterfly dance. Margaret Atwood describes Joan's character as a fat girl in the novel; it questions male attitudes to women's body thereby presenting her "as a victim of sexist social pressure".[25] According to Molly Hite, "Fat is a feminist issue and 'excess' of body becomes symbolic of female resistance to a society that wishes to constrict women to dimensions appropriate."[26]

In high school she plays "kindly aunt and wise woman" character because of her obese appearance, slim girls in her class feel that Joan is neither envious nor flirts. Joan says, she suppressed her own interest in sex as there was no available 'role for her'.

Joan believes that she can change herself by changing her body. Her body has always been her weapon in the struggle with her mother who both over-identifies with her daughter and sees her as an embodiment of the failure of her own "essential femininity". Joan's body is the commodity through which her mother desires to renegotiate her position in the world, for to bear a "pretty" daughter is to reinforce one's own sense of femininity. As Joan's body expands, her mother comes to see it as a reproach to her, "the embodiment of her own failure and depression, a huge edgeless cloud of inchoate matter which refused to be shaped into anything for which she could get a prize" (67).

For Joan her fat body is both a refusal of the chic, controlled, denying femininity, which her mother desires and also protective Armour against the fear that she is essentially unfeminine and will, therefore, never please anyone. The mother's femininity represents for Joan both sexual attractiveness and powerlessness and denial of need. Her own enormous body, meanwhile, is experienced as both a triumph over and rejection of her mother's desire to be 'feminine' and as a horrible unleashing of an uncontrollable monstrous femininity associated with the flesh:

> I happened to glance down at my body.... I didn't usually look at my body in a mirror or in any other way I snuck a glance at parts of it now and then, but the whole thing was too overwhelming. There, staring me in the face was my thigh. It was enormous, it was gross, it was like a diseased limb, the kind you see in pictures of jungle natives; it spread on forever, like a prairie photographed from a plane, the flesh not green but bluish-white, with veins meandering across it like rivers. (120-21)

Once Joan visits the Canadian National Exhibition along with her Aunt Lou. The sensitive Joan feels very much upset by the sight of a freak show of fat lady. She is enraged by the attitude of the society towards woman's body "What a shame... how destructive to me were the attitudes of society, forcing me into a mold of femininity that I could never fit, stuffing me into those ridiculous pink tights, those spangles those outmoded, cramping ballet slippers" (103).

Lady Oracle is the portrait of the writer as a woman and a survivor in the phallocentric culture. It shows how the identity and individuality of woman writer is destroyed behind the mask of anonymous authority of male writers and her writing is gendered and classed by sex status. Ultimately, the protagonist emerges as a serious writer in Rome and leaves an optimistic note to the female writers whose voices are marginalized:

> .... Dark place is only a cocoon; we will rest there for a time, and after that we will emerge with beautiful wings; we will

emerge with beautiful wings; we will be butterflies and fly up towards the sun. (107)

Joan suffers an identity crisis, because she has too many identities. She is Joan Foster who pretends not to have a mind of her own because Arthur, her husband, does not like to have a woman with a mind of her own. She knows that he would not appreciate her writing:

> Arthur never found out that I wrote costume Gothics...why did I never tell? I was fear, mostly. When I first met him he talked a lot about wanting a woman whose mind he could respect, and I knew that if he found out I'd written *The Secret of Margrave Manor* he wouldn't respect mine. I wanted very much to have a respectable mind. Arthur's friends and the books he read, which always had footnotes, and the causes he took up made me feel deficient and somehow absurd, a sort of intellectual village idiot, and revealing my profession would certainly have made it worse. These books...would be considered trash of the lowest order worse than trash, for didn't they exploit the masses, corrupt by distracting and perpetuates degrading stereo of women as helpless and persecuted? They did and I knew it, but I couldn't stop. (33-34)

Joan's identity crisis starts with her name. She was named after Joan Crawford, a popular actress who was thin. She chooses "Louise K. Delacourt", her Aunt Lou's name as her pen name when she starts her adult life in England as a writer. In her will Aunt Lou gives one thousand dollars to Joan only when she loses one hundred pounds weight in her. It is, therefore, yet another identity crisis for her. Margaret Atwood exposes Joan's own complicity in her will to be a victim: She nonetheless, at the same time, relates Joan's passivity—"Miss Flegg Syndrome" as Joan terms it to the patriarchal structure of power.

Joan is a complex woman who has had more than her share of turbulent relationship during her life. From her childhood and teenage relationship with her mother, to her bond with her husband. Later in life, Joan's relationships are rarely free of turmoil and drama. These relationships definitely have an influence on Joan, impacting her as a person. Joan's relationship with her mother is antagonistic. Joan's identity becomes based on the opposite of what her mother expects from her. Joan's relationship with her father was quite different. They rarely spoke. In her novel *Lady Oracle* Joan narrates her relationship with the 'costumed' men. When Joan takes part time job to become independent, an Italian cook in Bite—A Bit restaurant proposes her. Instead of showing his heart and love for Joan, he shows his bank balance and says, "I will give you babies." He said, "Lots of babies, I see you like the babies. You are a good girl..." (100).

Joan rejects his proposal and feels sorry for the commoditization of women in marriage. After meeting Paul in London, Joan acts in a way that she will find acceptable, so as not to upset or appall him. This is a direct contradiction of the identity Joan assumed when dealing with her mother. Instead of going against Paul's wishes, she is acquiescent and passive as she allows him to take her virginity without saying a word.

Instead of voicing concern or an opinion of any kind, Joan simply let Paul does as he will. She is mindful of his opinion and always lets him have the final decision in matters. Her identity at this point is based on Paul. When Joan tries to break out of this pattern, Paul's tolerance and patience regarding Joan began to whither as she started to do more things for herself, instead of doing things that pleased him.

Joan wants to be an ideal wife for Arthur and making sure that he is not displeased with her. Joan repeatedly makes herself look silly by trying to cook and failing miserably, yet she continues because she thinks that Arthur enjoyed watching her blunder:

> Arthur enjoyed my defeats. They cheered him up. He loved hearing the crash as I dropped a red-hot platter on the floor, having forgotten to put on my oven mitt; he liked to hear me swearing in the kitchen; and when I would emerge sweaty-faced and disheveled after one of my battles, he would greet me with a smile and a little joke, or perhaps even a kiss, which was as much for the display, the energy I'd wasted, as for the food. My frustration and anger were real.... My

failure was a performance and Arthur was the audience. (234-35)

When Joan finally does something for her own satisfaction that is publishing of her book of poetry *Lady Oracle*, it is met with hostility by Arthur. Joan's act of doing something for her creates static in her relationship with Arthur. Further Joan has an affair, asserting her own needs and identity, instead of Arthur's. Throughout her life Joan has to transform her identity to please someone. Joan spends a great deal of her life pretending to be a person she is not. She puts on performances for the people in her life, so that no one really knows who she truly is. She often alters her behaviour and her way of thinking in order to better fit in with her surroundings.

In fact, she does so much pretending and role-playing throughout *Lady Oracle*, that one may become confused as to who Joan Foster really is.

The obsession with costumes in her novels spills over into her private life. Each time Joan sheds an identity, she discards the clothes associated with it and tries to transform herself into different person. Her romantic identification with Gothic heroines of her own invention leads her to expect a romantic rescues by a heroic figure from the self-created maze in which she is trapped and lost. Her fiction becomes real for her, when Joan receives threatening anonymous notes, phone calls, dead animals on the doorstep; she suspects that Arthur is trying to kill her. She also suspects other men with whom she has come across. Finally she concludes that every man has two costumes. She says:

> My father, healer and killer; the man in the tweed coat, my rescuer and possibly also a pervert; the Royal Porcupine and his double, Chuck Brewer; even Paul, who I'd always believed had a sinister other Life I couldn't penetrate. Why should Arthur be any exception.... The fact that I'd taken so long to discover it made it all the more threatening. (325-26)

Joan fails in her relationship with men primarily because she is unable to transcend the negative aspect of the animus archetype and see them as representing the basic contrasexual component of her own psyche.[27] The fact that she regards all men as killers emerges from her latest Gothic hero Redmond. Redmond is composite of all the men in Joan's life. Though, Joan has always desired love, she has, at the unconscious level of her psyche, always equated it with death. The moment she hits the reporter and knocks him out, she realizes that like men, she is also capable of violence and can cause death. Reporter who threatens to take away her fictional identities and expose her real identity, compels her to adopt yet another identity, that of dead Joan. Shunning the real, therefore, she escapes to Italy through her fake suicide. She is, as she says, "an escape artist" after all. In the end when she realizes that Aunt Lou was right: "You can't change the past" she decides to accept the past and make a new beginning by committing herself to act rather than enact, by returning to Toronto to save her friends who are falsely implicated in 'murdering' her.

Through *Lady Oracle*, Margaret Atwood declares that both men and women are equal as they have same human capabilities and, therefore, gender-based injustices should be fought against in the society. Margaret Atwood believes that "fiction is one of the few forms left through which we may examine our society not in its particular but in its typical aspects".[28]

Margaret Atwood in her fiction not only reflects society but also aims to reform it by exposing, as in *Lady Oracle*. Margaret Atwood's narratives of her women-protagonists' search for a distinctive feminine identity also constitute metaphoric analogues for Canada's similar quest. Joan's passivity relates to Canada's similar patterns of passivity and powerlessness *vis-à-vis* the dominating U.S. Culture and therefore Atwood's implicit indictment of Joan's 'Miss Flegg syndrome' constitutes, by analogy, her similar indictment of Canada's identical malaise.[29]

The message of the novel is that "the experience of all women everywhere becomes, in a sense, our communal property, a heritage we bestow upon each other, the knowledge of what it has meant to be female, a woman in this man's world".[30]

Lady Oracle is a highly satirical novel, and the satire results not from an invasion of the real by the conventions of the artificial but from the clash of conventions belonging to different discursive practices. It is not a novel in which the costume gothic stands in clear opposition to the naked truth. The unvoiced plea may appear ridiculous, making the novel an anti-gothic one. Nevertheless, *Lady Oracle* shares with the gothic some of its basic assumptions. The gothic vision does not attempt to solve any of the contradictions of this world and does not differ any absolute truth. Gothic is one that lacks faith in organic notions of wholeness. The use of suspense and doubt in a gothic fiction renders it difficult to draw a clear line between fantasy and reality.

The novel is preoccupied both with the gothic and with the female body, a conjunction of concerns suggesting a "sexual and aggressive center" that will be treated more self-consciously, perhaps even inscribed in a altogether different register in this novel.

Conflict between fathers and sons is well-known in literature but *Lady Oracle* shows how mother raises her daughter in rejection and turns her towards men. The basic conflict is with the "all-powerful, devouring mother".[31] Joan's relationship with her aggressive unhappy and emotionally insecure mother is both complex and changed with ambivalence. At the deeper unconscious level, Joan's mother like that of snow-white in the fairy tale wants to be the lovelier of the two of them. Joan adopts the role of snow-white that image of virtue and victimization that is the object of the wrath and envy of the evil stepmother. Joan's mother often imagines being her stepmother, like the evil queen in snow-white tale. She sits before her mirror and Joan is permitted to watch while her mother applies her make-up:

> I would stare at the proceedings, fascinated and mute. I thought my mother was very beautiful, even more beautiful when she was colored in. And this was what I did in the dream: I sat and stared.... My mother always had a triple mirror, so she could see both sides as well as the front of head. In the dream, as I watched, I suddenly realized that instead of three reflections she had three actual heads, which rose from her toweled shoulders on three separate necks. This didn't frighten me, as it seemed merely a confirmation of something I'd always known.... My mother was a monster. (66-67)

The supernatural events in *Lady Oracle* invariably take the form of appearances of a female body. This body is always aligned with the maternal, most obviously in the case of Joan's mother, she is being visited by an 'astral body' wearing a navy blue suit with a white collar and a pair of white gloves. This manifestation recurs three times in the novel. Leda Sprott who runs the Jorden chapel sees first Joan's mother astral body.

Second time this astral body appears, when Joan returns to the London apartment of her lover Arthur and his two roommates. Her mother was standing there, dressed in her 1949 navy blue suit and make-up and "crying soundlessly, horribly; mascara was running from her eyes in black tears" (173).

Five days later she receives the telegram of her mother's death and realizes that "she'd turned up in my front parlor to tell me about it". The last time Joan's mother appears in the same suit and make up but her behaviour is changed, "She pressed her face against the glass like a child..." what do you want? "I said, but she didn't answer. She stretched out her arms to me, she wanted me to come with her; she wanted us to be together" (320). Now Joan realizes that "she'd never really let go of me because I had never let her go" (320) but still Joan is unable to find her complicity in her relation to her mother.

Many of Joan's mythologically inspired identities, are derived from mirrors; even the fat lady image is one she sees reflected in a fun-house mirror as a child. Mirror becomes symbols of the fragmented self, providing a distorted image of the self, stealing one's sense of real or complete self, robbing one of an identity.

Joan's early fascination with her mother's kind of art practiced ritualistically before the three-way mirror is never dispelled; significantly the adult Joan also buys herself a triple mirror. Joan, in the novel plays with triple mirrors, which disrupt any temptation to dualism, opening up infinity of perspectives that eventually encompass all the characters of the novel within the expanding persona of the mirror, Joan's literary career as 'Lady Oracle' begins with the mirror. Joan starts her experiments with automatic writing:

> I stared at the candle in the mirror, the mirror candle. There was more than one candle, there were Three, and I knew

> that if I moved the two sides of the mirror toward me there would be an infinite number of candles extending in a line as far as I could see...the room seemed very dark, darker than it had before.... There was movement at the edge of the mirror. I gasped and turned around. Surely there had been a figure, standing behind me. But there was no one. I was wide awake now.... I looked down at the piece of paper. There, in a scrawl handwriting that was certainly not my own. (220)

Joan's triple mirror not only inspires her *Lady Oracle* but her later gothic novels as well. In Margaret Atwood's *Lady Oracle*, mirrors symbolize not the moral and psychological limitations of the female protagonist, but rather the crippling emphasis the society places on the female images as a consumer item. Margaret Atwood shows in the novel that the mirror is a literary symbol of female narcissism and childish self. Self-absorption, more truly reflects a culture where women are objectified and packaged for the consumer society. In the novel Joan fragments her personality through multiplication rather than division. Joan moves rapidly between first and third person as she alternates between event and hallucination. Within the novel movement between past and present, between Toronto and London, between Italy and ancient Greece as rapidly as Joan changes costumes as sentences.

Margaret Atwood's *Lady Oracle* is one of the few novels, which attempt a serious examination of the genre. Man and woman can establish better relationship in patriarchal order. *Lady Oracle* challenges the norms of fiction writing and reworks or the older ones, such as the Gothic, the sentimental, the picaresque novel and the fairy tales. The novel provides a locus where a plurality of styles and traditions visit. In her book Margaret Atwood successfully deconstructs the classical unities of space, time and character. The novel's 'plot' within a plot also interrupts the chronology of the main narrative, thus creating different temporal levels, with the intertextual references offering alternative temporal dimensions.

REFERENCES

1. Patton, Marilyn. "Lady Oracle: The Politics of the Body", *Ariel*, 22.4, Oct. 1991, 41-42.
2. Gilbert, Sandra M. and Susan Gubar. *The Madwoman in the Attic.* New Haven: Yale University Press, 1979, 13.
3. Cixous, Helene. "The Laugh of the Medusa", trans. Keith Cohen and Paula Cohen. *Signs*, 1.4, Summer 1976, 875.
4. Bok, Christian. "Sibyls: Echoes of French Feminism in 'The Diviners' and 'Lady Oracle'", *Canadian Literature*, 135, Winter 1992, 80.
5. Howells, Coral Ann. *Margaret Atwood.* London: Macmillan P. Ltd., 1996, 67.
6. Patton, 32.
7. Rosowski, Susan J. "Margaret Atwood's Lady Oracle: Fantasy and the Modern Gothic Novel", *Critical Essays on Margaret Atwood,* ed. Judith McCombs. Boston: G.K. Hall, 1988, 197.
8. Freibert, Lucy M. "The Artist as Picaro: The Revelation of Margaret Atwood's Lady Oracle", *Canadian Literature*, 92, Spring 1982, 23.
9. Rosengarten, Herbert. "Urbane Comedy", *Canadian Literature.* Spring 1977, 84.
10. Vincent, Sybil Korff. "The Mirror and The Cameo: Margaret Atwood's Comic/Gothic Novel, Lady Oracle", in *The Female Gothic*, Juliann E. Fleenor (Montreal: Eden Press, 1983), 153.
11. Schreiber, Le Anne. "Motley with Method", *Time*, 108, 1 October 1976, 54.
12. Atwood, Margaret. "What's so Funny? Notes on Canadian Humour", *Second Words.* Toronto: House of Anansi, 1982, 175-89.
13. Freibert, 26.
14. Rao, Nageshwar T. "Male Mapping and Female Trapping: Parodic Deconstruction in Atwood's Lady Oracle", *Perspective on Canadian Fiction,* ed. Sudhakar Pandey. New Delhi: Prestige Books, 1994, 114.
15. Prabhakar, M. "Lady Oracle: Prophecy for a Brave New World", *Feminism/Postmodernism Margaret Atwood's Fiction.* New Delhi: Creative Books, 1999, 53.
16. Weitzman, Lenore J. "Sex Role Socialization", *Women A Feminist Perspective*, ed. J. Freeman. California: Mayfield Publishing Co., 1975, 106-07.
17. Atwood, Margaret. "On Being a Women Writer: Paradoxes and Dilemmas", *Second Word Selected Critical Prose.* Toronto: Anansi, 1982, 196.

18. Atwood, Margaret. "Witches", *Second Words.* Toronto: Anansi, 1982, 331.
19. Scicff, Roberta-Zamaro. "The Re/membering of the Female power in Lady Oracle", *Canadian Literature,* 112, Spring 1987, 37.
20. John, Thieme. "A Female Houdini: Popular Culture in Margaret Atwood's Lady Oracle", *Kunapipi,* xiv, 1, 1992, 78.
21. Oates, Joyce Carol. Comp., *First Person Singular: Writers on their Craft.* Princeton: Ontario, Review Press, 1993, 85.
22. Srinivasan, Padma. Atwood's 'Lady Oracle': A post-modernist text "*A Essay on Canadian Literature*", ed. K. Balachandran. Bareilly: Prakash Book, 2001, 75.
23. Grace, Sherill E. "More than a very Double life", *Violent Duality: A Study of Margaret Atwood,* ed. Ken Norris. Montreal: Vehicule, 1980, 111.
24. Freibert, 30.
25. Parsons, Ann. "The Self-Inventing Self: Women who lie and pose in the Fiction of Margaret Atwood", *Gender Studies: New Directions in Feminist Criticism,* ed. Judith Spector. Ohio: Bowling Green State U. Popular P., 1986, 107-08.
26. Hite, Molly. *The Other Side of the Story.* Ithaca and London: Cornell University Press, 1989, 131-32.
27. Vevaina, Coomi S. "The Mirror which distorts: Atwood's Lady Oracle", *Re/membering Selves: Alienation and Survival in the Novels of Margaret Atwood and Margaret Laurence.* New Delhi: Creative, 1996, 70.
28. Atwood, Margaret. *Second Words.* Toronto: Anansi Press, 346.
29. Salat, M.F. "Canadian Nationalism and Feminist Ideology: Margaret Atwood", *The Canadian Novel: A Search for Identity.* New Delhi: B.R. Publishing, 68.
30. Millet, Kate. "Prostitution: A Quartet for Female Voice", *Woman in Sexist Society,* eds. Vivian Gornick and Barbara K. Moran. New York and London: Basic Books, 1971, 23.
31. Fleenor, Julian E. "Introduction", in her *The Female Gothic.* Montreal: Eden Press, 1983, 16.

Bodily Harm

5

Bodily Harm is a different kind of therapy to gender victimization—"the kind of open conversation or consciousness-raising" session central to the development of the feminist movement.[1]

In *Bodily Harm*, gender-politics are contextualized within the frightening world of political intrigues and the novel depicts the process of self-discovery and re-humanization against the backdrop of cruelty. Thus, it succeeds both as a powerful psychological and political novel and is in no way the "immense failures"[2] as argued by J.A. Wainwright. As a psychological novel, it traces Rennie's movement from a superficial, alienated existence towards spiritual survival, which includes a deeper awareness of self and others.

Margaret Atwood is an active member of the Amnesty International so she is interested in gender/sexual power politics. By power politics she does not mean who votes for whom but "how power operates and who has power over whom".[3]

Sexual politics is often disguised, as 'love' is one more form of power politics. In her book of poems 'Power Politics', Margaret Atwood asserts that love is dominated by imperialistic intentions. Lovers wield love as a weapon rather than bearing it as a gift. As Howells says, "[In *Bodily Harm*] female bodies are all passive, distorted, dismembered or coerced witnesses to the sexual power politics of the Berger epigraph".[4] According to Lorna Irvine, the novel illustrates, "inscription of the female body and, by connecting hospital room and jail cell, dramatically presents the injury to the female body that results from its confinement".[5] Here female body becomes the metaphor for the weak and suppressed; Margaret Atwood says that a novel is "a vehicle for looking at society—an interface between language and what we choose to call reality,..."[6] thus, in *Bodily Harm* she states the moral function of writing which does more than "take what society deals out and makes it visible" (208). It is a profoundly moral, even a religious work which challenges the chauvinisms of class, culture, race and nation by emphasizing the need for mercy, pity and love in our power-mad world.

In *Bodily Harm*, the protagonist Rennie is a 'lifestyle journalist' who just had a mastectomy. Margaret Atwood traces her internal torment in dealing with this, her troubled childhood, her relationship with men and a violent society at large. Rennie tries to escape the traumatic experiences of her own past but unfortunately she escapes to an area that is politically abandoned by the British. As a journalist Rennie always carries a camera which becomes a symbol of "her tourist vision and identity".[7] It is a prison narrative with female subjects for whom marginality has become a condition of being. Howells calls the novel, "a prison narrative"[8] because during her visit Rennie gets imprisoned by the corrupt politicians of Caribbean island and she writes her travelogue in prison cell. In her travelogue Rennie includes all sorts of bodily harm perpetrated on women such as the pornographic violation of women as shown in the Toronto Policeman's Pornography museum; Jake her lover's sadism and the situation of rape; the humiliations she suffers in the prison, the torture she witnesses of the people crusading for human rights and civil liberties in the Caribbean Island; Rennie's mutilation by cancer; and Lora's "non-violent" rape by her vicious stepfather. "The most pathetic of all bodily harms is the brutality, torture, rape and heartless mutilation of Lora, Rennie's fellow prisoner in the Caribbean jail."[9]

Like the protagonists of Margaret Atwood's other novels, Rennie has broken out of the framed photograph and transcended camera vision, as well as other protective layers and distorting filters. She uses her pen as a "weapon" and exposes the position of women in prison cells and hospital beds. In her travelogue

Rennie writes about the wickedness of man and his brutality towards woman. As Gilbert and Gubar say, "for Rennie the pen is phallic, the page the female body".[10] *Bodily Harm* may seem to set a new direction in Margaret Atwood's work, it again presents a character who specializes in packaging experiences like torture, disaster and revolution for popular consumption and it is no closer to social realism and didacticism. It simultaneously externalizes an inner reality and personalizes nationalistic, cultural and metaphysical realities, revealing characteristics of romance.

Bodily Harm is about a woman's position in the society, for Rennie the Toronto journalist has to revise her image of herself as a middle-class Canadian exempt from the dangers that other people from other classes and other cultures have to face. The novel follows a character trying to break free from her past and grasp onto a brighter future. By criticizing and questioning the actions of westernized culture, the novel explores the problems of third world countries, as North American tourist. It is Margaret Atwood's most effective political novel and she does not shy away from criticizing Canada's own international political practices.

Margaret Atwood's work illustrates the degree to which her own language derives. *Bodily Harm* has Caribbean setting and its main concern is the restraint imposed on political articulateness by the 'circle game' of the small-town Loyalist inheritance in Canada. The thematic and metaphorical structure of the novel ingest on a paradoxical "rebirth" into the knowledge of death and of the things that death can symbolize. The plot of the novel is not complicated in itself, although some efforts must be expended in order to reconstruct the precise chronology of events from the intricately rough analeptic structure of the work.

The protagonist Rennie Wilford is a journalist, living in Toronto with her lover Jake. She spent her childhood in the narrow and repressive town of Griswold. This Puritanical town sees everything that happens as the will of God and believes that people get what they deserve. Rennie says that in Griswold, "everyone deserves the worst" (18). Rennie regards Griswold as a "backdrop" rather than as her background. In order to live a free life she escapes to Toronto as a university student. After college she starts her career as a freelance journalist specializing in "Lifestyles". After leaving Griswold she meets Jake. She is shaken as she is diagnosed of cancer requiring a partial mastectomy. Her operation is clinically successful still she continues to be haunted by the fear of recurrence. Before her operation, Rennie and Jake seem to be perfectly suited to each other but after operation Rennie realizes that Jake was all along packaging her according to his taste and pleasure till he realizes that packing was rotting from inside. She blames herself for allowing him to use her as a commodity and decides to leave him. At the same time, Rennie develops a crush on her surgeon, Dr. Daniel Luoma, but that too ends badly. She sees him as a substitute of Jake. He possesses the healing touch that Rennie comes to obsess about in his hand and her want and need for them to touch her. He saved her once from the cancer and Rennie thinks that he now reconciles herself with her body. But their sexual encounter does not tear her out of the darkness and insecurity that overwhelmed her after the operation. She feels violated, victimized, raped as Daniel manages to take something of her, which she had not expected. He too has "won". Her fantasy is unfulfilled. Shortly afterwards, in one afternoon she returns to her apartment to discover that somebody has broken into her home in her absence. The intruder has left a length of rope coiled on the bed and the police warn Rennie that he will probably return. This sinister incident prompts Rennie's decision to leave Toronto. She persuades Keith, the editor of *Visor* magazine to let her do a travel piece and ends up with an assignment "off the beaten track": a Caribbean island she "had never heard of" (22).

Rennie's experiences on St. Antoine and its neighbour Ste. Agathe, are the novel's present and constitute the unfolding of the plot. Essentially, the plot is about recovery. She recovers her capacity for sexual pleasure. Among the people she encounters here and on the neighbouring island of Ste. Agathe are Paul, an American involved in contraband activities and Lora, his former mistress who exploits Rennie to smuggle weapons into the country on Paul's behalf. St. Antoine is so far off the regular tourist path and because Rennie arrives during the first election since independence, her presence arouses suspicion. She is watched wherever she goes. The morning after her arrival on the island Rennie wonders whether she, like other cancer victims, will resort to faith healing, “the laying on of hands by those who say they can see vibrations flowing out of their fingers in the form of a holy red light” (60). Shortly afterwards she finds herself being pursued by a deaf and dumb man whose inexplicable attentions strike her as being “too much like the kind of bad dream she wishes she could stop having” (74). It is only when Paul explains that the man simply wants to shake hands with her in the conviction that “the gesture will bring her good luck” then Rennie realizes that “he’s only been trying to give her something” (75). Later Rennie falls in love with Paul. At first she is afraid that the scar left by her operation will repel him but these fears are dispelled when she perceives his actual reaction and understands that he’s seen people a lot deader than her” (204).

Rennie meets Dr. Minnow on the plane from Barbados. Rennie expects to be shown the local attractions but Minnow shows her the island’s poverty and the corruption of the present regime. He reveals that he is the major opposition candidate in the upcoming election. He shows the victims of hurricane huddle who did not benefit in anyway from the money sent for their rehabilitation by the “sweet Canadians”. By doing this he wants Rennie to write about them and feels that Rennie can, like him, “tempted to change things” (133). Rennie reacts badly and says politics is not her thing she does lifestyles. She says that the local politics of the island would not be of interest to Canadians. Later Dr. Minnow wins the election and is shot by the CIA agent on the island, now Rennie understands the reason behind his pleading.

After murder of Dr. Minnow, some of his followers attempt to overthrow the present government. Despite herself, Rennie becomes embroiled in the turmoil of a local election, a political assassination and is jailed as an outraged tourist. There she confined to a subterranean cell in an old fort with Lora who is accused of being involved with Prince the second opposition candidate. Here she is forced to witness various scenes of brutality, culminating in the sadistic beating of Lora by their prison guards.

Rennie regards as different from herself in every respect Lora is the child of poverty and abuse while Rennie is university educated. Lora is deeply immersed in the life of the island including its criminal aspects. These two women pass the time by recounting their personal experiences. Listening to her companion Rennie discovers that Lora has better stories than herself.

Lora has picked up certain tricks for survival in the course of her adventures and Rennie is disgusted to learn that she is prostituting herself in order to supply of cigarettes, a comb, a package to chewing gum from the prison guards. For Rennie "it isn't decent". To the hardened Lora it is simply a survival tactic.

Things seem to become hopeless for Rennie when she sees a number of prisoners are tortures by police guard in a courtyard. One prisoner, who turns out to be the deaf and dumb man she met earlier, is treated with particular ferocity: "The man fall forward, he is kept from hitting the pavement by the ropes that links him to the other man" (289-90). As Rennie witnesses this orgy of gratuitous cruelty, she is overwhelmed by a dark revelation of universal complicity in evil:

> She's seen the man with the rope, now she knows what he looks like. She has been turned inside out, there's no longer a here and a there. Rennie understands for the first time that this is not necessarily a place she will get out of, ever. She is not exempt. Nobody is exempt from anything. (290)

Shortly after this torture, Lora too is savagely beaten by the prison guards. The guards have promised to arrange her meeting with Prince. As the days go by, Lora becomes impatient and finally knows that Prince was never imprisoned, having earlier been "caught in the crossfire" (257).

When Lora feels that she has been used, her grief explodes, provoking the two guards. Lora's body endures their cruel beating and Rennie feels helpless. Now she feels pity for Lora. Her face is not:

> A face any more, it's bruise, blood is till oozing from the cuts...the mouth looks like a piece of fruit that's been run over by a car, pulp...it's the face of a stranger, someone without a name. (298)

Now she realizes that "it's the face of Lora after all, there is no such things as a faceless stranger, every face is someone's, it has a name" (299).

Lora's death is symbolic of the death of the helpless and weak self of Rennie. Rennie holds Lora's hands and trying to help her back to life. By doing so she rediscovers the hands she forfeited in the youth, "feel[ing] the shape of a hand in hers...there but not there.... It will always be there now" (300).

The consequence of this crucial act would seem to be that something is indeed "born" if not Lora herself then the new subversive reporter Rennie. This new Rennie is capable of seeing things not as society pretends they are but as they are in reality, "What she sees has not altered, only the way she sees it. It's all exactly the same. Nothing is the same" (300).

The novel ends with the anticipation of Rennie's release through the intervention of Canadian diplomatic authorities that she will not write about what happened to her. Rennie has become what they accused her of "a subversive. She was not once but she is now".

The narrative is told almost in the third person. At the end we realize that there is total break between her story and what is actually going on and that is how the world feels to one woman arbitrarily caught up in power politics.

In *Bodily Harm*, Margaret Atwood explores the inner life of the protagonist, Rennie Wilford, a young journalist. The novel gives us a peep as it were into the life of a tiny isle of St. Antoine with its politics, pathos, comedy and tragedy. But the focus is on the protagonist who works her way towards the goal of specialization through a life of tensions and conflicts.

It centers round the interior landscape of the protagonist's consciousness. Rennie is brought up in the, "Sterile, hypocritical, sexless"[11] Southern Ontario small Town called Griswold by her Grandparents. Her childhood is suppressed by her grandmother's rules of do's and don'ts. She is never allowed to think and feels independently. Rennie says:

> As a child I learned...how to be quite, what not to say, and how to look at things without touching them.... According to her, it was bad manners to ask direct questions. (54)

Rennie realizes that women relished sacrificing their lives, serving others, being subordinates. They are used in a negative way against their own selves. Her grandfather was a doctor, seeing her grandfather hero-worshipped by town; Rennie says that as a young child, she too wanted to be a doctor like him. However after a few years at school, she gave up the idea for by then she had become aware that "[m]en were doctors, women were nurses; men were heroes and what were women? Women rolled the bandages" (56). He grandfather is both the mixture of the heroic and kind doctor as well as the violent and brutal man. His father was an irresponsible man who leaves his family for a mistress. Her mother has sacrificed everything-husband, home and family to look after her aged parents. She is modest, and the praises gives her the necessary courage and confidence to negate her own existence, individuality. Rennie feels hurt as she is badly neglected by her mother. She hates the self-abnegation of her mother and chooses to break away from such an environment:

> I didn't want to be trapped, like my mother. Although I admired her—everyone was always telling me how admirable she was, she was practically a saint—I didn't want to be like her in any way. (58)

Thus, Rennie leaves Griswold in order to lead a life of freedom where there would be no fetters to bind to such an extent as to kill her own individuality and identity. Rennie begins her adult life as a versatile writer. She writes articles for *Pandora*, a woman-oriented magazine and for *Visor*, a male oriented magazine. During writing an article called "The Young and the Solven" for *Visor*, she comes in contact with Jake. Jake works as a designer for a packaging company. He is smart and keeps up with the latest trends in fashions. He lives according to the male images in the magazines he reads. Jake tries all his tricks to use and pack her just as he does thing. Rennie takes quite long to realize that Jake is a subtle exploiter. Rennie considers herself an intelligent and cautious one but she allows herself to be trapped in the evil designs of Jake. As Dorothy Jones says, "Jake, Rennie's foxy, saturnine lover is a trickster".[12] However underneath his self-assured, playboy mask, Jake is emotionally very insecure. For him love is a crude game intended to hurt women. As Rennie says:

> Jake liked to pin her hands down, he liked to hold her so she couldn't move. He liked that; he liked thinking of sex as something he could win at. Sometimes he really hurt her, once he put his arm across her throat and she really did stop breathing. (207)

Rennie soon learns that "people get trapped in things that are beyond their control..." (47), when she is diagnosed of breast cancer, she is shaken to know that Jake is now uncomfortable with her and she now seems like a faulty package to him. So she decides it is time for them to part. "Like David in *Surfacing* and Peter in *The Edible Woman* it would take a long time to scrape Jake down to where he was true." Jake who is tragically alienated from his inner self, is a classic wastelander figure and not at all the hero Rennie once thought him to be.[13]

Dr. Daniel Luoma, a male gynecologist, has performed a partial mastectomy on Rennie. Daniel takes his job very seriously and is earned in his effort to help his patients recover both physically and psychologically. Later Rennie engages in an abortive love affair with Daniel to "save her life" (197) by allowing him to touch her with his life giving hands. Daniel violates the professional ethics by taking advantage of her in her emotional state.

In her relationship with Daniel, Rennie wants something 'definite', the real truth, one way or the other. Then she will know what she should do next. It's this suspension, hanging in a void, this half-life she can't bear. "She can't bear not knowing" (60) but Daniel is, "afraid of emotional commitment, [and is] unable to offer her anything but platitudes".[14]

Ultimately, Rennie realizes that Dr. Daniel is a victimizer who exploits women in the guise of medicine and surgery. She says:

> May I'm not the only one...there's a whole line up of them, dozens and dozens of women, each with a bite taken out of them, one breast or the other...he tells us all he loves us. Anyway he gets off on it, its like a harem...he's the only man in the world who knows the truth, he's looked into each one of us and seen death. (142-43)

Rennie compares Daniel with her grandfather, a physician of violent temperament whose, "primitive life-saving methods uncannily resemble torturous mutilation of the body".[15] Rubenstein says that Daniel comprises, "the paradoxes of patriarchy: the opposing stances of healing and destruction as practiced in the characteristically male institutions of medicine and politics".[16]

After Jake's departure and the dead-end relationship with Daniel, Rennie comes in contact with Paul. Psychologically he is better balanced. Paul is a tourist guide in the Caribbean island. He lives on the edge, he deals drugs, and he rescues maidens in distress. Though he is a dope and gunrunner and a probable CIA agent, he cares for humanity. He helps Rennie to get rid of the political situation on the island and warns her against getting involved with Dr. Minnow. In his attempt to save Rennie, his mission fails and she remains imprisoned. For of rest of the novel nobody knows what happens to him, just as nobody knows where he had come from. Paul is a good substitute of Jake or Daniel as he shows extreme tenderness and is not repelled by the scar on Rennie's breast. Dorothy Jones says, "Unlike Jake, who tries to make her over into something else, or Daniel who sees her as the answer to his emotional needs, Paul accepts Rennie for what she is."[17] Her love experience with Paul gives Rennie a new meaning of life. In love scene which emphasizes the healing power of love:

> He reaches out his hands and Rennie can't remember ever having been touched before...this much is enough. She's open now, she's been opened.... She enters her body again and there's a moment of pain, incarnation...she's still here on the earth, she's grateful he's touching her, she can still be touched. (204)

But soon Rennie realizes that she is a sort of "house guest" (231).

Dr. Minnow is sixty years old and he is Rennie's mentor. He is like a Christ in many ways. When he introduces himself to Rennie, he says, "Dr. Minnow, like the fish" (31), which has been a traditional symbol for Christ. His physical appearance also resembles Christ. Being part Scottish and part native, he is "brown-skinned, spare-faced and tall with a high-bridged nose; [and] looks vaguely Arabian" (28). He is known for his rebellion against the tyranny of the government and one of the three candidates for the first local election since independence. Dr. Minnow believes in fair play, in democracy and does not mix politics with religion.

He wants Rennie to publish the truth about the island. He says, "Look with your eyes open and you will see the truth of the matter. Since you are a reporter, it is your duty to report" (134). By making Rennie conscious of her duty as a writer he succeeds fulfilling his role as a spiritual guide.

Ellis is also the candidate for the first local election and does not believe in fair play and democracy. Marsdon is the campaign manager of elections for Prince of Peace. He is mean spirited. Elva is Prince's grandmother and the owner and the manager of Sunset Inn. She is self-righteous and ill-wishing Englishwoman. Elva is deliberately unkind to Rennie and does all she can, to make Rennie's stay at her hotel uncomfortable. She does not like Rennie's relationship with Dr. Minnow who, in her opinion "stirs people up for nothing" (138). When the policemen arrest Rennie in her hotel room, the vicious and cold hearted Elva has "a look of pure enjoyment on her face". Elva seems very much like Rennie's grandmother who often punished her for making a noise.

Jocasta, a feminist activist, is Rennie's friend in Canada. She is a liberated woman. For Rennie, Jocasta represents a complete and complex socio-gender system. Jocasta believes that men are desperate to assert their superiority over women one way or another. Her theory is that "[t]hey don't want love and understanding and meaningful relationships, they still want sex, but only if they can take it" (167).

During her visit on the Caribbean island, Rennie has to face some political situations. She is accused of massive involvement in the island's current political affairs. Rennie is arrested for about two-week in a Central America prison where she comes in contact with Lora Lucas, a fellow prisoner. Lora tells Rennie the story of her life. When she was a child, her stepfather raped her. Lora says, "He hit me because he could get away with it and nobody could stop him" (114).

Her mother is a helpless victim and she lives her life as the will of destiny. Her life with her husband is much like an accident. Her mother occupy the victim position number two that is to acknowledge the fact that you are a victim, but the acceptance of it as something inevitable "an act of fate".

Lora belongs to the lower class, loose, disheveled women who get what they deserve by Griswold's standard. Lora attacks her stepfather and escapes from home. She has started working in a boat and she is shocked to know that all men around expect her to sleep with them and the condition is either to comply or to lose the job.

The social and sexual oppression that Lora experiences are different from Rennie's. In a male-dominated society, her voice remains unheard. Lora is exploited by the prison guard for sex in return for news about her lover Prince of Peace. She is finally the silenced, victimized woman as she is beaten and killed by the policemen. She accepts Lora's humanity; Lora now becomes a symbol of the weak and helpless mass of humanity.

Another victim Rennie finds in prison is a "deaf and dumb man" whom she encounters several times. He is homeless, victimized beggar. Rennie first sees him lying on the steps of her hotel. She is frightened as he ran after her to shake her hands. The next time she sees him being beaten by the police in the street. Though he "has a voice but no words" (290), he manages to convey the truth to others. His physical condition and the expression in his eyes gains sympathy from Rennie. He represents "the vast mast of people in the world crippled by poverty whom ignorance and political tyranny have deprived of their capacity to proclaim the suffering and injustice of their plight".[18]

Another character is, the faceless stranger who leaves a coil of rope on Rennie's bed in Toronto. With his lack of identity, the man with the rope takes different forms from the sadistic island police to the various men with whom Rennie is romantically involved. But every attempt that Rennie makes at actually identifying the man with the rope fails her. She tries to identify him as Jake, as Daniel, as Paul until, terrifyingly, she begins to realize that this facelessness is the possibility of any male in society: he is an "agent of male oppression" (10). He represents the potential in all men to brutalize women. This is not the individual brutality of a certain person inflicted upon another but the patriarchal structure. It is the need for male dominance and female subordination.

Rennie, is like a typical Atwood woman. She shares many of the traits of Atwood's early heroines. She fantasizes like Lesje; fabricates like Joan Foster; allows herself to be subjugated like Marian; and like all Atwood's heroines seeks 'magic transformations' and "wants to be cured miraculously of everything, anything at all".[19] Rennie represents all women who, through the influence of culture, have become passive and allowed themselves to be taken advantage by men whom they are anxious to please. She allows herself to fulfil the male desire, that exhibitionist object to fill the man's gaze. She is in fact observed and feels observed by the intruder who seems to know her and once again turns her into an object of desire, an attempt to visually control her feminine sexuality.

Margaret Atwood presents these realities as horrific, for they include a recent mastectomy and the possible death sentence of cancer. The disease begins to restore in the most brutal way possible the severed contact between Rennie and her body in which she has up to then merely been a tenant. Rennie has been treating her body as a machine and for her, the damaged breast is like a "diseased fruit". Daniel tells her that while "the mind isn't separate from the body neither can the body and its ailments be regarded merely as a function of the mind. He says cancer "isn't a symbol, it's a disease" (83). Rennie finds it increasingly difficult to live at the same level as before. Her evolving view as to the relative importance of her relation with two men when represents real or potential aspects of herself: her companion Jake and her physician Daniel. Jake, an adept in the field of advertising inhabits the plane of disembodied appearance alone, manipulating images, which bear no relation to the world of substance. "He was a packager" by profession and Rennie eventually discovers that "she was one of the thing Jake was packaging" (104). He enjoys sex as a pretended rape, "pretend I just came through the window. Pretend you're being raped" (104). Rubenstein says, "Jake—a man with canine teeth and predatory desires—prefers sex that includes bondage and sadism".[20]

He is an exploiter of female sex and a woman is just an object of sex for him. In the woman's objectification, the female is nothing but the body and the female body is representative of sexuality. From this stems Jake's need to reshape Rennie into the image of what is taken to be the eroticized female. After killing her plants, remodeling her apartment and her look, she stages the ultimate erotic object: the perfect sexual poses as she parades in sensual lingerie. Everything seems to underline the power relations between male and female: he asks and she complies. He hung posters in Rennie's bedroom showing, "brown-skinned woman wound up in a piece of material that held her arms to her sides but left her breasts and thighs and buttocks exposed" (105) and "a woman lying feet first on the sofa and her head up at the other end of the sofa, was tiny, featureless and rounded like a doorknob. In the foreground there was bull" (105-06). This shows Jake's rapist fantasies.

It is very close to, "the early 1980's feminist antipornography position which asserted strong links between pornography as misogynist power fantasy and male violence against women".[21]

Rennie's passive behaviour to Jake's every whim eventually drives him away. After her mastectomy, things begin to go sour between them. Jake does not lose interest because of her mastectomy as she believes, but because of her remarkable acceptance of his oppressive and abusive nature. She reacts to her abandonment with predictable passivity and tries to embody the victimized woman, the innocent one in a perverse world of wrongdoers. She seems to manifest the victim psychology which

Margaret Atwood announces as her subject in the epigraphs to the novel taken from John Berger's *Way of Seeing*: 'A man's presence suggests what he is capable of doing to you or for you. By contrast, a woman's presence...defines what can and cannot be done to her.'

After her mastectomy Jake feels uncomfortable with Rennie and sees the scar on her breast as "the kiss of death on her" (201). Now Rennie is emotionally disturbed by her operation and feels that she has her malignancy uncured, Rennie regards the operation very little in terms of a salvation but more as evil and violation by man, her body and self cut away from each other are marked by male 'probers' the labelers and cutters. It is significant that the surgery and removal is that of the breast—an eroticized body part thus enforcing the idea of man preying on the female as sexual object only. She has no more hopes of becoming a mother and breast-feeding her future child. As Rubenstein says:

> Some of Rennie's anxieties about invasion and violation can be understood through the cultural attitudes towards both the female flesh and cancer; Rennie is a double victim, of both disease and male exploitation. Men worship the breast, and woman internalize the male overvaluation of this aspect their anatomy. Because it is also associated with the actual and symbolic qualities of nurturance, the loss of part or all of a breast effects a woman's sense of her procreative capabilities, after her operation, Rennie wonders and worries whether she will able to bear a child.[22]

The partial mastectomy on her breast reinforces the idea of Rennie's incompleteness and her fractured identity. She feels "raw-material, violated and doctored"[23] by her surgeon Daniel. Now she understands the feelings of a woman who has undergone Daniel's surgery, "...holding the hand of a blonde woman whose breasts he has recently cut off. Who wants to cure, who wants to help, who wants everything to be fine you're alive, he says to her, with kindness and duplicity, compelling as a hypnotist. You're very lucky. Tears stream silently down her face" (283-84). Daniel can be parallel with the man with the rope and later in her dreams, the man with the knife, double to the anonymous would-be rapist.

Rennie's relationship with Paul is also not satisfactory, she realizes that falling in love with Paul, a mysterious stranger is "the biggest cliché in the book of her life" (222). She does not enjoy being in love but she requires being with a man to satisfy her bodily needs. As she says, "being in love was running barefoot along a street covered with broken bottles. It was fool hardy, and if you got through it without damage it was only by sheer luck...it gave [people] power over you. It made you visible, soft, penetrable; it made you ludicrous" (102).

She fails to establish a meaningful relationship with men and does not want another relationship, which is meaningless, and loveless, "I should take my body and run. I don't need another man. I'm not supposed to expect anything" (227). This shows her female passivity. Finally, Rennie realizes that all the men in her life are, in reality, one man, and that she herself has chosen him, created him in her own image his face, "...familiar, with silver eyes that twin and reflect her own" (287).

Rennie's friend Jocasta explains that for men woman is but a sexual object to be completely possessed. "Their prime concern is to take sex from the woman in a sadistic manner. The woman can be somewhat consenting but not too much so in order for the man to feel like he is some sort of a battle for what he desires and that he will ultimately leave the woman with a feeling of defeat" (6).

Rennie seeks to detach herself by trying to turn the event into "pieces" for a magazine, when she is in personal crisis. After her mastectomy and shocking incident of a man who breaks into her apartment leaving a rope with coil, she tries to attempt an article on pornography. She visits the studio of a male porn artist Frank with Jocasta. Frank depicts pornography as an art. In his studio Rennie sees life-sized mannequin tables and chairs featuring women muzzled and locked in demeaning position. There she understands the position and place of women in society and realizes how art is used to describe women as an object in a male dominated society. As Frank says, "what art does, it takes what society deals out and makes it visible, right?" (208).

Rennie also visits the Toronto policemen's Pornography Museum along with Jocasta. There she encounters with the evidence of male brutality and violence against women. She is shocked to see the film clips of nude women, different postures of naked women. Films clips of women copulating with animals make her physically ill. There Rennie see all ugly and horrible films to display bodies of women as maps of violence. She realizes the abuse of woman in so-called civilized society. She feels that men destroy women's individuality in a subtle and invisible manner with the help of cultural codes. She finds herself unable to complete this article and opts for another that is a travel article on a 'paradise' island.

Rennie association with Jocasta raises her feminine consciousness. Now she understands the exploiting and victimizing nature of the males. According to Jocasta women think that they are liberated but in reality it is like a distant dream. Nothing has really changed with women. Men still are interested in having full control over women. They consider women as rentable objects for the pleasure of men. Sexual exploitation is everywhere. Jocasta gives a fantastic idea of reversing the role of men and women:

> I think it would be a great deal if all the men were turned into women and all the women were turned into men, even just for a day. Then they'd all know exactly how the other ones would like to be treated when they got changed back, I mean. (156)

During her visit to the Caribbean island, Rennie discovers another awareness that life is unstable, one's body is erratic and unpredictable. There she feels that people are shocking in their attitude towards other. The bodily harm done by other people, are victimized by those who have power. Women are treated as object and humiliated by men. Rennie finds that women are powerless and abuse and their condition is not very different from common people. As Jaidev says, "woman becomes a metaphor for all those who are damaged and abused only because they are powerless".[24]

Rennie discovers that women are still where they were a century ago. Their freedom and identity are only delusions.

People enjoy torturing others especially women. A man can be disloyal to his woman but a woman dare not. People look at the cruelty on the women as silent spectators but they do not like to interfere, explaining it away as a man woman thing and not anyone else's business. There she sees Marsdon who tortures woman in a very brutal way:

> ...he made her take off all her clothes,...and then he covered her with cow-itch. That's like a nettle, it's what you do to people you really don't like a whole lot. Then he tied her to a tree in the back yard, right near an ant hill, the stinging kind. He stayed in the house, drinking rum and listening to her scream. He left her there five hours, till she was all swollen up like a balloon. A lot of people heard her but nobody tried to untie her.... (214-15)

Rennie is shocked to know that in the Caribbean robbery is greater crime than murder. If a man kills a woman it is linked with passion and that man is forgiven by the society:

> If you get angry and chop up your woman, that is understandable, a crime of passion you might say. But stealing you plan before hand. (225)

Things become horrifying for Rennie when she comes to know the violence done to Lora. Lora's tales further go to completely shatter her attitude towards the high voltage feminism. Rennie includes Lora's tale in her travelogue. Lora thinks that condition of women is not satisfactory in the society. Lora used to live in a cellar with her stepfather and lead a life of complete terror under the gross exploitation of him. When Lora begins to tell her tales, Rennie wishes she could not hear her. She fixates on Lora's opening and closing mouth. Rennie's attitude is much like that of her society, which marginalizes women like Lora. By Lora's tale, Rennie learns that in this society there are many more who are eager to exploit, if she is willing to be weak and give in. Lora says, "They think if there're renting the boat they're renting everything on it. May be I'm for sale, I'd tell them....I'm not for rent" (213-14).

This shows that in a post liberated age; man's attitude towards woman has not changed. They think that woman is for rent smacks of male arrogance. Lora's brutal experiences in Canada and Caribbean Island shock Rennie's feminist sensibility. The heartless mutilation of Lora is symbolic of the limited gender-specific role of women in society. The brutality done to Lora is the real "bodily harm". When prison guards beat up Lora, Rennie wishes that someone would cover her eyes, something she achieves for herself through fantasizing about her own release from prison. She realizes that women are victimized by male power and understands that no one is exempt:

> ...nothing is inconceivable here, no rats in the vagina but only because they haven't thought of it yet, they're still amateur...she has been turns inside out, there's no longer a here and a there. Rennie understands for the first time that this is not necessarily a place she will get out of, ever. She is not exempt. Nobody is exempt from anything. (290)

As she witnesses the gratuitous cruelty, Rennie is shocked by a dark revelation of universal complicity in evil. She finally understands that she is not afraid of cancer or amputation. Her scar has no significance and it is a very minor accident of her like, instead she comes to see men in the light of the power they wield, through violence as well as through language, "She is afraid of men and it's simple. It's rational, she is afraid of men because men are frightening" (290).

Now she becomes, "a sadder but wiser person".[25] Lora's death compels her to think in terms of some kind of positive action against cruelty on women. She emerges as a new human being, as her name suggests, "Renata Wilferd" means "born again".[26] She has begun to see things differently. As Howells says:

> Rennie's effort to tell the story is, like her effort to save Lora, an exercise of the moral imagination, being both reportage and invention.... As she is a reporter she determines to 'report', offering her interpretation of contemporary lifestyles in two different countries but now with an edge of moral engagement...[she] does more than report; she tries to imagine things differently and better than they are....[27]

Throughout the novel, Margaret Atwood uses literal and metaphoric camera images. Camera images in *Bodily Harm* include actual cameras and photographs, commercial illustrations and products, pictures or other non-commercial art, camera-like instruments or reflectors (including telescopes binoculars, sunglasses, mirrors) and films.

The camera narrator is a "Snapshots" the present by doing mental "pieces" on the order of her actual lifestyle journalism for *Visor* magazine. She also carries an actual camera bag throughout her trip to the Caribbean. It symbolizes her tourist vision and identity.

The picture of a cut-open melon in Rennie's room, at the Sunset Inn is, like most of the other pictures and products, apparent as an image Rennie and, in one sense, all women. When she waits at the airport to pick up a package, later revealed to be a machine gun, she would like to use the "photo machine" (109). She images Jake as a "packager" (103). Having been surgically as well as sexually "opened" or "violated" by men and she fears that the scar on her breast will, split open "like a diseased fruit" (60).

Painful events are often disguised with comic book images, for e.g. she pictures Daniel as Rox Mergan, M.D., Paul as Tarzan and herself as Paul's con-do-book date. She cannot picture Daniel's wife or Jake's "new lady".

When Lora tells her life story, Rennie "switches off the sound and concentrates only on the picture" turning it into a magazine "still" she arranges Lora "into a makeover piece, before and after, with a series of shots in between showing the process" (82-83).

Lora's tale is like "a movie with the sound gone". Rennie imagines her grandmother and mother: "Her hands are cold, she lifts them up to look at them, but they elude her. Something missing" (238-43).

In *Bodily Harm* Camera and photographs have been instrumental in the protagonist's metamorphosis. She makes connection among past, present and future, between background and foreground. It is narrated with a deceptive double vision and

Margaret Atwood does a brilliant job creating a narrative that combines first person with third person that very smoothly moves between the past and the present, as well as bits of a possible future. This novel is very effective on this level, in that it explores Rennie's own personal journey as a survivor of Breast Cancer. In this "massive involvement" situation, only through fantasy can Rennie distance herself from her intolerable position.

In *Bodily Harm*, Rennie's cancer is a metaphor for a malignant world. Her disease results her journey to the Caribbean. The disease really to be feared, Rennie comes to realize, is the capacity to take pleasure from another's pain. When police arrests her, she recognizes on the hotel manager's face "a look of pure enjoyment" (232) and in prison she watches a guard with a bayonet menacing a group of bound prisoners. She thinks, "he is doing it because he enjoys it. Malignant" (255). Margaret Atwood points that we all are somehow guilty of being human being and that malignancy is quite possible, a metaphor for the human conditions. Now "massive involvement" has a different meaning, for Rennie it is a term with positive action. She makes the one truly generous gesture of her life; she takes the injured Lora's hand and holds it with all her strength, willing her back to life, "Surely if she can only try hard enough, something will move and live again, something will get born" (299).

"It shows Rennie's feminist consciousness and she is struggling into a new awareness of herself as a morally responsible human being."[28] Rennie emerges as a bold and subversive journalist who is bold enough to narrate her experience in the form of travelogue called *Bodily Harm*. She uses "pen as a weapon"[29] and ends up as an activist. She realizes her duty to write, to report the truth; "she will pick her time: then she will report". As Helene Cixous says, Rennie puts women, "into the text—as into the world and into history by her own movement [of travelogue]".[30]

Rennie's story emerges as a warning that, "negative innocence ...is the most appalling characteristic of evil when it appears in the actual world".[31] *Bodily Harm* challenges us, "to become human".[32] Margaret Atwood says:

> Oppression involves a failure of the imagination: the failure to imagine the full humanity of other human beings. If the imagination were a negligible thing and the act of writing a mere frill, as many in this society would like to believe, regimes all over the world would not be at such pains to exterminate them.[33]

As *Bodily Harm* is written in the aftermath of an over-conscious women's liberation it forces one's attention on the horrifying status of women. But in this book, Rennie refuses to be a victim that is position number three—to acknowledge the fact that you are victim but to refuse to accept the assumption that the role is inevitable, described by Margaret Atwood in *Survival*. Rennie exposes that in society...holding her up (301).

Rennie exposes that in society 'bodily harm' is everywhere in prison, in civilized and uncivilized country, in political and personal life. There is no limitation of 'bodily harm'. As Prabhakar says, "Rennie's body which has been maimed, dismembered, altered and fragmented stands as a testimonial to the depravity and decadence of the society that is predominantly patriarchal."[34]

Rennie rejects her submissive role as a woman and is ready to speak out the truth about the exploited women. It is Rennie's new optimism, which dictates the ending:

> She will never be rescued. She has already been rescued. She is not exempt. Instead she is lucky, suddenly, finally, she's overflowing with luck, it's this luck holding her up. (301)

Rennie's story emerges as a warning against disabling female fantasies of innocence and victimization, which displace women's recognition of the dangers of the real life.

REFERENCES

1. Hansen, Elaine Tuttle. "Fiction and (Post) Feminism in Atwood's Bodily Harm", *Novel*, 19.1, Fall 1985, 11.
2. Wainwright, J.A. Rev. "Bodily Harm", *Dalhousie Review*, 61, Autumn 1981, 58.
3. Vevaina, Coomi S. "I tend to see symbols", *Times of India, Sunday Review Section*, 20, March 1988, 8.
4. Howells, Coral Ann. *Margaret Atwood*. London: Macmillan P. Ltd., 1996, 120.

5. Irvine, Lorna. "The Here and Now of Bodily Harm," *Margaret Atwood: Vision and Forms*, ed. Kathryn Vanspanckeren and Jan Garden Castro. Carbondale: Southern Illinois University Press, 1988, 96.
6. Atwood, Margaret. *Margaret Atwood: Conversations*, ed. Earl G. Ingersoll. London: Virago, 1992, 246.
7. Wilson, Sharon R. "Turning Life into Popular Art: Bodily Harm's Life-Tourist", *Studies in Canadian Literature,* 1985, 137.
8. Howells, 111.
9. Prabhakar, M. "Bodily Harm: Writing as Exposure", *Feminism/ Postmodernism: Margaret Atwood's Fiction*. New Delhi: Creative Books, 1999, 68.
10. Gubar, Susan. "'The Blank Page' and the Issues of Female Creativity", *Critical Inquiry*, 2, 1981, 247.
11. Blaise, Clark. "Tale of Two Colonies", *Canadian Literature*, 95, Winter 1982, 111.
12. Jones, Dorothy. "Waiting for the Rescue: A Discussion of Margaret Atwood's Bodily Harm", *Kunapipi*, 6.3, 1984, 91.
13. Vevaina, Coomi S. "We're all in it together: Atwood's Bodily Harm", *Re/membering Selves: Alienation and Survival in the novels of Margaret Atwood and Margaret Laurence.* New Delhi: Creative Book, 1996, 187.
14. Wainwright, 58.
15. Rubenstein, 264.
16. *Ibid.*
17. Jones, 93.
18. *Ibid.*, 96-97.
19. Salat, M.F. "Canadian Nationalism and Feminist Ideology: Margaret Atwood," *The Canadian Novel: A Search for Identity*. New Delhi: B.R. Publishing, 71-72.
20. Rubenstein, 261.
21. Howells, 12.
22. Rubenstein, 262.
23. Wilson, 140.
24. Jaidev. "Women as Metaphor: A Note on Atwood's Feminism", *The Indian Journal of English Studies*, 25, 1995, 111.
25. Thomas, Audrey. "Topic of Cancer", *Books in Canada*. Oct. 1981, 9-12.

26. Carrington, Ildiko de Papp. "Another Symbolic Descent", *Essays on Canadian Writing*, 26, 1983, 61-62.
27. Howells, 125.
28. Quoted from Atwood's Address delivered at a conference "Imagined Realities in Contemporary Women's Writing", held at Dyffryn House near Cardiff (Oct. 1982).
29. Prabhakar, 80.
30. Cixous, Helene. "The Laugh of the Medusa", trans. Keith Cohen and Paul Cohen. *Signs*, 1.4, Summer 1976, 875.
31. Woodcock, George. "Recent Canadian Novels (1) Major Publishers", *Queen's Quarterly*, 89, No. 4, Winter 1982, 748.
32. Suallivan, Rosemary. "Margaret Atwood", in the *Oxford Companion to Canadian Literature*, ed. William Toye. Toronto: Oxford University Press, 1983, 31.
33. Atwood, Margaret. "Amnesty International: An Address", *Second Words*, 397.
34. Prabhakar, 79.

The Handmaid's Tale

6

> *The Handmaid's Tale* is a Science-fiction fable and a futuristic feminist nightmare. It warns that if we cease to judge this world, we may find ourselves, very quickly in one, which infinitely worse.[1]
>
> Margaret Atwood

It is Margaret Atwood's sixth novel published is 1985. It is an international best seller, which won the prestigious Governor General's Award. *The Handmaid's Tale* has been made into a film directed by Volker Schlonderff in 1990, with a screenplay by Harold Pinter. This novel shows Margaret Atwood in her most radical light as she has revised the categories of 'Canadian and female' through which her own identity is constituted. Like most of her novels, *The Handmaid's Tale* is also a canon of feminism. The basic theme of the novel is still the examination of patriarchal structures of domination and power and the woman's quest for meaningful identity. As Sherill E. Grace says, "Atwood's vision has not essentially changed, but has expended and deepened".[2] It is a postmodern feminist novel in which Margaret Atwood explores how the protagonist Offred react to, "oppression in all its manifestations, both physical and psychological".[3] It is a dystrophic novel in the tradition of George Orwell's *1984*, Aldous Huxley's *Brave New World* and Zamyatin's *We*. W.H. New says:

> It speculates about present day trends: the verbal controls that commercial advertising exerts over roles and expectations, the legal controls that society claims over women's lives and bodies; the active will to assert power,

> the passive wish for anonymity that leads many people to surrender authority to institutions, the existence of economic structures more powerful that legislative ones, the resurgence of influential fundamentalist groups that impose preconceived boundaries around the design of truth.[4]

Lucy M. Freibert calls it, "political-science fiction".[5] In an interview Margaret Atwood said, "the political to me is a part of life. What we mean by political is how people relate to power structure and *vice versa*".[6] *The Handmaid's Tale* is set in 21st century in the U.S.A. which is now the Republic of Gilead. This is Margaret Atwood's first novel set in future but it is different from futuristic fantasy. As she says, "It is no science fiction. There are no space ships, no Martians nothing like that I didn't invent a lot. I transposed to a different time and place but the motifs are all historical motifs."[7]

It is written from a woman's point of view and predicts, "the horrors of a culture so frightened by normal sexuality that it codified and prescribed all such procreation and created hierarchies of life and death around it. It is a brutal horrifying culture".[8]

The Handmaid's Tale is dedicated to Margaret Atwood's ancestor Mary Webster and Perry Miller-her teacher whose books on the puritans have informed American history and who taught her to read national literatures when she was a student at Harvard. Wester was a rebellious colonial American, hanged for a witch in connecticut. Mary Webster's story is one of persecution and escape even if but short-lived. Like Webster the protagonist in the novel too escapes from Gilead, a dystopian misogynistic society.

In the novel Margaret Atwood offers a different perspective on the relationship between men and women. She expresses the complex relationship between sexuality and power and argues how power dominates on sex, Michel Foucault says:

> To deal with sex, power employs nothing more than law of prohibition. It's objective: that sex renounce itself. Its instrument: the threat of punishment that is nothing other than the suppression of sex. Renounce yourself or suffer the

> penalty of being suppressed; do not appear if you do not want to disappear. Your existence will be maintained only at the cost of your nullification. Power constrains sex only through a taboo that plays on the alternative between two nonexistences.[9]

Offred, the Handmaid who is the main character of the novel, is victim of theocracy. She narrates her own tale and concentrates on the fate of women in Gilead who are seen and used as mere means of procreation".[10] She lives with the commander and his wife Serena. Her job is to get pregnant by the Commander, give birth to the child, then give it up so that the wife can raise the baby as her own. The novel follows the thoughts of suicide, scandal and betrayal that Offred has throughout the journey. As Mario Klarer says, "In Gilead, being a woman means to become preliterate and to follow the prescriptions of men."[11]

Under the guise of religious salvation, the Gileadean regime builds a social structure that is rigid, oppressive and above all, misogynistic, "Women in Gilead are as, *unintelligent matter* in the reproduction process which is like everything else in this dystopia, dominated by men".[12] By exaggerating some existing misogynistic attitudes and interwining them with an affecting plot and characters, Margaret Atwood finds success in her endeavours to shed light upon and caution against a horrific social treatment of women.

The protagonist of the novel Offred, escapes from the Republic of Gilead to tell her story of victimization. She uses, "languages as a means of communication to unlock her inner feelings and bitter experiences as well as a 'Subversive weapon' to raise her voice against the marginalization of women".[13] The novel also offers, "a variant version of gothic"[14] which has female fear of male power at its center.

Margaret Atwood insists that women should become, "fully liberated individual". It is her conviction that "three attributes that power-mad regime cannot tolerate are a human imagination, the power to communicate and hope".[15] In *The Handmaid's Tale* Offred reclaims power/liberty by utilizing the three attributes and in the process defeats the destructive manipulation of the power brokers.

There is strong religious stand in the narrative as quotations from the Bible find their place in the text, especially in the title. The place is named the Republic of Gilead after the biblical land where Jacob went into the Handmaid Billah because his wife Rachel was infertile. The Handmaid is a substitute sex object required by the elderly barren wife to facilitate the continuation of her husband's lineage. With reference to this aspect, Margaret Atwood remarks:

> A new regime would never say, we are socialist, we are fascist. They would say they were serving God. You can develop set of beliefs by using the Bible.[16]

In the novel Commanders regard themselves as latter day Jacob and use their Handmaids in a similar way in this new Gilead. It justifies its, "sexist policies with the social-biological theory of natural polygamy and legitimizes its racist and sexist policies as having biblical precedent".[17] The title of the book, suggests a shared experience of a class of women in Gilead. Offred is in this sense a spoke person for the Handmaids of Gilead.

The Handmaid's Tale deals with questions, problems and predicaments, which have a universal rather than cultural specific validity. With no Canadian setting, the landscape of the novel is not geophysical or cultural but interior. It deals in patterns of oppression and victimization based on sexual difference. As a woman's story of resistance it is far more concerned with gender politics than with nationality. While giving a shocking treatment to the theme of sex, procreation and love, "this novel takes on the character of grim prophetic vision of a future world where male chauvinism would have, once and for all destroyed the finest chords of wifehood, motherhood and womanhood".[18]

The novel begins with the chapter entitled "Night" and ends with "Night". Every alternate chapter is entitled "Night". Paradoxically, Night is the only time during which the protagonist is free to think, recollect and crystallize her thoughts and memories. It is finally in the night that she perhaps escapes.

The time frame of the narrative is not too-distant future when everything that we would recognize as familiar has been relegated to "the other time, the time before" (55). The United States has undergone a coup defeat. The President has been shot, congress, "machine gunned" and the constitution "suspended" (183). Conservative Christians take control of the United States and establish a dictatorship.

Most women in Gilead are infertile after repeated exposure to pesticides, nuclear waste, or leakages from chemical weapons, "nuclear plant accidents...leakages from chemical and biological warfare stockpiles and toxic waste disposal sites...the uncontrolled use of chemical insecticides, herbicides and other sprays" (317). The few fertile women are taken to camps and trained to be Handmaids. The Handmaids are women with viable ovaries are forced to bear child for the childless commanders. In this new regime, the word, "sterile" is banned. There are only women who are fruitful and fruitless:

> The Handmaids are desexed, dehumanized and are forbidden choice and desire. They are not supposed to think and feel. Thus Offred says, "I try not to think too much. Like other things now thought must be rationed". (7)

Infertile lower-class women are sent either to clean up toxic waste or to become "Marathas" house servants. No women in the Republic are permitted to be openly sexual; sex is for reproduction only. The government declares this a feminist improvement on the sexual politics of today when women are seen as sex objects. *The Handmaid's Tale* focuses on one Handmaid, Offred. Like all Handmaids, her name denotes her possession by the high status male in whose home she is currently posted that is of Fred, Offred became a Handmaid after an attempt to escape with her daughter and husband from Gilead. Struggling to retain some vestige of her former personality, Offred hoards her memories. Offred's willed excursions into the "distant past" (94) along with her nightmares flesh out the narrative. In these sequences, we learn something of her personal history—her relationship with her husband Luke, her daughter and her feminist mother. We also get her fragments of knowledge about the coup and the changes gradually instituted in the months of following. When her marriage with Luke is decreed invalid because of Luke's prior marriage, they attempt escape. But at the border crossing the guard suspicious behaviour convinced them that their plan has been discovered, and they fled back into Gilead. Luke is shot; her daughter is given away to needy woman in the upper circle and Offred captured. In the worst of her nightmares, Offred can still see her daughter, "...holding out her arms to me, being carried away" (85). She never sees her daughter again, nor does she know, whether her husband is alive or dead. Following the capture at the border, her memory lapses, "there must have been needles, pills, sometimes like that. I couldn't have lost that much time without help" (49). When Offred regains full consciousness, she is at the Leah and Rachel center, the training center of handmaids. Here in a flashback sequence the novel opens. Now Offred is in the service of the Commander and his wife, Serna Joy. She is unable to produce children and hates Offred for taking her husband's seed. If Offred does not become pregnant, she will undoubtedly take revenge by sending her away, possibly to the toxic colonies. Offred does not become pregnant, but she does develop an unexpected relationship with the General. He plays games of scrabble with her, gives her gifts of cosmetics and old fashion magazines, which are officially denied. One night he dresses her in a cocktail dress and takes her to an illegal nightclub where Offred meets an old female friend Moira, now a prostitute in the club. Finally Offred escapes, with the help of Nick in the Black Van kept to cart dissidents away. "The van waits in the driveway, its double doors stand open...whether this is my end on a new beginning. I have no way of knowing: I have given myself over into the hands of strangers, because it can't be helped. And so I step up, into the darkness within; or else the light" (307).

Offred's voice is the most anguished in Margaret Atwood's fiction to date and the most self-conscious. She struggles with the process of telling, trying out different versions—inventing, then recanting scenarios that might show her in a better light.

Offred is permitted neither to read nor to write so she has no reader or listener to witness her suffering in Gilead, "I'll pretend you can hear me. But it's no good, because I know you can't"

(50), so she records her story. "By telling you anything at all, I'm at least believing in you, I believe you're there, I believe you into being...I tell, therefore you are" (279). She has no choice but to take a leap of faith and will her audience into being.

We learn in Historical Notes that the journal tapes were enclosed in a box, apparently buried, and sealed with postal packing tape. Professor James Darcy Pieixoto addresses an academic conference on 25 June 2195. He and his collaborator Professor Knotly Wade discuss the manuscript called *The Handmaid's Tale*. Gilead no longer exists but in its make the map of North America has been radically redrawn. Offred has been consigned safely to history. Her document is merely additional evidence for fleshing out a context that no longer exists. As Pieixoto put it, "Our author...was one of many, and must be seen within the broad outlines of the moment in history of which she was part" (317).

In Gileadean society men are rulers and women their subjects. The men are divided into Commander, those who exercise power and Guardians, those who form the second level of authority and perform the function of police and finally functional ones like doctors and drivers.

Offred's Commander though hungry for power is pathetically human. Previously he regards Offred as nothing more than his official Handmaid but soon he makes use of her as his unofficial scrabble partner and club companion. He plans private meetings with Offred and supplies her books, magazines and hand lotions, which are banned for the Handmaids. The Commander sees polygamy as natural and regards women as inferior beings. At times he looks at Offred sheepishly while at other times he appears as a caring human being. The thinking Fred and the feeling Fred appear to be two different persons.

Offred's lover Nick is a passionate one and seems to genuinely care for her, he does not part with any information about himself and remains as good as a stranger to her. Nick redeems all men by his act of saving Offred, although it may mean his own death. He is Commander's chauffeur. He shifts her from, "being a helpless victim to being a sly, subversive survivors".[19]

Offred's husband Luke is only depicted through her fragmented memories. When Gilead first deprived women of their job and economic independence—their money and property were transferred to the control of husbands or male relative. Luke expressed no particular outrage at the new laws. Offred however feels this lack of independence as another physical disjunction, "I feel like somebody cut off my feet but Luke doesn't mind this.... He doesn't mind it at all. Maybe he ever likes it. We are not each other's any more. Instead, I am his" (191). He thinks "its only a job". All the men in the novel attempt to legitimate and enhance their own power through the violent and social repression of women.

In Gilead women's identity is repressed by men, they are reduced to being men's possession, mere objects. Gileadian society is highly alienated especially for women. They are segregated from one another and divided according to their functions. They all wear uniforms colour coded to their functions. We can say that the novel posits, "a future culture in which such feminist dreams have been replaced by fundamentalist patriarchy that divides women into rigid categories based on function".[20]

The Wives are infertile. They help their husbands during the insemination, commonly known as "Ceremony". They are incharge of household discipline. They wear blue dress, which resembles virgin. The Marathas act as maids and housekeepers. When they become weak and sick and cease working, they are deported to the Colonies. They dressed in dull green. The wives of poor men called Econowives. They have to do everything "if they can" (34) i.e. waiving, housekeeping and childbearing. They wear striped dresses in red, blue and green. There are also the women who work in clubs and offer excitement outside these defined roles: they are prostitutes and called Jezebles.

The Aunts, the policewomen of Gilead wear paramilitary khaki dress with cattle prods slung on thongs from their leather belts. They are rigid, middle-aged women who have internalized patriarchal values and are used to impose them on other women. They run their re-education centers with cattle prods, torture techniques, and brain washing slogans. It is believed that, "the best and most cost effective way to control women for reproductive and other purposes was through women themselves" (320). The Aunts betray other women in order to "escape redundancy and consequent shipment to the infamous Colonies..." (290).

"They are like feminist and believe in a women's culture" (137). They see men as the enemy, "men are sex machines, said Aunt Lydia, and not much more. They only want one thing. You must learn to manipulate them" (153). They also believe that in Gilead the Handmaids are safe and protected. As they walk down the street, "...no man shouts obscenities at us, speak to us, touches us. No man whistles" (24). Aunt Lydia who regards the Handmaids as pampered and spoiled girls in privileged position, says that there is more than one kind of freedom, "Freedom to and freedom from. In the days of anarchy it was freedom to. Now you are being given freedom from. Don't underrate it" (24).

The Aunts in Gilead press the idea of the degeneracy of sex-love on the Handmaids. Aunt Lydia says, "They can't help it.... God made them that way but they did not make you that way. He made you different. It's up to you set the boundaries. Later you will be thanked" (43). It shows their feministic consciousness. The Aunts occupy victim position number one that is "Denial of the fact that one is a victim", described by Margaret Atwood in *Survival.*

The Handmaids are childbearer and they are young women whose possession of "viable ovaries" (153), make them an important and scarce "natural resource" (61). They wear red dress, which resembles religious habits. Their faces are obscured by peaked hats, which also function to prevent their seeing anything but what lies immediately in front of them. As Susan Jacob says, "Women's dresses in Gilead are meant to resemble both Christian nun's habit and the Muslim woman's purdah."[21] Margaret Atwood in her poem "The Red Shirt", describes red as a highly significant, "Young girls should not wear red./ In some countries it is the colour/ of death; in other passion,/ in others war, in others anger,/ in others the sacrifice of shed blood/ Dancing in red shoes will kill you".[22]

In Gilead, the Handmaids role is the most dehumanized. They act as a substitute biological mother and bear a child for the aging Commander. They are childless as result of their wives infertility: As Offred says:

> ...We are two legged wombs, that's all: sacred vessels, ambulatory chalices. (146)

The Handmaids are allowed three chances of two years each with different Commander to produce a child. If the Handmaid becomes pregnant, the child is taken over by the Commander and his wife and she move on to another Commander. Carole Pateman argues that the notion of, ownership of one's body can lead to a variety of social relations of subordination[23] including prostitution and surrogate motherhood. If the Handmaids do not succeed, they are declared 'Unwoman' and sent to the colonies to clear up toxic wastes. Compared to colonies, their present status is a paradise. There is the 'solitary' zone where they are tortured:

> They figure you've got three years maximum, at those, before your nose falls off and your skin pulls away like rubber gloves. They don't bother to feed you much, or give you protective clothing or anything, it's cheaper not to. Anyway it's mostly people they want to get rid of.... It's old women.... And Handmaids who have screwed up their three chances and incorrigibles.... Discards, all of us. (260-61)

Amin Malik says that, "the dictates of state policy in Gilead thus relegate sex to a salable commodity exchange for mere minimal survival".[24]

Male infertility is unthinkable in Gilead, as Offred says, "There are only women who are fruitful and women who are barren, that's the law" (57). So the Handmaids are defined, "not even by the category of gender, but quite narrowly by that of female fertility".[25]

The Handmaids are not supposed to talk with each other. When the Handmaids meet each other they greet by saying 'Blessed be the fruit" not a "Hello" and the accepted response, "May the Lord Open". So the silence and powerlessness go together in their lives. The power of body languages is also seized from the Handmaids. Despite the restriction, the Handmaids communicate in different way, "We learnt to whisper almost without sound. In the semidarkness we could stretch our arms when the aunts were not looking and touch each other's hands across space. We learned to lip read.... In this way we exchange names from bed to bed: Alma Janine Dolores, Moira, June" (14).

Gileadean society is faced with the complete loss of freedom; women have to lead a life bound by slavery. They are stripped of their identities by taking away their names from them. The Aunts are given the names of popular brands of cake-mixed and cosmetics. The Handmaid's name indicates the male they are currently rendering service. Offred name indicates that she is the Handmaid of Fred", her Commander. It's a kind of tag. As Offred says:

> My name isn't Offred, I have another name, which nobody uses now because it's forbidden...name is like your telephones number, useful only to others. (94)

Similarly Warren's Handmaid is Ofwarren, Glen's Handmaid is Ofglen. The destruction of the individual name is part of the attempt to destroy the past and force woman to live in the present moment alone, in a two-dimensional existence. Jessie Givner says, "Indeed, the desire of the Gilead regime to remove name is as strong as the desire to remove faces. Just as the rulers of Gilead try to eliminate mirrors, reflections of faces, so they attempt to erase names."[26]

It is significant, that out of all the women mentioned, only Moira-Offred's, college friend-seems to keep her real name. She is a rebel and appears both in narrator's pre-Gileadean past and in the dystopian present. Moira makes two attempts to escape from the Rachel and Leah Re-education Center. Both the time she fails and captures. Her escapade does not inspire other Handmaids instead they frightened, "At any moment there might be a shattering explosion, the glass of the windows would fall inwards.... Moira was like an elevator with open sides. She made us dizzy already we were finding these walls secure. In the upper reaches of the atmosphere you'd come apart, you'd vaporize, there would be no pressure holding you together" (143). She represents an ideal for Offred but also a source of guilt, for she accomplishes what Offred is too frightened to attempt.

The other rebellious woman in the novel is Offred's mother. She never appears directly but it made real for us through Offred's memories. She is "the kind of old woman who won't let any one but in front of her in a supermarket line" (130). She was independent and strong-minded. She was an active feminist of the early heady days of the women's movement, taking part in pornographic book burning demonstrations. She denies the power of the feminine in Offred by encouraging her individualism and independence from men but Offred's response, to her mother shows both her rejection of her mother's value and a longing (with the benefit of hindsight) for their return:

> I admired my mother in some ways, although things between us were never easy. She expected too much from me, I felt. She expected me to vindicate her life for her, and the choices she'd made. I didn't want to live my life on her terms; I didn't want to be the model offspring, the incarnation for her ideas. We used to fight about that. (132)

In Gilead, there is some groups of women who intent to survive at any costs. Janine and Serna Joy are two of them. Janine serves as a foil to Offred since she exists only on the physical level and does not aspire for anything beyond bare survival. She is classic example of an individual completely co-opted by the system.

Serena Joy is Commander's wife. In pre-Gilead she was known as Pam. She is neither serene nor joyous. She was a lead singer in Church choirs and later appeared on T.V. shows giving speeches on "the sanctity of the home, about how women should stay home" and presented her failure to do so "as a sacrifice she was making for the good of all" (55).

In new Gilead her life as the wife of a Commander would seem to be the enviable leisured life of the high class society but she too has been robbed of her identity and judged worthless, "damaged, defective" because of her infertility. She is forced to take part in the impregnation ceremony and she has to accept the extra-marital affairs of her husband. She treated Offred very harshly and makes it very clear that she is to treat her stay as a job, a business transaction, and not cause trouble of any sort with her husband. Serena arranges Offred's affair with Nick in the hope of freeing Commander from Offred but when she comes to know her relationship with Commander she is deeply hurt.

Serena Joy suffers from a divided self. Her repressed sexuality breaks out in her garden, where she grows a range of, "subversive flowers tulips, irises and bleeding hearts".[27] So female in shape it was a surprise they'd not long since been rooted out (161).

Offred, the protagonist of *The Handmaid's Tale* is trapped in a repressive and regressive society. In pre-Gilead time she was a well-educated happy person with her husband and her daughter. In Gilead she suddenly finds herself as nothing more than a child-producing machine. Her job as a Handmaid, as was the job of Rachel's Handmaid in the Old Testament, is to offer her body as a vessel for procreation. Love, romance and emotion are all taken over by single-minded obsession with the physical act of sex performed with the sole purpose of producing child. Offred knows that in Gilead women are treated as things and for her as a Handmaid only the inside of her body, which is important for reproduction, is essential. The Commander, who attempts to impregnate her once in a month, has no interest in her face. Her red dress covers her fully in many layers. It is specially designed to hide body contours and veil is meant to prevent her from seeing and also being seen. She lies almost fully clothed in red dress between the open things of the wife and the Commander does his duty to impregnate her. Offred says, "Copulating too would be inaccurate, because it would imply two people and only one is involved" (104-05).

There is no sense of privacy since appearance is unimportant, she is not given face cream or hand lotion and like other Handmaids, she also steals butter from her food tray, as substitute. Her bath is regulated by Maratha. Around her ovulation time, on the night before the "Ceremony", she is given bath by Maratha. After that she waits for the ceremony, feeling completely dehumanized, "I wait, washed, brushed, fed like a prize pig" (79).

Like other Handmaids, Offred is fed only with what the authorities regard as healthy food. As Emma Parker says, "One of the main ways the system of oppression is enforced is through food."[28]

Like other Handmaids, Offred is forced into pregnancy tests every month. Having already failed at two previous postings, she experiences anguished disappointment; "I have failed once again to fulfil the expectations of others, which have become my own" (83). Her alienation from her body is clearly reflected in the lines, "Now the flesh arranges itself differently. I am a cloud, congealed around a central object, the shape of pear, which is hard and more real than I am" (84).

Offred is so alienated from her body that it does not seem to be hers any longer. She is forced to do everything what the authorities wanted. She surrenders, "I resign my body freely, to the uses of others. They can do what they like with me. I am object" (268).

Her experience of sexual intercourse with the Commander leaves her totally alienated even from her body. It is her awareness of her body, which prevents her from getting completely anaesthetized:

> I sink down into my body as into a swamp, fenland, where only I know the footing. Treacherous ground, my own territory. I become the earth. I set my ear against for rumours of the future. Each twinge, each murmur of slight pain, nipples of sloughed off matter, swellings and diminishing of tissues, the drooling of the flesh, these are the things I need to know about. (83)

Above lines are filled with sheer, earthy images of the female body, rich and mysterious with a will of its own.

In Gilead, the women feel they are kept in prison like rooms, constantly watched and guarded, allowed going for a walk only in twos. Offred's room is like a prison cell and she is "a prisoner in solitary confinement, confined to an upstairs room in the attic, allowed no companion or friend, hers is the "minimalist life" (104). In her room there is a chair, a table, a lamp, a framed picture without glass, and a single window that can open only partially. The use of mirrors, glass window panes, hooks have been dispensed with her safety purposes because Offred's predecessor had hanged herself from the light fixture: "The room is white. Curtains and spreads are the white. On the white ceiling is relief ornament in the shape of a wreath...they've removed anything you could tie a rope to (17).

In the bathroom razors are removed and the windowpane glass is shatter proof so that there is no "cutting edge". Being a Handmaid, Offred is allowed to do is to go shopping with a neighbouring handmaid and buy only those things for which she has been given tokens. The rest of the day she is supposed to do nothing. She is not allowed to knit, sew, read, write, embroider, smoke, wave, and listen to music. She says, "here time is measured by bells, as once in nunneries" (18). She thinks that the Commander's wife is more fortunate, she can do all these things. Offred's dead routine is very boring. She says, "I am like a room where things once happened and now nothing does, except the pollen of the weeds that grow up outside the window, blowing in as dust across the floor" (104).

In her room her previous occupant had scratched a coded message: "Nolite te bastardes carborundorun" (Don't let the bastard's grind you down). Since there is no other writing except the word 'FAITH' embroidered on her cushion. Offred feels she can communicate with this message. "It pleases me to ponder this message. It pleases me to think that I am communicating with this message. It pleases me to think that I am communicating with her...they give me a small joy" (62). This gives her state of mind, "an excessive preoccupation with the resonance and sounds, of words as facts in themselves make sense, particularly since reading and writing are forbidden".[29]

The women who accept by the strict laws of Gilead are allowed some recreations from time to time. These recreations act as safety valves, which serve to release pent-up emotions and frustrations. Gilead's aim is the total annihilation of woman as a person. Then women are allowed to see dead bodies of men hung up on the wall, and are supposed to feel hatred and scorn for them.

Since reading and writing is prohibited in Gilead, arms and legs are ruthlessly chopped off for reading and writing. Speaking freely in Gilead is a capital offense like most other things. Women are denied books, paper, and pens. Only ruling class has right to read books. The Handmaids are required to recite the Biblical injunctions, which are distorted to reinforce their submissiveness. As Klarer says:

> Women from all classes of society are excluded from any kind written discourse. These measures aim at giving the male leadership all the advantage of highly developed text-processing culture and of using these advantages purposefully against the women who are condemned to orality.[30]

The shops of Gilead are identified by pictures and there are no written signs for public, all are replaced by pictographs. As Offred says, "they decided that even the names of shops were too much temptation for us" (24). Klarer says that by doing, "this form of enslavement, the man of Gilead use pictographs and visual signs as a means of documenting their claims to ownership and power".[31]

Offred is aware that the fruition of the survival wish is possible only through a communication with the outer world that is debarred to her. She manages to communicate with her friend Moira, Ofglen and Cora, one of the housekeepers.

Cora develops a liking for her. Offred says "It pleased me that she was willing to lie for me, even in such a small thing, even for her own advantage. It was a link between us" (160).

Later Commander invites her to play a word game Scrabble with him. The game of scrabble, a symbol of reading and writing is forbidden for women, "Now it's forbidden for us, now it's dangerous: Now it's indecent" (149). For Offred playing Scrabble has all the excitement of a forbidden pleasure. It functions, "as a signifier of the power (games) of language, the power of the word, as does Offred's play with language throughout the tale".[32]

Commander and Offred meet several times in the greatest secrecy and do many forbidden things together. He takes her out to his private club. This behaviour of Commander brings out the loopholes or weaknesses in any repressive regime. The human spirit can never be subjugated completely by any ideology, Commander really wants friendship and intimacy but Offred experiences mixed feelings towards him and at no stage does she feel love for him. When Commander asks her to kiss him "as if she meant it" (150). She says, "I think about the blood coming out of him, hot as soup, sexual, over my hands" (131).

When Commander takes her out, he tells her that they have quite a "Collection" (meaning whores) at their club. Offred who is excited at the idea of getting out of the houses feels it "just another crummy power trip" (242). There she knows that the leisure pastimes of the Gileadean elite is not very edifying.

Later Commander secretly presents her copies of women's magazines like *Vogue*. She finds them very interesting though she realizes that at one time she took such magazines very lightly.

The commander also allows her the use of pen to write a line in Latin on a note pad. For the Handmaid "Pen Is Envy" now she realizes the power of pen. She says:

> The pen between my fingers is sensuous, alive almost, I can feel its power, the power of the words it contains.... Just holding it is envy. I envy the Commander, his pen. It's one more thing I would like to steal. (174)

Debarred from language, she symbolizes women who have been silenced though the centuries. According to Helene Cixous, when women write, their writing includes, "the possibility of charges, the space...can serve as a springboard for subversive through, the precursory movement of a transformation of social and cultural standards".[33]

Offred also enjoys the news on T.V. and looks forward to birthing, prayvaganza (an extravaganza of mass wedding conducted by males), and other such outings. But night is the time for private exchanges when arbitrary distinctions are dissolved. This is the time when she remembers her past life, memories of her husband Luke, her daughter and her mother. It is also the time when she meets her Commander and later she meets Nick. She says, "The night is mine, my own time, to do with as I will.... But the night is my time out. Where should I go" (147). She strongly desires escape from her present environment.

She is aware that she is in danger and not even free to die. When she comes to know suicide of her predecessor and Ofglen she realizes facts of a woman's destiny in Gilead. Offred decides to end up by hanging, "I could noose the bedsheet round my neck, hook myself up in the closet, throw my weight forward, choke myself off" (274) but she has faith and it feels a sense of hope. She says, "As long as we do this.... We can believe that we will some day get out, that will be touched again in love and desire" (91).

She recalls memories of her better past. She remembers her husband and daughter:

> Nobody dies from lack of sex. It's lack of love we die from. There's nobody here I can love, all the people I could love are dead or else where...where there are or what their names are now? They might as well be nowhere, as I am for them. I too am a missing person.... (113)

However, while Offred is clearly a victim, the most disturbing feature of dystopia is the power exercised over women, not by men but by one group of women over others. The control agency in this novel is not the Commanders but the Aunts. It recalls the 'total women' mentality, popularized in the early 60s to counteract emerging feminism. Offred remembers her feminist mother who has involved in many "antiporno" and "antiabortion" movements in the hope of creating a 'women's culture', "Mother, I think. Wherever you may be. Can you hear me? You wanted women's cultures. Well now there is one. It isn't what you meant, but it exists. Be thankful for small mercies" (137).

Offred's mother believed in women's economic and emotional independence but the Aunt indicates that some radical feminist position run the risk of being appropriated by the dominant power group and then exploited as a new instrument for female oppressions. The novel can be interpreted as a metaphor of the condition of women, which has changed minimally over the centuries. Perhaps only the justifications used for keeping them subjugated have changed. The forms of oppressions and their external manifestations may differ at different periods in history but the fact remains that women have been and still are victims of patriarchy. Margaret Atwood concentrates on the problems of women's survival in a hostile male dominated world through her protagonist's refusal to be a silent victim. Offred develops her feminist consciousness towards the slavery syndrome and with the help of her lover Nick she escapes from Gilead. Howells says, "Stubborn survival continually subverts the regime's claims to absolute authority, creating imaginative spaces within the system and finally the very means of Offred's escape from Gilead".[34] Out of the four victim positions, Offred occupies number three that is "acknowledgement of the fact of being a victim, but a repudiation of the victim role. The average women who accept their victim position as something inevitable, dictated by Biology are the Wives, the Maratha and the Handmaids. There are a few like Moira and Ofglen who rebel against the role of the victim but they are pushed for denial of their roles. Offred, in taking up secret creativity at the imaginative and then the oral level, perhaps does the only possible thing that is her reduced circumstances, towards evolving to the non-victim position.[35]

At the structural level, *The Handmaid's Tale* may be viewed as Margaret Atwood's strategy for creating female space out of patriarchal structures. She becomes successful through the novel's structure, the narrative mode of oral reconstruction, the use of language and symbols. It is not presented as history but as Offred's story narrated by herself. The whole novel is supposed to be orally narrated by Offred because reading and writing is forbidden in Gilead. She says: "It's also a story I'm telling in may head as I go along. Tell, rather than write, because I have nothing to write with and writing is in any case forbidden" (49).

Margaret Atwood, "knows the strength of language and its vulnerability...such is the case in Gilead and Offred's narrative.... It stands as a probe that true language means survival".[36] It is language that enables Offred to survive in Gilead and becomes the medium through which she defines herself. She realizes the centrality of language to the process of self-realization and struggles for equality. She knows that communication is imperative so she works her way to freedom through language, which is forbidden in Gilead. Her association with Nick and underground May Day Resistance group helps to escape from Gilead to the underground female road to tell her story. Carol Beran says, "Offred's power is in language".[37] She finds an antiquated artifact, a tape recorder, and over the music of Montavani, Elvic Presly and Twisted Sister, she records her message while she is in process of escaping from Gilead. She believes that the system can be evaded and that there is still a world outside Gilead:

> I keep on going with this sad and hunger and sordid, this limping and mutilated story, because after all I want you to hear it.... By telling you anything at all I'm at least believing in you.... Because I'm telling you this story I will your existence. I tell, therefore you are. (279)

Offred emerges as a rebel and fights by breaking the silence by using language. As Verwaayen says, "she 'acts' through the power of her words, through her memory and voice which resist the ideology of repression".[38]

Margaret Atwood frequently uses metaphors, symbols and images in her novel. Offred plays scrabble, which is symbol of reading and writing. The Scrabble game functions as a spatial metaphor of the freedom and restrictions existing for Offred in the novel, for she can write but not communicate by writing, and choose her moves, but only within the confines of the board and the Commander's room, with his complicity.

She often plays language games by which perhaps, Margaret Atwood tries to breath new life into the existing fossilized patriarchal language, "I sit in the chair and think about the word chair. It can also mean the leader of a meeting. It can also a mean a mode of execution. It is the first syllable in charity. It is the French word for flesh. None of these facts has any connection with the others" (120).

Her empty room, she sits in, becomes a symbol of her own empty inner space, "I am like a room where things once happened and now nothing does, except the pollen of the weeds that grow up outside the window, blowing as dust across the floor" (98).

Margaret Atwood uses pearl/oyster references in *The Handmaid's Tale* to provide character clarification as well as illuminate central issue of the text.[39] Aunt Lydia clichés glorification of the Handmaid's role:

> A thing is valued, she says, only if it is rare and hard to get. We want you to be valued, girls. She is rich in pauses, which she savors in her mouth. Think of yourselves as pearls. We, sitting in our rows, eyes down, we make her salivate morally. We are hers to define we must suffer her adjectives. I think, about pearls. Pearls are congealed oyster spit. (145)

Pearl theme's echo occurs when Offred divulges the contrasting emotions entangling her lust for Nick, "It's Nick, I can see him now; he's stepped off the path; onto the lawn to breathe in the humid air which stinks of flowers...like oysters spawn into the sea" (234-35).

The pearl theme also underscores the corruption of the Gilead. Offred relates the Commander's decree at the women's Prayvaganza, "I will that women adorn themselves in modest apparel" he says, "with shame face dress and sobriety; not with braided hair, or gold, on pearls, on costly array" (286).

Margaret Atwood is more a poet than a fiction writer and her initial orientation as a poet has enriched her style. In 'The Handmaid's Tale' every symbol, every image like that of wall, square, Church, shops and the use of biblical references demonstrates a poet's control of structures and world.

As a woman's story of resistance, *The Handmaid's Tale* also incorporates Margaret Atwood's nationalist concerns with regard to Canada's female posture *vis-à-vis* America's male. This is Margaret Atwood's first novel, which is set entirely outside Canada, in the United States of America. The Americanization of Canada as a result of its colonial outlook, has been of great concern to nationalist like Atwood for whom imperialism in any form, is offensive. Margaret Atwood regards the United States of America as, "a tragic country because it has great democratic ideals and rigid social machinery".[40]

Therefore, the repressive regime of Gilead is implicitly America and Canada is the Handmaid. As Anna Swan says, "Indeed, to be from the Canada's is to feel as women feel—cut off from the base of power." On this basis, *The Handmaid's Tale* can be comprised of Margaret Atwood's anti-American nationalistic concern within the framework of her feminist polemics.[41] Thus the novel can be read both as a feminist and nationalist work.

The Handmaid's Tale is built up from extrapolations of current attitudes, trends and events. Though set in a future it is far from fantastical literature. As Atwood says, "I made rule to myself that I would put nothing in the book that hasn't already been done in some from or another, that isn't already happening now or for which we don't have the technology".[42]

It can be read as a cautionary tale about the effects of excessive adherence to "norms" already existing in our world. By watching the characters grappling with the effects of this excess, we are supposed to learn how to avoid them and their consequences. It is clearly a novel in this genre. As Malashri Lal says:

> *The Handmaid's Tale* is a warning against essential biologism which for women must create the most terrible disjunction between body and spirit. For society as a whole, the warning is against the tendency to see all human endeavours as economic production thereby causing a corresponding neglect of earth-based spirituality.[43]

Offred the protagonist challenges the traditional values and tells as that we need "Canonization of feminism" for survival and to know about the human capacity.

REFERENCES

1. Atwood, Margaret. "Witches", *Second Words*, 333.
2. Grace, Sherill E. "Articulating the Space Between: Atwood's Untold Stories and Fresh Beginnings", *Margaret Atwood: Language, Text and System,* eds. Sherill E. Grace and Lorraine Weir. Vancouver: University of British Columbia Press, 903-04.

3. Rigney, Barbara Hill. "Politics and Prophecy: Bodily Harm, The Handmaid's Tale and True Stories", *Margaret Atwood, Women Writer Series*. London: Macmillan Education, 1987.
4. New, W.H. *A History of Canadian Literature*. London: Macmillan Education, 1991, 294.
5. Freibert, Lucy M. "Control and Creativity: The Politics of Risk in Margaret Atwood's The Handmaid's Tale", *Critical Essay on Margaret Atwood,* ed. Judith McCombs. Boston: G.K. Hall, 1988, 280.
6. Atwood, Margaret. "An Interview with Margaret Atwood", conducted by Elizabeth Meese. *Black Warrior Review*, 12.1, Fall 1985, 96.
7. Davidson, Cathy. "'A Feminist 1984': Margaret Atwood Talks About Her Existing New Novel", *Ms* 14, No. 8, February 1986, 24.
8. Wagner, Linda W. Martin, "Epigraphs to Atwood's The Handmaid's Tale", *Notes on Contemporary Literature,* 17.2, March 1987, 4.
9. Foucault, Michel. *The History of Sexuality, Volume I: An Introduction,* trans. Robert Hurley. New York: Vintage Books, 1980, 84.
10. Klarer, Mario. "Orality and Literature as Gender-Supporting Structures in Margaret Atwood's The Handmaid's Tale", *Mosaic* Spl. "Media Matters: Technologies of Literary Production" 28/4, 1995, 131.
11. Klarer, 132.
12. *Ibid.*, 131.
13. Prabhakar, M. "The Handmaid's Tale: Language as Subversive-Weapon", *Feminism/Postmodermin: Margaret Atwood's Fiction.* New Delhi: Creative Books, 1999, 86.
14. Howells, Coral Ann. *Private and Fictional Words: Canadian Women Novelists*. London: Methuen & Co. Ltd., 1987, 58.
15. Atwood, Margaret. *Second Words, Selected Critical Prose.* Toronto: Anansi, 1982, 145.
16. Davidson, Cathy, 25.
17. Vevaina, Coomi S. "Wastelanders in this New Gilead: An Analysis of Margaret Atwood's The Handmaid's Tale", *Ambivalence Studies in Canadian Literature*, eds. O.M.P. Juneja and Chandra Mohan. New Delhi: Allied Publishers Ltd., 1990, 224.
18. Ramamurti, K.S. "The Canadian Women Novelists in a Multicultural Context", *Commonwealth Literature: Themes and Techniques*, eds. P.K. Rajan et al. Delhi: Ajanta, 1993, 186.

19. Malak, Amin. "Margaret Atwood's The Handmaid's Tale and The Dystopian Tradition", *Canadian Literature,* 112, Spring 1987, 13.
20. Walker, Nancy A. *Feminist Alternatives: Irony and Fantasy in the Contemporary Novel by Women.* Jackson: University Press of Mississippi, 1990, 69.
21. Jacob, Susan. "Woman, Ideology, Resistance: Margaret Atwood's The Handmaid's Tale and The Third World Criticism", *Margaret Atwood: The Shape Shifter*. New Delhi: Creative Books, 1998, 27.
22. Atwood, Margaret. "The Red Shirt", *Two Headed Poems.* New York: Simon & Schuster, 1978, 101.
23. Pateman, Carole. *The Sexual Contract.* Starford: Standfort University Press, 1988, 148.
24. Malak, 9.
25. Marta, Cominero-Santangel. "Moving Beyond The Black White Spaces: Atwood's Gilead, 'Postmodernism, and Strategic Resistance'", *Studies in Canadian Literature*, 19.1, 1994, 27.
26. Givner, Jessie. "Names and Signatures in Margaret Atwood's Cat's Eye and The Handmaid's Tale," *Canadian Literature*, 133, Summer 1992, 58.
27. Jacob, 34.
28. Parker, Emma. "You Are What You Eat: The Politics of Eating in the Novels of Margaret Atwood", *Twentieth Century Literature*, 41.3, Fall 1995, 354.
29. Judith, Fitzgeraled. "A Necessary Allegory", *Canadian Forum*, October 1985, 30.
30. Klarer, 131.
31. *Ibid.*, 137.
32. Verwaayen, Kimbedy. "Re-examining the Gaze in the Handmaid's Tale", *Open Letter*, 4, Fall 1995, 48.
33. Helene, Cixous. Qtd. In Tonq, Rosemarie, *Feminist Thought: A Comprehensive Introduction.* London: Routledge, 1992, 131.
34. Howells, 69.
35. Gomez, Christine. "From Being an Unaware Victim to Becoming a Creative Non-victim: A Study of Two Novels of Margaret Atwood", *Perspectives on Canadian Fiction*, ed. Sudhakar Pandey. New Delhi: Prestige, 1994, 91.
36. Pinard, Mary. "A Cautionary Tale", *New Directions for Women*, Vol. 15, No. 3, May-June 1986, 15.

37. Beran, Carol L. "Images of Women's Power in Contemporary Canadian Fiction by Women", *Studies in Canadian Literature*, 152, 1990, 71.
38. Verwaayen, 46.
39. Dymond, Erica Joan. "Atwood's The Handmaid's Tale", *The Explicator*, Vol. 61, No. 3, Spring 2003, 181.
40. Sandler, Linda. "Interview with Margaret Atwood", *Malahat Review*, 41, January 1977, 22.
41. Swan Anna. Quoted in *The Canadian Postmodern: A Study of Contemporary English-Canadian Fiction*, Linda Hutcheon, Don Mills: Oxford University Press, 1988, 120.
42. Vevaina, Coomi S. "A Conversation with Margaret Atwood", Parts of the interview were published under the title "I Tend to See Symbols", *Times of India*, Sunday Review section, 20 March 1988, 8.
43. Lal, Malashri. "Inheriting Nature: Ecofeminism in Canadian Literature", *Postmodernism and Feminism: Canadian Contexts*, ed. Shirin Kudchedkar. New Delhi: Pencraft International, 1995, 318.

Cat's Eye

7

> The cat's eyes are my favorites. If I win a new one I wait I'm by myself, then take it out and examine it, turning it over and over in the light. The cat's eyes really are like eyes, but not the eyes of cats. They're the eyes of something that isn't known but exists anyway; like the green eye of the radio; like the eyes of aliens from a distant planet.[1]
>
> Margaret Atwood

Margaret Atwood's seventh novel *Cat's Eye* published in 1989 is a fascinating and immensely detailed work that deals with interaction between adulthood and childhood, as well as the relationship between art, artists and interpretation. Unlike the "allegorical misery" of the women in most of Margaret Atwood's earlier works, the present novel "gives way to recognizable landscapes and more plausible grief" and is Margaret Atwood's most emotionally engaging fiction so far.[2] This novel offers an alternative art history which foregrounds women's achievements as artists. Before publication of this novel, the female protagonist discovered herself and her place only in marriage and submission to patriarchal norms but this novel focuses on the issues of women through art, for the first time in history. As Prabhakar says, "*Cat's Eye* is Atwood's attempt to expose male prejudices against women's creativity and talent and shows how art can be used as a weapon against tyranny in all its manifestations. Thus, the novel is like on oasis in a desert for those whose creativity is prevented from blooming."[3]

Cat's Eye questions and challenges the gender bias of male art history which condemns a woman painter to a passive role on account of her femininity. The male centered ordered in art practices is displayed with the moustaches-worn portrait of Elaine displayed at the entrance of the Art Gallery. It shows the feeling of woman's revolutionary power as a painter and ridicules and deflates the chauvinistic male-art world. It also adds a dimension of heroism to woman painter. It drives home the message that:

> Talent is not something you are born with, any more than is genius. It is something, which is acquired by dint of effort, if you have to face up to difficulties, and if you struggle to overcome them, you are forced to excel.[4]

Cat's Eye deals with the uncomfortable subject of childhood bullying, and the psychological wounds that it inflicts on later stages of life. The novel's main character Elaine, is a conflicted and insecure painter whose friendship with Cordelia has marked her through childhood adolescence and adulthood. Margaret Atwood explores complex childhood issues like the difference between boys' and girls' play and the effects of having a brother, and of course, the bullying itself.

This novel also deals with the problems of growing up as well as the various anxieties of a mother. The narrator recalls incidents from her childhood and the relationships she had with the members of her family. Now as a married woman, she worries about her own children and the problems, which will beset them when they start out in life. She considers the different influences including family, relationships and education, which mould a person and make them what they are in adulthood. The importance of the past and past memories and the need to deal with this in order to cope with present reality seems to be the overall vision or viewpoint presented in this novel.

Cat's Eye explores in its examination of the growth and development of the woman-as-artist/artist-as-woman in a society where both these roles are marginalized. It is the story of Elaine Risley, the middle aged painter, who returns to Toronto, after many years of absence for a Retrospective show of her paintings. "The Retrospective becomes the novel's central metaphor"[5] since what the novel depicts is Elaine's retrospection of her own life from her school days to her present career as a painter. Her early involvement with a feminist art show leads us to call her, "a sociocultural agitator who seeks to change oppressive or stagnant language and laws"[6] through her paintings. It shows how art promotes feminism and freedom for women. She wants to break up the patriarchal art history in order to produce new spaces. With her artistic creations she demolishes the myth that art is the privilege of men and seems to assert that, "art must belong to all human beings, not alone to a traditionally privileged segment; every endeavor, every passion must be available to the susceptible adult, without the intervention of myth or canard".[7]

The novel begins with a definition of time. This is essential, as the novel is really an extended treatise on the relationship of the past to the present and how this influences our perceptions of others and ourselves. She says, "time as having a shape, something you could see, like a series of liquid transparencies, one laid on top of another" (3). It continues an exploration that is common to Margaret Atwood's work that is, the exploration of a not too strong female protagonist who is delving deeply into her past, trying to make sense of her place in the world. Specifically, the backdrop of the novel focuses on the first person narrative of Elaine Risley a successful painter at fifty who returns to her childhood city Toronto for the opening of an art exhibition featuring her own painting at a gallery named Sub-Versions. The dull, provincial city of her youth has become world class in the intervening years, "New York without the garbage and muggings".

Elaine's first eight years are spent on the road with her family, as her father, an entomologist (one who studies about insects), tracks infestations across northern Canada. For Elaine and her brother it is an enchanted existence "irregular, and slightly festive", a life of motels and housekeeping cottages and tents, but it little prepares her parents, move to Toronto, to a new and only partially completed tract house.

It is a world that Margaret Atwood portrays with deadly accuracy, a lonely, terrifying place where time is marked by the endless procession of paper pumpkins and snowmen and tulips that are hung in classroom windows, and the future, with all its repulsive, distinctly feminine mysteries, is only threat. In her childhood Elaine draws girls "in old fashioned clothing, with long skirts, pinafores and puffed sleeves, with big hair bows on their head" (30-31). She uses "silver paper" of cigarette packages to draw figures of woman and cuts coloured figure of women, cookware, and furniture out of the book and paste them in her scrapbook. She plays the scrapbook game with her brother Stephen and friends: Grace, Carol and Cordelia.

Cordelia and her two friends surround Elaine throughout her day, pointing out her failings, her weakness, mocking the way she walks, the way she eats, the way she laughs. They torment her with her own image, ostracize her, and in terrible bit of play-acting, bury her alive. Cordelia starts victimizing Elaine almost as soon as they are introduced. She experiences mixed feelings towards them and cannot understand their love for her, as is seen when she confusedly says, "with enemies you can feel hatred, and anger. But Cordela is my friend. She likes me, she wants to help me, and they all do. They are my friends, my girlfriends, my best friends, I have never had any before and I'm terrified of losing them. I want to please" (120). Her teasing shatters Elaine's self-esteem and leads her to adopt neurotic habits, such as peeling her skin, biting her nails, and chewing her hair. Her mental anguish becomes so great that she forgets how to laugh, begins to feel secure when ill, contemplates suicide, desires invisibility and faints at will. "Fainting", she says, "is like stepping sideways, out of your own body, out of time on into another time. When you wake up it's later. Time has gone on without you" (171).

In exploring the world of childhood female friendship, Margaret Atwood broke new ground. The world of eight to twelve year-old girls had never been examined so thoroughly and with such unflinching insight. It intricately examines the relationship children develop with all the interval strife, emotion and politics that accompany growing up.

Cordelia's torture tactics and Elaine's anguish come to an abrupt end after the three girls abandon her in icy water in the dangerous ravine. Leaving Cordelia behind, Elaine begins to study drawing, has an affairs with her teacher Josef Harbik. As Stephen Ahern says, "her art teacher Josef is a walking catalogue of patriarchal myths of femininity. He feels women should live for him only and has an objectivizing, Pre-Raphaelite vision of women as 'helpless flowers, or shapes to be arranged and contemplated' (318). He is a demon lover of the Health cliff variety...."[8]

Elaine comes to know the true nature of Josef as a manipulator and leaves him. Later Elaine comes in contact with Jon, a fellow art student. They come together by accident and get married but she is not satisfied with her married life. As Elaine says, "I don't yet see Sarah as a gift I have given him, but one he has allowed me. It's because of her that we got married...for the oldest of reasons" (356).

With her marriage and childbirth Elaine's dreams of establishing a balanced and healthy relationship with a fellow-painter turns sour. Soon after her divorce, Elaine marries Ben, a travel agent. As against Josef and Jon who are indiscipline, selfish and irresponsible, Ben seems a mild-mannered trusting and caring person. In Vancouver Elaine begins her career, as a painter and takes part in several women's conference and group shows organized by women. She deals with the torment of her early life in her art and exerting power in paint over the people who had condemned her. Empowered by her success as an artist, Elaine returned to Toronto for a show of her work, able to resist the pleas of her former tormentor, Cordelia, now a pitiful patient in a psychiatric facility. In a dream, Elaine surpasses her desire for revenge and offers Cordelia Christian charity, "I'm the stronger.... I reach out my arms to her bend down.... It's all right, I say to her. You can go home" (419). Elaine is reinforced by the very words spoken to her in the vision that saves her life years before. Her work fosters her liberation. By projecting her rage outside of herself, she confronts her demons and exalts herself as a divine redeemer.

Finally *Cat's Eye* is not only about memory, nor is it the chronicle of a particular life, it is a novel of images, nightmarish, evocative, heartbreaking and mundane, that taken together offers us not a retrospective but an addition. The novel portrays the inner development of the main character Elaine Risley by means of a backward look over her life. Her father influences her.

Elaine's parents frown upon religious and radical fanaticism and are friendly with people of other races and faiths. As a scientist her father believes that science can help make the world a better place to live in. He is impatient and concerned about ecology and so passionately interested in Biology that he wants his children to share his excitement about the subject. He believes that science is "the only universal language" (248). He is shocked when he knows that his East Indian colleague Mr. Banerji is not given the promotion he deserves. Elaine says, "my father's view of human nature has always been bleak but scientists are excluded from it, and now they aren't. He feels betrayed" (287-88).

When Elaine decides to be a painter, her father acts supportive but secretly thinks that her, "talent for drawing is impressive but wasted. It would have been better applied to cross-sections of stems and the cells of algae. For him I am a botanist-manqué" (287).

Elaine's mother is fully aware of the presence of the power-hungry beast within all human beings but chooses not to talk about it. Elaine's mother is a very hard-working, tolerant and sensible woman who makes the best of even the worst situations. When she comes to know that her daughter is tortured by Cordelia and other she asks her to either stop associating with the girls altogether or else cease acting spineless. As Elaine grows older she comes closer to her mother as she realizes that she acts very like her mother who lived a life of moderations and defied categorization till her death. She never says "what will people think?" (214). Elaine feels that her parents are unconventional and complains:

> My parents are like younger, urchin-like brothers and sisters whose faces are dirty and who blurt out humiliating things that can neither be anticipated nor controlled. I sigh and make the best of it I feel I'm older than they are, much older. I feel ancient. (239)

Like her parents, Elaine's brother Stephen, an astrophysicist is so completely involved in his intellectual system that he keeps, as far away as possible, from social interaction which involves power politics. As a child, Stephen acts in accordance with the gender stereotype he encounters in the books and comics he read. His passions change periodically. He begins by collecting milk-bottle tops, then marbles and later comic books. For a short period he feels interested in chemistry and finally in stars. He introduces Elaine to scientific concepts and helps her in developing her mental perception and vision of painting by means of the various dimension of the universe and the idea of space-time. He says, "We're limited by our own sensory equipment. How do you think a fly sees the world?" (219). He teaches her how time and space go hand in hand in the universe. He says, "Time is dimension. You can't separate it from space. Space time is what we live in" (219). Howells says that Stephen's scientific enthusiasms shape, "Elaine's imagination, so that her paintings and his theories come to occupy the same area of speculation on the mysterious laws which govern the universe...." His discourse from theoretical physics provides the conceptual framework for her paintings, for Elaine is "painting time".[9] He teaches Elaine how to explore the freedom of imagination beyond the constraints of time. As Sharpe says:

> Elaine unwittingly participates in this process when she embraces her brother's ideas about space-time and combines them with the symbolization of her private experiences in her paintings. She asserts no feminist political strategy, however, and claims simply to paint what she could see. But the combination of science with private symbolizations in her paintings challenges the language and conventions of linear time and challenges the limits placed upon women's communication. "Elaine's paintings bridge the gaps between herself and other women; they communicate visually instead of verbally by depicting the objects and symbols of her own world or space-time."[10]

Elaine's association with her brother encourages her to improve her painting skill and teaches her how to see in the dark. Stephen's serio-comic arrest while observing butterflies in military testing zone in California and his sudden death at the hand of terrorists, reveal the extent to which he lived his life divorce from society.

The most revealing aspect of the novel centers on not just relationships in general, but the relationships between women. Specifically, the novel focuses on one key relationship that between Elaine and childhood friends Cordelia, Carol and Grace. Cordelia represents the best and the worst in people. She is the chief tormentor. Cordelia's family environment is unhealthy. Cordelia's mother is a tiny and fragile woman, an actress in her youth. She names her daughters Perdita, Miranda and Cordelia after Shakespeare's heroine "as though its something we should all recognize" (73). Presenting herself as an artist, she cleverly leaves the household work to a cleaning lady, takes painting classes and arranges flowers in Swedish glass vases wearing gardening gloves.

Cordelia's father too seems to suffer from a split personality. His craggy, charming external self is at variance with his power-hungry, brutish inner self. It is largely on his account that Cordelia is the kind of person she is. After many years she tells Elaine, "I wanted some place that was all mine, where nobody could bug me. When I was little, I used to sit on a chair in the front hall I used to think that if I kept very still and out of the way and didn't say anything, I would be safe...I used to get into trouble a lot, with Daddy when he would lose his temper. You never know when he was going to do it" (252). Since violence begets violence, Cordelia tortures Elaine as she "finds in Elaine a perfect foil for her own apprehensions".[11]

Cordelia grows up as an alienated person totally unaware of her inner self. She feels that she is neither as beautiful nor as "gifted" as her elder sisters. When Cordelia is young, Elaine feels that her sisters are the only ones "who have any real power" (117) over her. She tries hard to imitate their way of talking, their pretentious mannerisms like rolling their eyes upward and blowing out smoke through their nose. Hungry for power, Cordelia starts victimizing Elaine. She acts as she knows everything and tells Carol, Grace and Elaine about plays, ballets, menstruation, male anatomy, fresh kisses, poisoning with the deadly nightshade and the stream of dissolved dead people in the ravine under the wooden bridge. Cordelia and her other friends torture Elaine by making her believe that she is not normal and they want to improve her personality. Elaine says, "the expression on my face how I walk, what I wear, because all of these things need improvement. I am not normal; I am not like other girls. Cordelia tells me so, but she will help me. Grace and Carol will help me too. It will take hard work and a long time" (118).

Overcome with self-hatred and fear of them, Elaine peals off the skin from her toes as far as the blood and says, "the pain gave me something definite to think about, something immediate. It was something to hold onto" (114). After abandon her in icy water in the dangerous ravine, Elaine feels angry for having been a willing victim. She also feels guilty about not helping Cordelia and sees her shadow even when she returns to Toronto after many years.

Elaine's other friend Carol Campbell is an Anglican by faith. She is a stubby girl with frequent laugh. Like Cordelia's parents, Carol's parents too seem to have split personalities. As Carol tells Elaine, "her mother sings on a radio programmed under a different name...her father takes some of his teeth out at night and puts them into a glass of water beside his bed" (48). Carol reports to her other friends the detail of Elaine's unfinished house not with scorn, but as exotic specialties. Elaine says, "She wants me to be marveled at. More accurate; she wants herself to be marveled at, for revealing such wonders. It's as if she's reporting on the antics of some primitive tribe: true, but incredible" (49).

Grace Smeath is a year older than Carol, Cordelia and Elaine. She is taller than Carol with dark thick coarse hair. Her skin is extremely pale. Taught to control her emotions, Grace is terribly repressed and acts prudish, hypocritical and manipulative even as an eight-year-old child. The things they play are mostly Grace's ideas, because if they try to play anything she doesn't like, she says she has a headache and goes home, or else tells her friends to go home. Grace does not raise her voice, gets angry or cries. As Elaine says, "She is quietly reproachful, as if her headache is or fault.... She gets her way in everything" (52). She always insists on being the teacher and forces them into doing spelling tests and sums of arithmetic. Elaine and Carol always use only those colours, which Grace specifies in her movie star colouring books, "made-up stories don't interest her unless they contain a lot of real things: toasters, ironing boards, the wardrobes of movies stars. Cordelia melodramas are beyond her" (74). She feels that she knows everything about God and regards God as a punishing old man who can be appeased with pleas, prayers and nickels. She is incapable of laughter and there is no trace of naturalness in her.

Once Cordelia, Carol and Grace torture Elaine by lowering her into the hole dug in the ground and arrange the boards over the top. After that she starts avoiding them and make a new friend whose name is Jill. She is interested in other kinds of games, games of paper and wood. Later Elaine joins Art College because of her deep interest in painting. She realizes during her final Grade Thirteen exams that she will be an artist rather than a biologist:

> In the middle of the Botany examination it comes to me, like a sudden epileptic fit, that I'm not going to be a biologist, as I have thought. I am going to be a painter. I look at the page, where the life cycle of the mushroom from spore to fruiting body is taking shape, and I know this with absolute certainty. My life has been changed, soundlessly instantaneously. (255)

Her art teacher Josef Hrbik is in his mid-thirties, with dark thickly curled hair, a moustache, and eagle nose, and eyes that look almost purple, like mulberries. He has a habit of staring without saying anything and it seems, without blinking. He is sly and manipulative and regards women, as mannequins to be shaped in accordance with his will. During his art class he arranges the picture of live naked woman, especially for girl students to draw for fluidity of line. Here Elaine comes to know how art is being used by male artist as "a vehicle for sexual wish fulfilment—a way of making women an object for man's contemplation and erotic desire".[12] Elaine is frightened by the image of the massiveness of body such as "lot of flesh...below the waist; there are folds across her stomach.... Breasts are saggy and have enormous dark nipples.... She is not beautiful, and I am afraid of turning into that" (269). Elaine discovers that her art teacher wants to have sexual relationship with his students.

They learn to draw objects very well but fail to draw life on canvass. They receive his constant encouragement with his desires for sex. As he says, "You are an unfinished woman", he adds in a lower voice, "but here you will be finished" (273). Molly Hite comments: "Her drawing instructor Josef's dicta that she is both an 'unfinished woman' who needs to 'be finished' and artistically 'nothing...we will see what we can make of you' (272), suggest that in so far as she remains sexually female, she remains subject to the goal of 'improvement'."[13] Elaine falls in love with Josef and is delighted with his unpredictable lovemaking. He tells her that she should remain untouched by others as he sees her as his property and tells that "a woman belongs to a man: if a man finds his woman with another man, he kills both of them and everyone excuses him" (316). He regards women as "helpless flowers, or shapes to be arranged contemplated" (318). Elaine knows the true nature of Josef in the victimization of Susie. Susie is her fellow art student who commits suicide because of her illicit pregnancy. After Susie's abortion Elaine realizes that women were not real to Josef and that he is a weak, narcissistic, unfeeling, dirty two times, incapable of love. Elaine identifies with her so deeply that she feels, "At the same time I know that in her place I would have just as stupid. I would have done what she has done, moment by moment, step by step" (312).

As time passes, Josef's disappearance leaves Elaine to begin her affair with Jon, a fellow art student in "Life Drawing". The relationship between Elaine and Jon is dependent upon the situation, "the two constantly change from victim to bully positions".[14] Elaine accepts that they come together by accident, "a lot like traffic accident, but we do share it. We are survivors, of each other. We have been shark to one another, but also lifeboat. That counts for something" (17). Their married life is almost lethal and she becomes a silent buried mother within the confines of house. Elaine says:

> If I were to win them, the order of the world would be changed, and I am not ready for that. So instead I lose the fights, and master different arts. I shrug, tighten my mouth

in silent rebuke, turn my back in bed, and leave questions unanswered. I say, 'Do it however you like'. (341)

Jon seems to have split personality. As Jon begins to paint "very swiftly, in violent eye-burning acrylics reds and pinks and purples, in frenzied loops and swirls" (317) and says that "they are a moment of process, trapped on the canvas. They are pure painting" (317). After a short period he starts painting straight lines or perfect circle and dismisses his earlier style as "too romantic, too emotional, too sloppy, too sentimental" (325). He calls these paintings things like *Enigma; Blue and Red, Variation: Black and White* and *Opus 36*. A few years later he paints pictures that look like commercial illustrations and says "the necessity of using common cultural sign systems to reflect the iconic banality of our times" (335) and finally he stops painting.

Jon feels that, "sexual possessiveness is bourgeois, and just a hangover from notions about the sanctity of private property. Nobody owns anybody" (324-25) though he continuously reminds Elaine that she does not own him, he somehow feels that he owns her. Before marriage he has pretended to offer Elaine equality, now he doesn't like her working at night because it disturbs his sleep. He wants her to stop painting. Elaine now realizes that her own husband crushes her creativity and individuality. She starts developing her personality as an independent painter and comes across with, "limitation and immurement, training in menial and frustrating tasks, restrictions of the intellect and limitation of erotic activity".[15] Her husband never supports her instead he thinks that she is mad because she is an woman. Elaine refuses to accept gender stereotyping saying that, "once it was a shaming thing to say, and crushing to have it said about you, by a man. It implied oddness, deformity, sexual malfunction. I'm not mad because I'm a woman I'm mad because you're an asshole" (346).

She is aware how male painter's sexist attitude and professional envy humiliates women's talent. She feels amazed at, "all those explosions, that recklessness, that Technicolor wreckage" (265) they caused. Elaine's experiences of male reactions to her paintings often echo Atwood's own. In "Paradoxes and Dilemmas, the woman as writer", she points out what Elaine to discovers for herself, how only too often woman's artistic accomplishments are reviewed only by women and only as women's work rather than for its own intrinsic merit, and is often dismissed as being feminine in style and sensibility. She says:

> Good equals male, bad equals female and there is no critical vocabulary for expressing the concept good/female. I call it the Lady Painter syndrome...when she's good we call her a painter, when she's bad, we call her a lady painter.[16]

Elaine's realization of the harsh reality of this world, its cruelty and destructiveness, its politics of power, leads to a loss of innocence and to her dreams of isolation, death and destruction. Blind obedience to patriarchal demands make people move like bright animated dolls, with her realization she feels that the artist/woman has the power and the ability to arrange her own life. She feels enlightened and rebels against the attitude of her husband and refuses to "conform to the socially approved role of wife and mother, the only role to which every social institution consigns her automatically, simply by virtue of her birth".[17] She leaves Jon and goes to Vancouver with her daughter Sarah and marries to Ben, a travel agent.

As against Josef and Jon, Ben does not cherish popular images of womanhood and accepts Elaine as she is and respects her decisions. He encourages her and gives her a lot of moral and financial support. She participates in the 'Women Artists' conference on "anger" towards men. During her close association with women's group, she comes in contact with many kind of women artists, most of them are lesbians. Elaine finds herself on the periphery of groups of radical feminists. They believe that women's oppression is the deepest form of human oppression. In order to be liberated from sexual oppression, radical feminist prescribe a strategy to "create an exclusively female sexuality through celibacy, auto-eroticism, or lesbianism".[18] They are against heterosexuality. Lesbianism is demanded and is seen as courageous. Some of them believe that "it's the only equal relationship possible for women. You are not genuine otherwise" (378).

Elaine fears to turning into a lesbian. She says:

> I am ashamed of my own reluctance, my lack of desire; but the truth is that I would be terrified to get into bed with a woman. Women collect grievances, hold grudges and change shape. They pass hard, legitimate judgments, unlike the purblind guesses of men, fogged with romanticism and ignorance and bias and wish. Women know too much, they can neither be deceived nor trusted. I can understand why men are afraid of them, as they are frequently accused of being. I am unorthodox, hopelessly heterosexual, a mother, quisling. I still shave my leg. (378-79)

She appreciates lesbians for their conviction, optimism and comradeship but labels herself "timid" even while she is moving in the direction of feminism. She says:

> I am like someone watching from the sidelines, waving a cowardly handkerchief, as the troops go boyishly off to war, singing brave songs. (379)

This statement established Elaine's stance as a feminist who cannot be pigeonholed into any specific category.[19] For Elaine, artist is an "overblown, pretentious theatrical" (15) person who neglects the labour and the pain of creativity of painter. She says:

> The world artist embarrasses me; I prefer painter; because its more like a valid job. An artist is a tawdry, lazy sort of thing to be.... (15)

As a painter Elaine is seen pouring her energy into her paintings so that they can materialize, "whatever energy they have came out of me; she notes, I'm what's left over" (409). She starts painting and emerges as a painter who paints for social values. Art becomes a source of inspiration and power for her. Her experiences teach her how women can be cruel to each other. Her relationship with Cordelia is betrayal of sisterhood. She paints the defiant, almost belligerent stare of Cordelia in her picture *Half a Face*.

Falling Women is her another painting which is about men like Josef and Jon who caused women to fall. It shows the innocence of women and male's domination over them. In her picture Elaine shows, "the women, three of them, falling as if by accident off a bridge, their skirts opened into bells by the wind, their hair streaming upwards. Down they fall, onto the men who were lying unseen, jagged and dark and without volition, far below" (268). It warns women to protect themselves from victimization and survive with dignity as human beings.

Elaine's series about her mother called *Pressure Cooker* shows the suffering of women in kitchen. Elaine says that she did this painting soon after her mother died and that it was her way of wanting to bring her mother back to life. It is also about female slavery and depicts a stereotyping of women in negative and trivial domestic roles. This series contain "six images, six panels, like a double triptych or a comic book, arranged in two groups" (150).

This first image depicts her mother in her city house kitchen in her late forties dress of "a bib apron, blue flowers with navy piping, even she wore it, from time to time" (150). The second one shows "the same figure in college, made from the illustrations from an old *Ladies' Home Journals* and *Chatelaines* (150). The third image is of the same figure, "white on white, the raised parts pipe-cleaners contoured side by side and glued onto a white cloth-covered backing. It looked as if my mother was slowly dissolving, from real life into a Babylonian bas-relief shadow" (150). The bottom set of images goes the other way with the image made of "pipe-cleaners first, then the same in college then the final one in full-colored realistic detail" (150). But this time depicting her mother in slacks making chokecherry jam over the outdoor fire Charna says about her paintings, "Early forays by Risley into the realm of female symbolism and the charismatic nature domestic objects" (404). Elaine paints things like the toaster, the coffee percolator, her mother's wringer washer, sofas, and the silver paper. Prabhakar says about these paintings:

> They reveal the anxiety and insecurity lying in those things themselves, which symbolize feminine roles. They are suffused with the anxiety of women. Even in the context of modern technology the burden of the roles of women is not lessened. Elaine makes an attack on the attractive kitchen gadgetry

> while even while promising more comfort to women do not cease to be symbols of women's oppression.[20]

Her painting *Life Drawing* is about the abuse of women by male painters. She paints Josef and Jon in "stark naked but turned with a twist half away from the viewer...the ass end, then the torso in profile" (365). Their bodies are luminous with "wonderful bums". Each of them is painting a picture on an easel. Josef's is of a voluptuous model, her face is Pre-Raphaelite, brooding, consciously mysterious. Jon's painting is a series of intestinal swirls, in hot pink, raspberry-ripple red and burgundy cherry purple. This painting questions and challenges the gender bias in male art history.

In *Pico Seconds* she draws her parents making lunch outdoors standing on a platform under which are gas pumps emblems. Charna says about this that it, "takes on the group of seven and reconstructs their vision of landscape in the light of contemporary experiment and postmodern pastiche" (405).

Three Muses depicts the three persons who were kind to Elaine in her childhood namely, Mrs. Finesterin, the Jewish neighbours Mr. Banerji the scientist from India; Miss Stuart, the teacher from Scotland. All the three appear as presenting their gifts of love—an orange, a globe of the world, a slide with spruce budworm eggs. By painting two female muses and one male Elaine deconstructs gender power. As Charna says, "Risley continues her disconcerting deconstruction of perceived gender and its relationship to perceived power, especially in respect to numinous imagery" (406).

Elaine also paints a picture for her brother after his death named *One Wing*. It is a triptych. A man is falling from the sky, wearing a world war two RCAF uniform. It is a statement about men, and the juvenile nature of war.

Elaine also paints a series of virgin. The vision of the virgin helped Elaine regains her courage and confidence, which she had lost while under the power Cordelia. The first painting celebrates the power of the virgin and depicts her as a lioness "fierce, alert to danger, wild" (345). The second one is called *Our Lady of Perpetual Help* humanizes and modernizes the virgin by showing her tiredly descending to earth with winter coat and purse carrying two brown paper bags of groceries from which an egg, an onion and an apple have fallen out. The third painting called *Unified Field Theory* depicts the virgin of lost things dressed in black walking above the top railing of the bridge with on oversized blue cat's eye marble in her hand.

Her painting *Cat's Eye* shows the retrieval of the dignity of women's life. It's her "self-portrait". Top half is Elaine's face and behind half head, "in the center of the picture, in the empty sky, a pier glass is hanging, convex and encircled by an ornate frame" (408). Roberta White says that convex mirror symbolizes "the power of an eye that sees things whole and a mind that comes to terms with the world through words or through art".[21]

Elaine in her childhood believes that some objects have great hidden power. Her blue cat's eye marble is such an object. She feels that the marble has the power to protect her. *Cat's Eye* used as a metaphor for the survival. For cat's eyes grow in the dark, as Elaine's art does for her. Atwood changes it into a positive symbol by referring to its eyes, which can seen in darkness. It is this extraordinary visual capacity, which she endows her protagonist with to help her see and expose the truth, tucked away under the darkness of patriarchal ideologies dominating the world. Since she takes upon herself this task with greater objectivity it is difficult to pigeonhole her.[22]

The cat's eye vision of Elaine helps her to focus on the victimization of women and turns them over and over in the light of truth through her painting. Elaine's paintings are true to life and she emerges as a feminist painter. Elaine is so successful as artist that a 'Retrospective' of her paintings is organized in Toronto, once her home. The return to Toronto is an important stage in Elaine's journey towards selfhood. The Retrospective arouses memories that helps Elaine to exist in two places at the same time for "You don't look back along time but down through it, like water. Sometimes this comes to the surface, sometimes that, sometime nothing. Nothing goes away" (3). Her use of the present tense throughout the novel suggests the interpenetration of the past and the present indicated by this water image. Water is associated with femininity, birth and rebirth. Elaine's story is like water, transparent but fluid, changing its implications and focus. Her struggle towards achievement of identity as woman and as artist is obviously harder, more painful because she is a painter. The cat's eye vision guides Elaine towards the creation of surrealistic paintings, which are luminous. Thus, the art has an air of soothing, retrieving and transforming existing gender relationships. As Elaine flies back to Vancouver at the end of the Retrospective, therefore, victorious over the new Toronto and her memories of the past, sure of her survival in a world that will always be hostile, she looks out of the plane window, sees the stars in the night sky glowing like the cat's eye and leaves an optimistic message:

> If they were sounds, they would be echoes, of something that happened millions of years ago: a world made of numbers. Echoes of light shining out of the midst of nothing. It's old night, and there's not much of it. But it's enough to see by. (412)

Thus she sums up as "a portrait of the artist as a woman and a survivor".[23] She wishes for a society, which will come together as human being. Margaret Atwood's feminist vision is much broader than that of her contemporary women writers. She is not a liberal feminist nor is she a Marxist, radical, psychoanalytic, existentialist, socialist and postmodern feminist. She uses one or more than one theory according to social issues and theme of her novel. In *Cat's Eye* she had gone through radical and socialist feminist theory. Radical theory is chiefly concerned with the issues arising out of "pornography, prostitution, sexual harassment, rape and women battering"; they support lesbianism and reject most or all forms of collaboration with men or organization containing men.

Socialist feminists analyze women's oppression in terms of gender, class, race, and sexual orientation. This theory challenges the power relations in patriarchal capitalist system and argues that equality of opportunity can never be possible in society as long as there are fundamental differences in wealth privilege and power. In *Cat's Eye*, the protagonist Elaine as a woman and an artist makes art the possibilities of better and healthy relationships between men and women. With the help of her paintings she advocates human rights of women and gives a clarion call for the destruction of gender-based social system.

REFERENCES

1. Atwood, Margaret. *Cat's Eye*. London: Virago Press, 1990, 62-63.
2. Stefan, Kanfer. "Time Arrested", *Time*, 6 February 1989, 70.
3. Prabhakar, M. "Cat's Eye: A Vision in the Dark", *Feminism/ Postmodernism: Margaret Atwood's Fiction*. New Delhi: Creative Books, 1999, 114.
4. Beauvoir, Simone de. "Women and Creativity", *French Feminist Thought: A Reader*, ed. Toril Moi. Basil Blackwell, 1987, 19.
5. Salat, M.F. "Canadian Nationalism and Feminist Ideology", *The Canadian Novel: A Search for Identity*. New Delhi: B.R. Publishing Corporation, 76.
6. Sharpe, Martha. "Margaret Atwood and Julia Krishteva: Space Time, the Dissident Woman Artist, and the Pursuit of Female Solidarity in Cat's Eye", *Essays on Canadian Writing*, 50, Fall 1993, 175.
7. Ozick, Cynthia. "Women and Creativity: The Demise of the Dancing Dog", *Woman in Sexist Society*, eds. Vivian Gornick and K. Moran. New York, London: Basic Books, 1971, 320.
8. Ahern, Stephen. "Meat Like You Like It": The Production of Identity in Atwood's Cat's Eye: *Canadian Literature*, 137, Summer 1993, 12.
9. Howells, Coral Ann. *Margaret Atwood*. London: Macmillan P. Ltd., 1996, 152-53.
10. Sharpe, 177.
11. Dermott, Alice Mc. "What Little Girls are Really Made of", *New York Times Book Review*, 5 February 1989, 35.
12. Brown, Lyvia Morgan. "Sexism in Western Art",*Women A: Feminist Perspective*, ed. Jo Freeman. California: Mayfied Publishing Co., 1975, 312.
13. Hite, Molly. "Optics and Autobiography in Margaret Atwood's Cat's Eye", *Twentieth Century Literature*, 137, Summer 1993, 12.
14. Vevaina, Coomi S. "The Trick is to Walk in The Spaces Between The Words: Atwood's Cat's Eye", *Re/Membering Selves: Alienation and Survival in the Novels of Margaret Atwood and Margaret Laurence*. New Delhi: Creative Books, 1996, 246.
15. Pratt Annis. *Archetypal Patterns in Women's Fiction* (Bloomington: Indiana University Press, 1981), 29.
16. Atwood, Margaret. "Paradoxes and Dilemmas, the Woman as Writer", *Feminist Literary Theory: A Reader,* ed. Mary Eagleton. Oxford: Basil Blackwell, 1988, 74-77.

17. Nichlin, Linda. "Why Are There No Great Women Artists", *Women in Sexist Society*, eds. Vivian Gornick and K. Moran. New York, London: Basic Books, 1971, 361.
18. Bunch, Carlotte. "Lesbians In Revolt", *Women and Value*, ed. Marilyn Pearsall. Belmont, Calif: Wadsworth, 1986, 128.
19. Prabhakar, 120.
20. *Ibid.*, 121.
21. White, Roberta. "Margaret Atwood: Reflections in a Convex Mirror", *Canadian Women: Writing Fiction,* ed. Mickey Pearlman Jackson: University Press of Mississippi, 1993, 53.
22. Prabhakar, 123.
23. Barat, Urbashi. "Cat's Eye: Margaret Atwood's Portrait of the Artist as a Woman and a Survivor", *Canadian Literature Today,* ed. R.K. Dhawan. New Delhi: Prestige Books, 1995, 185.

The Blind Assassin

8

Margaret Atwood's tenth novel *The Blind Assassin* published in 2000 is winner of the Booker Prize and the International Association of Crime Writers Dashiell Hammett Award. It is a Canadian postmodern metafiction that is deliberately deceptive. It is a novel within a novel within another novel. The tales nested perfectly in Russian doll style. The three narratives are interspersed with newspaper clippings, a letter and society announcements. As Linda Richards says: "It's initially dizzying, then dazzling and—finally—very compelling to watch Atwood weave her brilliant tapestry."[1] Reviewer Billy J. Hobbs observes: "Atwood's style of writing,...is anything but convoluted, it is straightforward, but complicated, with expertly created characters".[2]

"*The Blind Assassin* takes the novel within a novel" idea to new heights, the elderly Iris Chase Griffen writing her record of the past, side by side with her late sister's book *The Blind Assassin* which is an account of two surreptitious lovers meeting in seedy room and eateries, plotting a strange science/ancient world story. As well, Iris looks at her slowed down world of the present, in the fictional Ontario town of Post Ticonderoga. The three stories are all separate yet slowly come together in such a skilful and subtle way. It is also a snapshot of the first half of the 20th century, with two world wars, the depression and the social realities of the time.

The Blind Assassin is set in the tumultuous period between the wars. Margaret Atwood nails these details beautifully; the optimism in the 1920s, the fear and hunger of the depression, the enthusiasm and political unrest into the late 1940s. Margaret Atwood brings us physical details as well; meals, clothing styles and the general modes of life, etc. The pragmatic focus in the novels is significant because the stories dealing with life provide enlightenment as to how to live with truth. As Margaret Atwood herself says,

> "the past no longer belongs only to those who once lived in it, the past belongs to those who claim it, are willing to explore it, and to infuse it with meaning for those alive today. The past belongs to us, because we are the ones who need it."[3] In *The Blind Assassin* historical scope is wide.

It is a novel subtle and dangerous as a spider web—its surface simple as water, its depth complex as the teeming, hungry sea. Three stories are intertwined in this complex novel, in the end, they become one. As Margaret Atwood's most ambitious work unfolds—a tricky process, in fact, with several nested narratives, we're reminded of just how complicated the familial game of hide and seek can be;

> "What had she been thinking of as the car sailed off the bridge, they hung suspended in the afternoon sunlight, glinting like a dragonfly, for that one instant of held breath before the plummet? Of Alex, of Richard, of bad faith, of our father and his wreckage, of God, perhaps, and her fatal, triangular bargain". (4)

The First narrative of the novel is the fictional autobiography of a Canadian women whose life spans over century. It is a self-reflexive memoir of Iris Chase's life in Port Ticonderoga and Toronto, Canada. In the novel's present, this is in her 80s and living simultaneously in three time periods, the past of the two narrative's events, the present of the writing, and the future of the science fiction.

It is a tale of two sisters, one of whom Laura dies under ambiguous circumstances in the opening pages. Iris, the elderly protagonist who narrates this story of her family life starts with a dispassionate observation: "Ten days after the war ended, my sister Laura drove a car off a bridge" (3).

Iris initially seems a little cold blooded about this death in the family. She knows the actual reason behind her death. When a police officer suggests that the brakes failed; Iris thinks: "It wasn't the brakes, I thought. She had her reasons. Not that they were over the same as anybody else's reasons. She was completely ruthless in that way" (3).

Iris sets out to write the true story of Laura's life and death and in this process, she tells her own life history. Laura and Iris spend their childhood in Avilion a "merchant's palace" and like princesses in a fairy tale. They are virtually untouched by the outside world. Her grandmother named her mansion after an island valley where king Arthur went to die (64). Their grandfather is considered as a wealthy industrialist whose rise and fall reflects shifts in Canada's ruling class over the last century.

Her childhood experiences are not happy as her mother dies of miscarriage and due to her father's escape to alcoholism. Father always wanted boys to carry on the family business. Iris' father Norval returns from military service with one good eye and one good leg from the World War I; where he has lost his two brothers. He becomes alcoholic after being shattered by these tragic deaths. He suns, Chase industries, a button factory but problems start in the button factory and shut down was announced and the interior thunder storm struck when the factory caught fire apparently set by Alex Thomas, the radical labour agitator. After this incident, the sisters managed to hide Alex Thomas in the family attic before he escaped to Spain. They both fell in love with him but at the age of nineteen, Iris is forced to enter a joyless marriage to thirty-five years old wealthy Richard Griffen out of obedience to her father who hoped that this union would save his factory and his daughters. He says:

> I have to consider your future. In case anything should happen to me, that is Laura's future, in particular.... I have to consider the factories as well.... I have to consider the business. It might still be saved, but the bankers are after me. They're hot on the trail. They won't wait much longer. (231)

Iris sells herself into marriage. She immediately finds herself and Laura thrown into a pit of snakes—Richard and his sister Winifred are the ones with the sharpest fangs.

We gradually discover that defiance and maternity allow Iris to carve out her own space within the confines of the social situation. Later Laura becomes Richard's victim of blackmail and seduction and sent to an "asylum" where she has an abortion. Upon her release the sisters reconnect and hurt each other with painful revelations. Iris tells Laura that she has had secret affair with Alex.

She pushed Laura towards suicide by telling her why she and not Laura, received the telegram announcing Alex's death. This story ends in tragedy because Iris alone knows who is the real culprit of Laura's death; and yet, at the same time, Iris is aware that she is nearing her journey's end, so she wants to tell the truth though it is difficult:

> The only way you can write the truth is to assure that what you set down will never be read. Not by any other person and not even by yourself at some later date. Otherwise you begin excusing yourself. You must see the writing as emerging like a long scroll of ink from the index finger of your right hand; you must see your left hand erasing it. (291)

The second narrative also called *The Blind Assassin* supposed to have been written by Laura Chase. The manuscript was found after her death and published by Iris. It becomes a cult classic of Canadian literature. Although the protagonists are identified only as "He" and "She" we are led to believe that it records the secret love affair of Alex and Laura. Later we come to know that it is authored by Iris. As she writes, "As for the book, Laura didn't write a word of it, But you must have known that for sometime. I wrote it myself, during my long evening alone, when I was waiting for Alex to come back..." (529).

The Blind Assassin describes the risky affair in the turbulent thirties between a wealthy young woman and a man. During their meetings in the cramped dirty and rented rooms, the lover tells a science fiction to entertain his girlfriend. This third narrative is a pulp fantasy set on the planet Zycron which is, "located in another dimension of space, there's a rubble strewn plain. To the north is the ocean, which is violet in colour. To the west is a range of mountains, said to be roamed after sunset by the voracious undead female inhabitants of the crumbling tombs located there, "Zycron has a flourishing city, Sakiel-Norn, roughly translatable as the pearl of Desting" (17). It has elements of beauty and advance thinking, but is in other ways an archaic and brutal 'civilization' sacrificing its people ruthlessly to achieve its aims—or rather, the aims of its aristocrats, the Snilfards.

In Sakiel Norn, aristocrats are called the Snilfards. They are skilled metal workers and inventors of ingenious mechanical devices. Male Snilfards wear masks of woven platinum while female Snilfards veil their faces in a silk like cloth made from the cocoon of the chaz moth. They are fond of music. They fall elaborately in love with one another's wives; "Duels were fought over these affairs, though it was more acceptable in a husband to pretend not to know" (18).

The slaves are called the Ygnirods. They wear shabby gray tunics with one shoulder bare, and one breast as well for the women, who are fair gain for the male Snilfard.

The Ygnirods are resentful of their life but they conceal it. The lowest among them are Slaves, they are prohibited by law from reading and have secret codes that they scratched in the dirt with stones. If a Snilfard becomes solvent, he is demoted to an Ygnirod. He can avoid this by selling his wife or children.

The culture of Sakiel-Norn is based on ancient Mesopotamia. It's in the code of Hammurabi, the laws of the Hittites (19). It was renowned for its handicrafts, especially its weaving. The slave children weave the carpets because their fingers are suitable for such intricate work. But this labour caused them to go blind by the age of nine and their blindness is the measure of the cost of carpet; "This carpet blinded ten children.... This blinded fifteen, this blinded twenty" (24). Aflin that these boys are sell off to brothel-keepers and they become assassins, as their sense of hearing is acute:

> There are lots of Gods, who are carnivorous. They require human sacrifice. It is believed that nine devout fathers offered their own children to be buried and in honour of the nine girls buried at the city gates, nine girls are offered every year. This is known as "the Goddess's Maidens".

According to law the noblest Snilfards must sacrifice at least one of their daughters. They should not feel blemished so the Snilfards begin to mutilate their girls by cutting their small body part. Now they adopt the offspring of female slaves and use them to replace their legitimate daughters. It shows how weak and helpless mass of humanity are damaged and abused only because they are powerless, "It was cheating, but the noble families were powerful, so it went on with the eye of authority winking" (30).

The Snilfards simply send these girls to the Temple of the Goddess where they brought up and trained to fulfil their duties happily.

The dedicated girls were shut up inside the temple compound, fed the best of everything to keep them sleek and healthy and rigorously trained so they would be ready for the great day-able to fulfil their duties with decorum, and without quailing, "The ideal sacrifice should be like a dance,...stately and lyrical, harmonious and graceful" (31). Some of girls try to revolt and escape too. It became the practice to cut out the tongues of the girls three months before they were due to be sacrificed. This was not a mutilation...but an improvement...for the servants of the Goddess of Silence (31).

The night before her sacrifice, every girl must undergo a visitation from the Lord of the Underworld, it is for if "her soul will be unsatisfied, and instated of traveling to the land of the gods, she will be forced to join the band of beautiful nude dead women with azure hair, curvaceous figures, ruby-red lips and eyes like snake filled pits, who hang around the ancient ruined tombs in the desolate mountains to the West" (119).

There is one open secret that the Lord of the Underworld isn't real, but one of the courtiers in disguise.

The High Priestess receives bribe and excuses herself that she uses the money for charitable purposes. The girls cannot complain as being without tongue or even writing materials. The girl must be killed by a blind assassin.

In the story, the blind assassin X moves through the palace and intends to kill the sacrificial maiden but falls in love when he touches her; "Touch comes before sight, before speech. It is the first language and the last, and it always tells the truth. This is how the girl who couldn't speak and the man who couldn't see fall in love" (262).

They assist each other to escape and are mistaken for divine messengers (277) and are taken to the servant of Rejoicing. There is two different endings of this story. According to "She" after helping the leader, the assassin and maiden escaped to the foothills and lived happily. In "his" ending, however, "Not one escapes alive.... An entire culture is wiped from the universe...our two romantic leads are wolf meat" (356). He says "I'm not incurable, but I like my stories to be true to life, which means there have to be wolves in them, wolves in one form or another" (356).

Within *The Blind Assassin* there is another story with happy ending. It is about lizard man of planet Xenor and peach women of planet Aa'A.

Lizard man wears flammable shorts and, "their plan was to capture a large number of Earth women and breed a super race half human half Xenorian Lizard man" (362). They attack on earth and "had made parts of Eurasia and South America their slave colonies, appropriating the younger women for their hellish breeding experiment and burying the corpses of the men in enormous pits" (362-63).

Earth fighter pilots want to wipe out the Xenorians entirely. During this war two young men Will and Boyd are shot to hell. The zorch rays have put a hole in their tank and loose contact with earth control. They've been seized by a gravity field and find themselves on the Plant of Aa'A. There are no men except them and women are virgins. After some days they discover that there is no birth and death, "These women grow on trees on a stem running into the tops of their heads, and were picked when ripe by their predecessors.... When time came, each of a Peach women...would simply disorganize her molecules, which would then be reassembled via the tree into a new, fresh woman" (366).

These women are completely shameless and display the most whorish behaviours. At first both men find this entertaining but after a while it irritates them. They say, "It's all the loving you over dreamed of, in every shape and form. It's everything men think they want when they are out their.... It's Paradise, but we are can't get of it. And anything you can't get out of is Hell" (367).

Margaret Atwood subtly braids all these stories together and gradually reveals their buried secrets. She co-relates these stories with the help of a torn photograph. In the Prologue and Epilogue of *The Blind Assassin* and Iris memoir, there is a photograph of a man and woman on a picnic, showing just the hand of a third person in one corner, which evidently frames the whole novel. But actually, both are different photographs, one is tinted and other is black and white.

The mixing up of genres, blending of documentary materials with the main narrative , a memoir, makes the novel a postmodern fiction. Sharon Wilson says: "The novel seems to build a meticulously realistic portrait of Canada through the first and second world wars. Only to deconstruct it through postmodernist magical realism and the exposure of deceptive contradictions and gaps."[4]

The characters within Iris' memoir are superb recalling her life over the past seventy years is a long, tedious process, but characters make this novel a unforgettable piece of literature.

The main characters include Iris and Laura Chase and their parents, father Norval, Mother named only as "Our Mother" who sacrifices herself for others. Two sisters are brought up by their nursemaid Rennie. Her grandfather Benjamin, who built the button factory in the early 1870, and Grand Mother Adelia who was "married off" rather than married.

According to a book titled The Chase Industries: A History commissioned by her grandfather, "His forbears had come up from Pennsylvania in the 1820's to take advantage of cheap land and of construction opportunities—the town had been burnt out during the war of 1812, and there was considerable rebuilding to be done" (56).

Adelia's maiden name was Montfort. She was from an established family. She died in 1973 of cancer. Iris father was the eldest of three brothers. Two younger brothers Edger and Percival were killed in the war. Norval is a serious gentleman. He never shows his emotions for his daughters. As Iris says: "He rarely spoke to us...we worshipped him, of course. It was either that or hate him. He did not invite the more moderate emotions" (102).

Her Mother was a religious woman. She died of miscarriage and remains helpless victim throughout her life. Iris says of her mother's flickering love; "perhaps she loved us both equally.... Her love for us was a given—solid and tangible, like a cakes. The only question was which of us was going to get the bigger slice" (96).

After her mother's death, Iris' father meets Callista Fitzsimmons who is the sculptress of the weary soldier project. She is twenty years old woman and a read head. She is consulted like a man and strides around and shakes hands like one as well. She smokes cigarettes. In her company Iris' father "seemed happier, certainly he was drinking less" (150).

Miss Violet Groeham is the tutor of Chase sisters. She is forty years old woman with a wardrobe of faded cardigans that hinted at an earlier, more prosperous existence. The sisters called her Miss Violence.

In the place of Miss Violence, their father appoints a man, Mr. Erskine, who'd once taught at a boys school in England. He changed the whole system of their study and is a hair puller, and ear twister. He tries to exploit Laura so Mr. Norvel expelled him from his house.

In their teenage life, Iris and Laura meet Alex Thomas in the button factory picnic. He is an orphan and adopted by a Presbyterian minister and his wife. He is an European immigrant and a labour organizer. Suspected of Bolshevik Violence, and dodging the law, he is secretly sheltered by Laura and Iris when they are too young to understand his position and their own sexual pull. They supplied him food and drink; "Mornings and evenings were the times of our visits. We raided the pantry, salvaged and leftovers. We smuggled up raw carrots, bacon rinds. Half-eaten boiled eggs, pieces of bread folded over, with butter and Jam inside" (219). After his departure Laura gives a torn photograph to Iris in which she cuts herself out of it and she has another one is which she cuts Iris' photo. This is her love for Alex.

In Attic, Alex tried to make sexual relationship with Iris. She was shocked that time but later in Iris memoir we discovered that Iris and Alex have secret love affair and Aimee is daughter of Iris and Alex not of Iris and Richard as was believed earlier.

At the age of nineteen Iris' father "sells" Iris to Richard in Marriage. He is the owner of a successful firm called "Royal Classic Knitwear". His enemies "referred to it derisively as Royal Classic Shitwear, because Mr. Griffen was not only father's chief competitor, he was also an adversary of sorts" (180).

Iris marries Richard because of her father's hope that she can in this way save the now-failing button factory. Iris writes: "He was only doing what would have been considered—was considered, then—the responsible thing. He was doing the best he knew how" (232). But this proved to be a bitter pill saturated in sweetness. Iris is so busy trying to resist the imposition of monarchical authority, of the civilization for which Richard stands, that she fails to see how greatly her sister is being victimized.

Richard is very selfish kind of man, as he didn't tell Iris about her father's death because he doesn't want any disturbance during their trip, actually it was his business trip. He says to Iris "I know I ought to have, but I wanted to spare you the worry, darling. There was nothing to be done and no way we could get back in time for the funeral, and I didn't want things to be ruined by you" (317).

But Iris feels no emotional attachment with him. Their honeymoon trip is just a business for Richard. Iris writes: "Honeymoon's were said to allow the new couple the time to get to know each other better, but as the days went by I felt I knew Richard less and less. He was effacing himself, or was it concealment?" (312).

Later Iris finds that Richard "has a yen for young girls" (523). He seduced Laura and says: that he did nothing without Laura's consent. Iris says: "I suppose when he married me he figured he'd got a bargain-two for the price of one. He picked us up for a long" (522).

Iris leaves his house with Aimee and after that Richard is discovered dead in the sail boat "Water Nixie" because his political carrier is ruined by the scandal of Laura's book.

Richard's sister Winifred is an over ambitious and cunning socialite, a perfect manipulator. She is thirty years old and like to call her Freddie. She arranges parties' dinners and social events for Richard. She takes the helpless bridal Iris in her hand and arranges all her shopping according to her taste; "in one of my several brand new trunks were a tennis skirt although I didn't play, a bathing suit although I couldn't swim, and several dancing frocks although I didn't know how to dance" (240). Richard consults Winifred about everything because she is the one who encourages him. Iris recalls:

> They'd both deicide that Richard was the man of the future, and the woman standing behind him...was her. It certainly wasn't me. Our relative positions were now clear, hers and mine...she was necessary to Richard, I on the other hand could always be replaced. My job was to open my legs and shut my mouth. (341-42)

After Richard's death she blamed Iris and now there is open war. She does the worst thing to Iris and takes Aimee away from Iris.

Iris daughter Aimee died of drugs was self-neglected, alienated from her mother. She was resentful of Iris for having dragged her away from her former and considerably more affluent life. Iris says: "She was already deciding that I was unsatisfactory as a mother" (524). Richard takes advantage of long distance and develops sympathy for himself by giving gifts to Aimee. Throughout her life Aimee is hoping that her real mother is somehow Laura.

Laura Chase is the younger glamorous, strange sister, the artist and empathy a temple girl with no illusions about god's mercy. She is the girl who will never fit into the world's regulations and structures. She is spiritual, curious, uncompromising. She is not a woman with the organisational power or love of self-advertisement to write an autobiography or a novel—but she is both heroic soul and sacrificed female. Other who claims they don't understand her always uses her.

Richard uses her for his lust and Iris her own sister uses her by posting her story under Laura's name. Throughout her life Laura becomes a helpless victim. She confined to an asylum as an acknowledgement that she is not enough of this world and she is raving and hysterical. Winifred says to Iris that mental specialist suggests that she is jealous of Iris and it is better to send her to an asylum.

"Laura must be insanely jealous of you", said Winifred, "Jealous of everything about you—she wants to be living your life, she wants to be you, and this is the form it's taken." He said you ought to be kept out of harm's way (443).

But actually Richard whisks her out because Laura gets pregnant from him. Laura has more courage and dignity than Iris. Laura herself was more devoted to Alex; "I had to make the sacrifice. I had to take the pain and suffering onto myself. That's what I promised God. I knew if I did that, it would save Alex" (502). She escapes from asylum just to meet Alex:

> Because the war's over...and Alex will be back soon. If I wasn't here, he wouldn't know where to find me. He wouldn't know about Bella Vista, I went to Halifax. The only address he'll have for me is yours. He'll get a message through to me somehow. (502)

When Iris tells Laura about Alex's death, she kills herself by driving off a bridge. Here Iris functions as her sister's assassin. Iris Chase emerges from the story as one of Atwood's most memorable characters to date. She is a woman of ascetic life and acetic wit, sharp and bitter as old wine. In her childhood she was her father's substitute boy. Iris has moved through her life in a fog of other's expectations, incapable of identifying her own needs and responsibilities. The impulse to grab her by the shoulders and shakes her is strong, particularly when she sleepwalks into an arranged marriage and passively permits her sister's institutionalization in a mental hospital. Iris is a victim to whom fate has not been kind, but whose ills—like those of many victims of circumstance are largely of her own making, even if her contribution was often one of complacency.

Her marriage with Richard follows her and Laura's humiliation. She says about her honeymoon, "Why is a honeymoon called that? Lune de miel, moon of honey—as if the moon itself is not a cold and airless and barren sphere of pockmarked rock, but soft, golden, luscious—a luminous candied plum, the yellow kind, meeting in the mouth and sticky as desire, so achingly sweet it makes your teeth hurt. A warm floodlight floating, not in the sky. but inside your own body. I know about all of that. I remember it very well. But not from my honeymoon" (309).

Now Iris is a woman near the end of her life, reflecting on the path she's taken to old age. She says: "Nothing is more difficult than to understand the dead, I've found; but nothing is more dangerous than to ignore them" (525).

She has lived fifty years with the secret meaning of Laura's death, and her story. Now she is constructing her story as the more personal memorial to preserve her memories of the paradise lost of her love affairs with Alex Thomas. She writes: "I wanted a memorial that was how it began. For Alex, but also for myself" (529).

She adds: "The picture is of happiness, the story is not. Happiness is a garden walled with glass; there no way in or out. In Paradise there are no stories, because there are no journeys. It's loss and regret and misery and yearning that drive the story forward, along its twisted road" (534).

Iris memoir seems as the tragedy of a woman sold into a loveless marriage by her bankrupt father to preserve the family's social and economic standing, only to lose the man she loves, her reputation, and even the love of her daughter, a daughter fathered perhaps by the only man she loved.

The Blind Assassin explores how men can be convinced to sacrifice themselves in war for such dubious concepts as honour, courage and nationalism and about how women can be passively indoctrinated being marked with abuse. The novel's themes of sacrifice, loss, betrayal, assassination, blindness, amputation and silencing connect to the novel's mythic and fairy tale inter texts and allusions.

Iris is a victim of patriarchal society where her father sells her and her sister to the "devil" Richard. She feels helpless, tired and useless. Iris is the only survivor, who is recounting. Her story has to cope with the fact of her own survival, with a failing body and diminished powers in a world which is impatient of illness, weakness, vulnerability and death itself.

Iris is also an assassin, because she tells Laura about Alex's death. Iris, acting according to traditional female virtue, has tried to spare her father by marrying Richard, but that proves to be the road to her father's death and ultimately to Richard's also Iris wants to take revenge yet she is not triumphant but forsaken as her daughter died prematurely and her granddaughter has long been estranged from her.

The novel moves along, chronicling Iris' life, the young Iris is presented as so vapid, so unaware so stupid and the older Iris realize this, it is something for which she is quite apologetic and sad. She never fully understood the implications other people had on her life, on the lives of her sister and father. By the time she did, it was too late. The older Iris is batter and sad, but she never really descends into angst or insincere emotion—there are times when she chides herself for being melodramatic. She is very sympathetic, a sad, sorry woman. who demands and deserves respect and caring.

In presenting Iris' story, Margaret Atwood chooses from all the themes and styles she's explored in the past. There is a little of *The Handmaid's Tale* in the sci-fi dystopian novel within a novel and much of *Cat's Eye* in the protagonist's reflective journey back in time. *The Blind Assassin* is a dark masterpieces in which tension comes from the sharp juxtaposition of worlds and in which futuristic fantasy interrupts and reflects a disquieting reality.

The expert craftsmanship that Margaret Atwood possesses in *The Blind Assassin* is amazing. She also captures the 1930s-40s atmosphere quite well. The blending of real events and newspaper clippings with science fiction and strange photography and mythic and fairly take allusions builds. *The Blind Assassin's* magical realism and establishes come of its major themes. The novel constructs layer upon layer of desire; the desire to know finally why Laura Chase took her own life—if it was suicide or an accident. The novel is tiered at the end and Margaret Atwood explores each level, one by one, until the final page. She creates a world of astonishing vision and unforgettable impact.

Margaret Atwood is more a poet than a fictional writer and her initial orientations a poet has enriched her style. Her language in her novels is more closely aware of its urge toward the poetic. In *The Blind Assassin* the protagonist Iris seems influenced by Keats; "It's the first week of October season of woolen garments taken out mothballs; of nocturnal mists and dew and slippery front steps, and late-blooming slugs."

The novel reveals a skilled use of metaphors and similes. Here she is striking in her metaphors, "But long ago I made a choice between Classicism and Romanticism. I prefer to be upright and contained an urn in daylight."

As Margaret Atwood pointed out in *Survival* that Canadian literature tends to be about persisting in an environment not altogether adapted to human habitation, a beautiful but not sweet natural land; the sharpness of Canadian seasons and landscape are evoked in a continuous story of ruin and survival. *The Blind Assassin* is embedded in Canadian tradition. Iris' memoir covers approximately hundred years of Canadian history. Though there is faithful historical reconstruction, the focus is on the familial dissolution suffered by the Chase family.

Like Margaret Atwood's other works in *The Blind Assassin* too there is varying patterns of domination and subordination highlighted through the book. Margaret Atwood's texts are never simple. If Iris is a victim of patriarchal society, she is also an assassin. *The Blind Assassin* is more generally homicidal. Nobody gets away free, Alex whose crimes were merely union organizing, fell in World War II. Richard who is manipulator, committed suicide Iris who wants to take revenge, the surviving teller, dies.

REFERENCES

1. Richards, Linda. "Brilliant Tapestry" review article, file: 11A:/ Review The Blind Assassin by Margaret Atwood 8 htm 04/18/03, 1.
2. Hobbs, Billy J. "billhobbs" Tyler, TXUSA.
3. Atwood, Margaret. "In Search of Alias Grace: On writing Canadian Historical Fiction", *American Historical Review*, 103 (1998), 1503.
4. Wilson, Sharon. "The Blind Assassin", *The Literary Encyclopedia* at http://www.literncyc.com, 23 March 03, (3-4).

Conclusion

9

> What kind of world shall you describe for your readers? The one you can see around you, or the better one you can imagine? If only the latter, you'll be unrealistic; if only the former, despairing. But it is by the better world we can imagine that we judge the world we have. If we cease to judge this world, we may find ourselves, very quickly, in one, which is infinitely worse.[1]
>
> Margaret Atwood

Margaret Atwood is clearly concerned with the alignment of power that exerts physical, political, economical and social control over woman to fragment her. In her novels she proves, the things that man do, woman can do better. They are neither deficient physically nor intellectually. They hold the reins of power firmly in their hands. In her feminist novels progress of her protagonist is not very smooth yet they triumph ultimately through many tactical retreats. It becomes increasingly clear that man's powerful status has been destabilized and he is loosing out in the game of power as he is finding himself incapable of dwarfing, maiming, victimizing and threatening women for his personal gain. Her novels concentrate on woman's realization of power control and self-awareness.

Most of the novels of Margaret Atwood are replete with the theme of victimization and survival, the part of cultural life of Canada and actively engage with problems that are not just national concerns but are also the social, political and traditional issues that will determine the survival of their country. As the pervasive symbol of American literature, according to Margaret

Atwood, is the frontier, so the dominant image in Canadian fiction is survival, the un-heroic survival of victimization:

> ...The main idea is the first one: handing on, staying alive Canadian is forever taking the national pulse like doctors at a sickbed: the aim is not to see whether the patient will live well but simply whether he will live at all. Our central idea is one which generates not the excitement and sense of adventure or danger which the frontier holds out...but an almost intolerable anxiety. Our stories are likely to be tales not of those who made it but of those who made it back, from the awful experience—the North, the snow storm, the sinking ship—that killed everyone else. The survivor has no triumph or victory but the fact of this survival; he has little after his ordeal that he did not have before, except gratitude for having escaped with his life.[2]

As a writer she is aware of the dynamics between an artist and the society in which he operates. She writes:

> Far from thinking of writers as totally isolated individuals, I see them as in escapable connected with their society. The nature of the connection will vary—the writer may unconsciously reflect the society, he may consciously examine it and project ways of changing it and the connection between writer and society...becomes the 'subject' of the writer.[3]

As a novelist, Margaret Atwood discovers the anomalies of Canadian civilization in which women are not allowed to make any strategy of grabbing the male space. Her novels represent and reflect an important development in the post-sixties Canadian writing. The quest for identity, traditionally and by implication was with reference to the male in terms of the knight out/night out male-questers. The woman's quests were perceived in terms of marriage and 'happy ever afterwards' ends: not self-actualization or individuation but self-effacement and socialization. In her fiction she attempts to fictionalize the progress of the women protagonists' quest for distinctive feminine identity.

In *The Edible Women* Marian's progress as a strong individualist is evident from the fact that she rejects the conventional role that her society offers her as a woman and is more aware of her inner self and other than at the novel's outset. By creating her false image in the forms of the cake woman and consuming it, Marian indicates that she will henceforth attempt to live in accordance with her true self. By acting against the norms of her society, Marian seems to have started out on the path of mythic heroes. She chooses her own freedom and refuses to be the edible woman. At the end, she is aware of her own resilience, openness and her capacity to love and care for others.

The narrator of *Surfacing* experiences transcendence in nature, which heals the split between the conscious and the unconscious parts of her psyche. Finally she decides to refuse to be a victim. She returns to society determined to stop being a fake artist and there is a tremendous transformation is her personality for the better. The novel shows a new hope that a woman can emerge as a new woman with a new courage to lead an authentic life. All on her own, she can face the challenges of life and needs no god to help her now. The narrator has been able to revive and recover the part of herself she had lost and is returning as a wiser, saner being. Her journey has been indeed, a journey from death to life, from withdrawal to reintegration with society, from illusion to reality. She has learnt that survival is tough, yet she is prepared to struggle to survive not by an escape from reality but by a bold confrontation of it.

Joan in *Lady Oracle* as a wife takes recourse to extra-marital affairs. The novel shows how this dramatic choice affects her life. The consequences of her affairs are painful and she realizes that she has made a mistake in taking a short route to pleasure. Joan fails in her relationships with men and she regards all men as killers. Later she realizes that, like all men she too is capable of to live her life as she wants. She catches a few glimpses of her authentic self. Ultimately she emerges as a serious writer and offers an equal and better relationship between man and woman.

Rennie, in *Bodily Harm* is proud of her liberated and independent existence. But once she steps into the Caribbean Island she becomes aware of the still traditional male attitude. Like all the protagonists of Margaret Atwood's fiction, the central character of the novel also undergoes a major transformation. She rejects her submissive role as a woman. At the end of the novel she is prepared to speak out the truth about all exploited people and women. As a freelance journalist she uses pen as a 'weapon'. She challenges the male dominated society and hopes for a better and healthy relationship between man and woman. Thus Rennie's writing as exposure of bodily harm conducts us in a journey of the imagination, "to contemplate both the fact of individual mortality and the conditions under which the great mass of the world's population love to live, so that through the exercise of imagination [we] may be lead to a more aware, more compassionate politically committed view of life".[4]

In *The Handmaid's Tale* Margaret Atwood does not depict only men as the oppressors. Women, too, in the novel are presented as equally ruthless and dominating and are castigated for their complicity in the processes of victimization of fellow-woman. The novel proves that even women are not exempted from perpetrating crimes similar to those of men. Margaret Atwood's de-construction of patriarchal structures of power and dominion, therefore, is not gender specific but a comprehensive criticism of all power structures that inferiorize and de-humanize individuals, especially women. Offred, rebels against her society seem abortive, her covert rebellion against Gilleadian ideology is praiseworthy.

Cat's Eye shows the inner life and the sensibility of women. The emotional and intellectual development of the protagonist Elaine suggests both the limitations and the possibilities of life as lived by both women and men, for the women's experience, is a paradigm for human experience, the feminine sensibility for the human sensibility. As an artist she realizes the position of women painter in patriarchal society. Through her paintings she wishes a society, which does not disfigure and disqualify women from excellence.

In her novels, Margaret Atwood poses all present day feministic solutions and rejects them bluntly. Her protagonists learn through their experiences that imitating male attitudes do not lead them towards a complete and dignified life. They are forced to rethink and re-evaluate their decisions and choices.

They realize that they have long been exploited and they feel that it is time "to become human and men could do the same".[5] They refuse to be victim and merely survive giving in to the jungle rule of strong and powerful men. Margaret Atwood proves, that we all possess the talent and the strength to revitalize our lives and reject society's well-trodden paths that suppress the human spirit. They do not desire a matriarchal society to replace the patriarchal. In *The Handmaid's Tale* Offred says that, "if Moira thought that she could create an utopia by setting herself up in a women only enclave, she was sadly mistaken" (161). With this, Margaret Atwood claims "human equality" and "human freedom of choice" for women as "one is not born [a woman] but becomes a woman".[6] Thus, we can say that Margaret Atwood is neither a feminist nor an antifeminist but a humanist who proposes androgynous vision as against an either/or world-view.

In her feminist perspective Margaret Atwood is not limited by the regional or geographical boundaries. "Think globally, Act Locally" seems as the most appropriate message of her novel. She proposes the world where all women enjoy human rights and lead a stable, peaceful and healthy life. As a feminist thinker she is concerned with all the modes of victimization of women and their rebel from oppression. Her fiction deals with, "a comprehensive range of social issues and from such a variety of perspectives that it eludes the simplicity of any single 'feminist' position".[7] In her novels, Margaret Atwood has chosen to examine gender-based violence, which explores women's painful realities, their suffering and endurance of life's perversities. She questions and challenges the concept of gender because women's status in patriarchal society is ingrained as victims. She wants to protect the basic human rights of women through her fiction. In her fiction she explores various forms of gender victimization of women in the name of tradition, modernity, technology, and marriage. Her protagonists learn lessons from their lives and take truer control of their images of self and their future directions. They come to realize that women themselves have got to have faith in their own powers. Then alone can they achieve something. The fact that they can now refuse victimization implies that till now they have lived as a victim in the male dominated world, which threatens the freedom of women. They confront all the adversities with courage and fortitude. They no longer perceive themselves as a victim and attain the feminist consciousness—consciousness of women's own power and potential. They are involved in a grim struggle to attain "freedom and full human status after millennia of deprivation and oppression".[8]

Through her protagonists, Margaret Atwood has revealed not only the stereotyped perception of women and the traditional society's expectations from them but she has also shown the changing man-woman relationships. She has tried to shown how women are trying to redefine themselves. She also tries to establish the fact that the two sexes are complementary and neither is complete without the other. In *Second Words*, Margaret Atwood suggests the following strategy for women's liberation:

1. Ignore [your] victimization, and sing songs like "I Enjoy Being A Girl".
2. Think it's the fault of Biology, or something, or you can't do anything about it; write literature on How Awful It Is, which may be a very useful activity upon a point.
3. Recognize the source of oppression; express anger; suggest ways for change.[9]

In other words, Margaret Atwood teaches women to know the glory of their lives and realize the confidence and dignity in women. She advocates human rights of women and wants to create a favourable atmosphere to develop the personality of women according to their interests. She is a feminist writer who recognizes the oppression of women and her feminist approach is for equality of women and their human rights. Her feministic point of view is neither male-centered not female centered but equality between male and female.

Margaret Atwood in her fiction has pointed to shared themes of powerlessness, victimization and alienation as well as to a certain ambivalence or ambiguity. She does not just use language in a largely referential way, providing verisimilitude that is a staple of realist fiction and that authenticates the world and the world's relationship to it.[10] She uses and abuses the convention of both language and narrative in her fiction in an attempt to make us question any naive critical notion we might have about modernist formalism and about realist transparency. Her fiction subjects both language and its various discourses to 'psychoanalysis', in order to reveal the structures, which shape it, and to show the ways it can be used to victimize not only women but also men. Yet, throughout her exploration of language and discourse, she suggests that language is available either to entrap us or to liberate us, whether men or women. Margaret Atwood has searched to create a language, which does not fragment and debase either women or men. She has rejected the univocal statement or any concept of meaning or truth as single and determinate. She has explained that we must learn what is not said is often more important than what is said. She has developed further the literary convention of language as surfaces and depths, as a palimpsest, which hides what it means, and she has toyed with the deceptive devices of rhetoric and figures of speech, metaphors as essential to language. She has insisted that language is available as either a release or a transformative power or as a trap and a force of subjugation. Her fiction expresses these issues, after thorough powerful images and symbols. She has used journey metaphor, both as a quest for identity and unknown territories. She has also explored the various modes of gaining control over our lives, as she has shown that the past must be regained. She dismissed the sexist assumptions hidden in language, which prevent women from taking hold of words, and from writing themselves into new, powerful identities. Her texts show the historical and cultural nature of 'natural' phenomena and subject them to control by analyzing their hidden assumptions. Her novels often look like portrayals of a search for alternative roles of a more viable kind for both men and women seeking to escape the preferred, conventional, socially approved roles. Rejection of the victimization of negative role is explored, as is the difficulty of escape. These projects are concerned with cultural and social issues. Sociology and psychology are not separable for Atwood because the individual who escapes from victimization is also from the community.

Margaret Atwood has used mythology and folk tale in her writing to reveal the constraining effects of cultural heritage and social values. She used Greek and Latin mythology along with fairy tale and folklore element as images, characters or situations. Figures of Artemis, Diana, Hecate and Aphrodite or Venus abound, as she uses, these familiar archetypes to expose sexist assumptions and rewrite situations which involve either female figures avoiding traditional stereotype or male figures exposed as tyrannical. Through her systematic use of familiar images of mirror labyrinths, wolves she has engaged in self-conscious, self-referential gestures. By using mirror images, she reveals that art is not a mirror or representation of nature, but a reflection of process of writing, reading and interpretation. Margaret Atwood's narrative strategies draw systematically for structured unity upon familiar literary conventions, regenerated by theoretical gestures towards feminism, colonialism, theories of the gaze, the camera, the victim, psychoanalytic metaphors and images. Her novels constitute a powerful exploration of the labour involved in such psychic regeneration. Her heroines are depicted struggling to divest themselves of the social myths, which cripple their personal power. Atwood's novels not only reveal sexist, patriarchal assumptions hidden in language and culture generally, she has also built into her texts a level of analysis which explodes the myth of men as free, and has detailed the victimization of men which a patriarchal social system institutionalizes.

Margaret Atwood's other novel, which are not part of this study, are also concerned with social issues and her feminist approach.

In *Life Before Man* (1979), she examines the politics of power in interpersonal relationships between wife and husband. This novel articulates the existential despair of both men and women in contemporary urban society.

Marriage is believed to be the destiny of a woman within a patriarchal society but Margaret Atwood's protagonists are conscious of the victimization of women in marriage. Elizabeth, the protagonist is considered to be a frustrated, rebellious and an indifferent woman in regard to the institution of marriage. It is a story of three ordinary middle class people—Elizabeth and her husband Nate and Nate's lover Lesje, for whom he leaves his wife. The novel covers two years of their lives, "charting the development and deterioration of their relationships within the context of daily routine, miscommunication tawdry affairs and gray emotional struggles".[11]

Elizabeth, a special projects administrator at Toronto's Royal Ontario Museum, marries Nate, an unemployed law graduate, with the hope of getting safety and shelter for her life. But soon she discovers that it is Nate, who requires security because he depends on his wife for money. Their marital relationship does not based on love. They have never lived together as a real wife and husband, yet two daughters Janet and Nancy are born out of their wedlock. Nate feels that Elizabeth has made him to lead, "a termite's life" (285) and is fed up of acting in accordance with her numerous "rules, subrules, codicils, addenda, errata" (163). So he gets involved with Lesje and plans to leave his wife for Lesje, a paleontologist (one who studies of life in geological past) who becomes a victim of prehistory. Lesje has loved William but their relationships ends, as William does not want to have child by her. For Lesje, Nate is absolutely necessary to get pregnant. For Lesje, Nate leaves his wife and children for his mistress. Despite their unhappy marriage, Elizabeth and Nate live together because of their children. In the process of her struggle for survival, Elizabeth gets involved with Chris following Nate's path on the basis of equality. Unlike Nate, Chris demands deep and emotional involvement, but Elizabeth opposes the power of Chris over her life because of her strong bond with her children. Unable to get her to quit her job, home and children, Chris shoots off his head. After his death Elizabeth thinks about her own values and mode of living and wishes to lead a harmonious life with Nate. She says, "I don't know how I should live. I don't know how anyone should live. All I know is how I do live. I live like a peeled snail. And that's no way to make money" (11). Feeling both vulnerable and lost without her social mask she says, "I want the shell back, it took me long enough to make" (11).

But Nate's decision shatters her dreams as he is determined to leave his family for Lesje. Elizabeth's traumatic experience in married life turns her deaf and her deafness is the indifference she has towards hearsay about her marriage. She is so disturbed that has violent nightmares. Ultimately, Elizabeth and Nate agree to get divorce Elizabeth is pained to see her daughters act guilty rather than sad about her separation from Nate and does all she can to soothe and comfort them. She ends alone with her daughters and betrayed by Nate. She shows her reluctance to enter the institution of marriage again for:

> Marriage is not
> a house or even a tent
> it is before that, and colder
> the edge of forest, the edge
> of the desert....[12]

She accepts her life as it is and refuses to be a victim because "she's still alive, she wears clothes, she walks around, she holds down a job even. She has two children" (278). She decides to survive with dignity in society.

By depicting marital life of Elizabeth and Nate, Margaret Atwood drives home the message that marriage, as an institution, should help the personal growth and mutual respect of both wife and husband. They should be faithful to each other and they must show respect for this social conduct. She wants to teach us that:

> The married people should not be viewed as each other's property but as living, growing organisms...personal growth [is] commendable. You...have the right attitude and be honest with yourself. (113)

The Robber Bride (1993) is feminist thought provoking novel. It shows how one sex dominates and is a strategy for exercising power in society. Zenia, the protagonist of the novel is a whore who rebels against male sexual politics in patriarchal society. She rejects society's view of fallen women, oppressed by male and uses her body as weapon to humiliate men. Her power is the power of female sexuality. She calls men, seduces them and pulls them inside out like gloves and then abandons them. Zenia wants to take the position of man because man is the power. She drifts into prostitution as a temporary solutions to her unfavourable circumstances created by the male world. As all of Margaret Atwood's protagonists, Zenia is also not fortunate. Her background suggests an unhealthy, weedy soil that causes her young plant to twist and permutated. Zenia is a child of a victim of commercial sex. Being penniless, the life becomes very difficult for her mother so she rent herself and her daughter to men as the sexual commodities to be bought and sold in the open market. After the death of her mother and her aunt by whom she is brought up, Zenia goes to England and joins a magazine as a freelance journalist. There she suffers from same traumatic experience and once again dragged into prostitution. She becomes drug addict as exploited by men. She says:

> Men don't see you as a person, they just see the body, and so that's all you see yourself. You think of your body as a too, something to use God, I'm tired of men! They're so easy to amuse all you have to do to get their attention is take off your clothes. After a while you want a bit more of challenge.... (361)

Zenia's identity as 'The Robber Bride' is established through the stories of Tonny, Charis and Roz, who are tricked in their friendship by Zenia, an acquaintance from their university day. Each succumbs to Zenia's web of deceit. Playing the part of a confidant and thoughtful listener, Zenia encourages the three women to divest themselves of their tales of their traumatic childhoods. She learns their tortured secrets and uses their confidences to spirit away the men each woman believes to be the cornerstone in her life.

Tony is an undesired child of her mother's hasty wartime. She used to flirts with men and leaves her daughter for them. Tony suffers loneliness and alienation in a well-educated and wealthy family; later she marries West, a musicologist who is sensual and sex is the very breath of his life. When Zenia comes in contact with Tony, West develops an illicit relation with her. But Zenia as a revengeful bride exhausts him and shows the power of her sexuality. She uses him and leaves him because he is boring like "one women's meat was another woman's boredom" (403). West is so terribly frightened by Zenia's behaviour that thereafter he is afraid to look at other women.

Second character, Charis is fatherless, abandoned by her mother, is sexually violated by those who should have offered love and trust. Charis falls is love with Billy and marries him. Charis is a Yoga teacher and Zenia attends her classes for her feigned cancer. When Zenia discovers the true nature of Billy, she exhorts Charis to give him up. She tells her that he has lust for women and he has no love and sympathy for his wife. Billy wants to exploit her sexually. Hearing all about Billy's intention Charis loses her equilibrium and feels painful. Billy runs away with Zenia as he has been won by her. Charis thinks Zenia as a Jezebel who has ruined the life of her husband and has robbed him.

Roz, the third of the trio, is a successful managing editor of magazine, *Wise Woman World*. She marries Mitch, who is one of the boards of directors of the magazine. Zenia joins as a freelance journalist and takes charge as the editor. Later she develops sexual relationship with Mitch. He does not like Roz's feminist friend who are drug addict and lesbians. He likes Zenia but she never loves him. She robs him for the pleasure of winning and of taking him away from Roz in the game of sexual politics. She has made fool of him and kills him. Zenia also kidnaps Roz's son Larry to break family who becomes a drug addict under her spell. Later Zenia accepts that:

> I've been on the edge, I've been out there so long; I've had to do it alone. I can't work it out with men, they all want the same thing from me, I just can't make those kinds of compromises any more. I mean, you've got all this, you've got a home, a husband...our kids. You're a family, you've got solid ground under your feet. I've never had any of that. I've never fitted in. I've lived out of a suitcase, all my life; even now it's hand-to-mouth, that's what freelancing means, and I'm running out of energy.... There's just no base, there's no permanence! (362)

Zenia is a homeless, demonic woman who wants to revolt against male hegemony. So she adopts such tactics to seduce men and becomes 'The Robber Bride', Roz develops a kind of sympathy with Zenia and she transforms herself into a "new woman" playing the role of a saint. But soon Zenia leaves her.

Zenia is a representative of the power of female sexuality. As Howells says: "In this Gothic fairy tale retold from, a feminist perspective, Zenia is a very disruptive figure for she is the spectacle of desirable femininity a beautiful façade which hides, whatever is behind it."[13] *The Robber Bride* is "the tale of greed, violence, viciousness and lust for power" (458) and the war of the sexes. Margaret Atwood implies that men and women who adopt the male/female perversion lead them to degradation. Women cannot change the male chauvinistic and sexist world overnight. They need courage, patience of will to transform the society and attitudes of men towards women. The novel demands for the equality of both sexes and hopes for the world free from sexual exploitation and oppression.

Margaret Atwood's ninth novel *Alias Grace* (1996) is different from her earlier writing as for the first time the multiple selves are seen to exist within the protagonist herself and not as people in external reality. Margaret Atwood in her novel, examines crucial issues like the idea of an unified subject, the nature of truth, relations of power. She has shown that she is far more than single perspective as feminist would indicate, that her approaches to politics and literature are global and multifaceted and that she is enthusiastically involved in bringing about positive change.

Alias Grace is the story on the life of Grace Marks, a Canadian servant girl convicted in 1842 at the age sixteen for conspiring with a fellow servant, James McDermott (rumoured to be her lover) to murder her employer Mr. Thomas Kinncar and his housekeeper Nancy Montgomery. Her alleged accomplice in the crimes, James, paid the extreme sentence of the law and was hanged. But some thought Grace was innocent and her sentence has been commuted to life imprisonment. Margaret Atwood has chosen to tell Grace's story in fictional form although the major characters and events are as they happened. Atwood portrays the Victorian prison system and asylum life in detail, including issues Grace has with the wardens who escort her to her work in the Governor's house, other prisoners who see her receiving preferential treatment, and the governor's family. Simon Jorden is a doctor who is using the new science of psychology. He meets with Grace and listens to her story drawing her out about her life and her crime. A parallel plot involves Jorden's increasing obsession with Grace and the social, professional and psychological dangers into which it leads him.

A crucial point in the novel, and its virtual foundation, is that she cannot remember the actual killings. There is a space an absence, at the heart of her narrative, Doctor Jorden has been hired to solve this mystery and he slowly draws memories from Grace tracing her difficult life, her wretched childhood, her emigration from Ireland, her several jobs and day of Kinner's death.

The novel makes a profound point that Heaven and Hell, both exist on Earth. Myths form two different traditions point to the same truth. For Grace, the ultimate achievement is grasping the essential truth of life, which is that life contained the Good and the Evil. Grace also attains this self-awareness, which is a spiritual milestone. Mary Daly suggests, "the way out of imposed 'innocence' or lack of knowledge and choice, both the good and the bad women is through experiential knowledge, a "Fall from false innocence into a new kind of adulthood".[14] She insists that women have to forge new ways of living and renaming the world. This is in a sense, what Grace achieves. Margaret Atwood herself has said that she does not believe in the existence of a single female voice, but in several female voices. It can be argued that there are as many voices as there are women in the world, In *Alias Grace*, she considers all roles and conditions of women: mothers, daughters, wives, deserted women, women dying because of frequent childbirth and abortion. Atwood stresses the vulnerability of Victorian women, the way in which they were trapped, very often because of their compassion for children and because of male domination and lack of economic opportunity and equality.

Margaret Atwood challenges "postmodernist aesthetics" in respect of feminism along with contemporary women writer like Margaret Laurence, Alice Munro and Mavis Gallant who raised their voices against the gender-based injustices and proposed feminist alternatives through their writing. According to Margaret Atwood, society limits the choices of women, and she prefers to portray women who make clear-cut dramatic choices. Her protagonists are constantly engaged in the dialectics of survival. It is essential for them to redefine the term survival, which is not a mere continuance of life in the same old traditional fashion. It is for them a challenge to better their own personal existence. This gives birth to the concept of 'New woman'. This 'New woman' is not the ideal or best woman but a rebel against the general happenings of the patriarchal society, and in exploring her true potential, along with the struggle to fulfil her urges and needs.

Thus, the present study shows that the protagonists and other characters in the novels of Margaret Atwood, provide us with a map of the spiritual condition of modern Canadian fiction with specific reference to their physical and cultural milieu. The most interesting aspect of her novels is that her characters dilemmas and sufferings, desires and errors and their ability to consciously or unconsciously wound others, make her readers react to them not as fictional characters but as live human beings. Though she is certainly supportive of feminist issues like women's dilemmas and alienation caused by their marginal position in patriarchy, she refuses to go to war against men, instead she believes in equality of both sexes.

REFERENCES

1. Atwood, Margaret. Witches, *Second Words: Selected Critical Prose*. Toronto: Anansi, 1982, 333.
2. Atwood, Margaret. *Survival: A Thematic Guide to Canadian Literature*. Toronto: Anansi, 1972, 33.
3. Atwood, Margaret. "A Reply", *Signs: Journal of Women in Culture and Society* 2, No. 2, 1976, 34.
4. Hutcheon, Linda. "Margaret Atwood", *Dictionary of Literary Biography*, Vol. 53: Canadian Writer Since 1960. New York: Gale, 1986, 33.
5. Jones, Dorthy. "Waiting for the Rescue: A Discussion of Margaret Atwood's Bodily Harm", *Kunapipi*, 6.3, 1984, 91.

6. Sawyer, Jack. "On Male Liberation", *Female Psychology: The Emerging Self,* ed. Sue Cox. Chicago: Science Research Associates INC, 1976, 392.
7. Beauvoir, Simone de. *The Second Sex,* trans. H.M. Parshley. England: Penguin Books, 1972, 295.
8. Howells, Coral Ann. *Margaret Atwood.* London: Macmillan P. Ltd., 1996, 14.
9. Millet, Kate. "Sexual Politics: A Manifesto for Revolution", *Radical Feminism,* eds. Anne Koedt, et al. New York: The New York Times Book Co., 1973, 367.
10. Atwood, Margaret. *Second Words: Selected Critical Prose.* Toronto: Anansi, 1982, 145.
11. Grace, Sherill E. *Violent Duality: A Study of Margaret Atwood,* ed. Ken Norris. Montreal: Vehicle Press, 1980, 135.
12. Margaret, Atwood. *Selected Poems.* Toronto: Oxford University Press, 1976, 133.
13. Howell, 84.
14. Daly, Mary. "Beyond God the Father", *Toronto a Philosophy of Women's Liberation.* Boston: Beacon Press, 1973, 67.

Bibliography

PRIMARY SOURCES

Fiction

Atwood, Margaret. *The Edible Woman*. London: Virago Book, 1969.

——. *Surfacing*, London: Virago Book, 1972.

——. *Lady Oracle*. Toronto: McClelland and Stewart, 1976.

——. *Life Before Man*. Toronto: McClelland and Stewart, 1979.

——. *Bodily Harm*. London: Random House, Vintage, 1981.

——. *The Handmaid's Tale*. London: Random House Vintage, 1985.

——. *Cat's Eye*. London: Virago, 1988.

——. *The Robber Bride*. New York: Doubleday, 1993.

——. *Alias Grace*. Toronto: McClelland and Stewart, 1996.

——. *The Blind Assassin*. London: Virage, 2000.

Non-Fiction

Atwood, Margaret. *Survival: A Thematic Guide to Canadian Literature*. Toronto: Anansi, 1972.

——. *Second Words: Selected Critical Prose*. Toronto: Anansi, 1972.

SECONDARY SOURCES

Full Length Studies

Balachandranan, K. *Essays on Canadian Literature*. Bareilly: Prakash Books Depot, 2001.

Davey, Frank. *Margaret Atwood: A Feminist Poetics*. Vancouver: Talonbooks, 1984.

Davidson, Cathy N. and Arnold. ed. *The Art of Margaret Atwood: Essays in Criticism*. Toronto: House of Anansi, 1981.

Dhawan, R.K. *Canadian Literature Today*. New Delhi: Prestige Books, 1995.

Grace, Sherill E. *Violent Duality: A Study of Margaret Atwood,* ed. Ken Norris. Montreal: Vehicle Press, 1980.

Grace, Sherill E. and Loraine Weir. ed. *Margaret Atwood: Language Text and System*, Vancouver: University of British Columbia Press, 1983.

Hengen, Shannon. *Margaret Atwood's Power: Mirrors Reflections and Images in Select Fiction and Poetry*. Toronto: Second Story, 1993.

Kaur, Iqbal. *Margaret Atwood's Surfacing: A Critical Study*. Chandigarh: Arun Publishing House (P) Ltd., 1994.

McCombs, Judith, ed. *Critical Eassays on Margaret Atwood*. New York: G.K. Hall & Co., 1988.

Pandey, Sudhakar. *Perspectives on Canadian Fiction*. New Delhi: Prestige Books, 1994.

Rigney, Barbara Hill. *Margaret Atwood Women Writer Series*. London: Macmillan Education, 1987.

Rosenberg, Jerom. *Margaret Atwood*. Boston: Twayne Publishers, 1984.

Singh, R.A. *The Feminist Mode in Commonwealth Literature*. Bareilly: Prakash Book Depot, 2001.

Singh, Sunaina. *The Novels of Margaret Atwood and Anita Desai: A Comparative Study in Feminist Perspectives*. New Delhi: Creative Books, 1994.

Singh, Sushila. *Feminism and Recent Fiction in English*. New Delhi: Prestige Books, 1991.

Van Spanckeren, Kathryn and Jan Garden Castro, eds. *Margaret Atwood: Vision and Forms*. Carbondale: Southern Illinois University Press, 1988.

Vevaina, Coomie S. *Re/membering Selves Alienation and Survivals in the Novels of Margaret Atwood and Margaret Laurence*. New Delhi: Creative Books, 1996.

Vevaina, Coomie S. and Howells, Coral Ann. *Margaret Atwood, The Shape Shifter, In Memory of Iqbal Kaur*. New Delhi: Creative Books, 1998.

Wilson, Sharon Rose. *Margaret Atwood's Fairy-tale Sexual Politics*. Jackson: University Press of Mississippi, 1993.

Interviews

Gibson, Graeme. "Margaret Atwood", *Eleven Canadian Novelists*. Toronto: House of Anansi, 1973, 1-31.

Ingersoll, Earl G. "Waltzing Again", *Margaret Atwood: Conversations*. Princeton, N.J.: Ontario Review Press, 1990, 234-38.

Meese, Elizabeth. "The Empress No Clothes", *Margaret Atwood: Conversations*, ed. Earl G. Ingersoll. Princeton, N.J.: Ontario Review Press, 1990, 177-90.

Oates, Joyce Carol. "An Interview with Margaret Atwood", *New York Times Book Review*, 21 May 1978, 43-45.

——. "A Conversation with Margaret Atwood", *Ontario Review*, 9, Fall-Winter 1978-79, 5-18.

Sandler, Linda. "Interview with Margaret Atwood", *Malahat Review*, 41, Jan. 1977, 7-27.

Articles and Journals

Ahern, Stephen. "'Meat Like You Like It': The Production of Identity in Atwood's Cat's Eye", *Canadian Literature*, 137, Summer 1993, 8-17.

Anarson, David and Alice, K. Hale. eds. "Isolation in Canadian Literature", *Themes in Canadian Literature Series*. Toronto: Macmillan of Canada, 1975, 17.

Atwood, Margaret. *Power Politics*. 1971; rpt. Toronto: House of Anansi, 1973.

——. "What's So Funny? Notes on Canadian Humour." This Magazine, 8.3, Aug.-Sept. 1974, 24-27.

——. "Marrying the Hangman" in *Fiction of Contemporary Canada* ed. George Bowering. 1974; rpt. Erin, Ontario: Press Porcepic, 1975, 41-43.

——. "Paradoxes and Dilemmas, the Woman as Writer", *Women in the Canadian Mosaic,* ed. Gwen Matheson. Toronto: Peter Martin Associates, 1976, 256-73.

——. "A Reply", *Signs: Journal of Women in Culture and Society,* 2, No. 2, 1976, 34.

——. "Face to Face", *A Place to Stand On: Essays by and About Margaret Laurence*, ed. George Woodcock. Edmonton: Newest Press, 1983, 22-27.

——. "If You Can't Says Something Nice, Don't Say Anything At All", *Language in Her Eye: Views on Writing and Gender by Canadian Women Writing in English*, eds. Libby Scheier, et al. Toronto: Coach House P, 1990, 15-25.

Bailey, Nancy. "Margaret Laurence, Carl Jung and the Manawaka Women", *Studies in Canadian Literature*, Vol. II, No. 2, Summer 1977, 306-21.

Battiata, Marry. "Atwood's Handmaid's: Reawakening Vigilance", *International Herald Tribune*, 26 April 1986, 16.

Beauvoir, Simone de. "Women and Creativity", *French Feminist Thought: A Reader*, ed. Toril Moi. Basil Blackwell, 1987, 19.

Beran, Carol L. "Images of Women's Power in Contemporary Canadian Fiction by Women", *Studies in Canadian Literature,* 15.2 (1990): 54-766.

Bessai, Daiane E. "The Novels of Margaret Atwood", *Essays on Contemporary Postcolonial Fiction*, eds. Hedwig Book and Albert Wertheim. Munchen: Max Hueber Verlage, 1976, 389-406.

Bjerring, Nancy E. "The Problem of Language in Margaret Atwood's Surfacing", *Queen's Quarterly*, 83, No. 4, Winter 1976, 597-62.

Blaise, Clark. "Tale of Two Colonies", *Canadian Literature*, 95, Winter 1982, 110-12.

Bok, Christian. "Sibyls: Echoes of French Feminism" in "The Diviners" and "Lady Oracle", *Canadian Literature*, 135, Winter 1992, 80.

Bouson, J. Brooks. "The Anxiety of Being Influenced: Reading and Responding to Character in Margaret Atwood's The Edible Woman", *Style,* 24.2, Summer 1990, 230.

Broege, Valerie. "Margaret Atwood's Americans and Canadians", *Essay on Canadian Writing: Canadian-American Literary Relations*, 22, Summer 1981, 111-35, 14.

Brown, Lyvia Morgan. "Sexism in Western Art", *Women A: Feminist Perspective*, ed. Jo Freeman. California: Mayfield Publishing Co., 1975, 309-22.

Brown, Rossell M. "Beyond Sacrifice", *Journal of Canadian Fiction*, 16, 1976, 158-62.

Bunch, Carlotte. "Lesbians In Revolt", *Women and Value*, ed. Marilyn Pearsall. Belmont, Calif: Wadsworth, 1986, 128.

Burt, Sandra. "The Second Wave of Canadian Women's Movement", *Canadian Politics: An Introduction to the Discipline*, eds. Alain G. Gagnon and James P. Bickerton. Ontario: Broadview Press, 1990, 548-49.

Campbell, Joseph. *The Hero with a Thousand Faces*. 1949, rpt. Glasgow: Paladin Grafton Books, 1988, 35.

Campbell, Jossie P. "The Woman as Hero in Margaret Atwood Surfacing", *Mosaic,* No. 3, Spring 1978, 18.

Carrington, Ildiko de Papp. "Another Symbolic Descent", Rev. of Bodily Harm, *Essays on Canadian Writing*, 26, 1983, 61-62.

Chandra, Suresh. "Women' Liberation in the Fiction of Margaret Atwood and Shashi Deshpande", in *Meerut Journal of Comparative Literature and Language*, ed. Rajiv Sharma. 6.2, Meerut: Sushila Printers, 1993, 77-85.

Christ, Carol P. "Margaret Atwood: the Surfacing of Women's Spiritual Quest and Vision", in *Signs*, Journal of Women in Culture and Society, 2.2, 1976, 316-30.

Cixous, Helene. "The Laugh of the Medusa" trans. Keith Cohen and Paula Cohen, *Signs*, 1.4, Summer 1976, 875-93.

Cranny, Francis Anne. "Feminist Detective Fiction", *Feminist Fiction, Feminist Uses of Generic Fiction*, Polity Press, 1990, 185.

Daly, Mary. "Beyond God the Father", *Toronto: A Philosophy of Women's Liberation*. Boston: Beacon Press, 1973, 67.

Davey, Frank. "Margaret Atwood", *Profiles in Canadian Literature*, ed. Jeffrey M. Heath. Toronto: Dundurn Press, 1980, 57-60.

Davidson, Arnold E. and Davidson, Cathy N. "Margaret Atwood's Lady Oracle: The Artist As Escapist and Seer", *Studies in Canadian Literature*, 3, No. 2, Summer 1978, 166-77.

Davidson, Cathy. "A Feminist 1984: Margaret Atwood Talks About Her Existing New Novel", *Ms* 14, No. 8, February 1986, 96.

Doday, Anne Margaret. "Royal Classic Knitwear" *London Review of Books,* Vol. 22, No. 19, 5 Oct. 2000, 27-29.

Dymond, Erica Joan. "Atwood The Handmaid's Tale", *The Explicator,* Vol. 61, No. 3, Spring 2003, 181.

Eagleton, Mary. "Fictional Debates on the Woman Author", *Working with Feminist Criticism.* UK: Blackwell Publisher, 60-72.

Easton, Elizabeth. Review of the Edible Woman. *Saturday Review,* 3 October 1970, 40.

Fitzgeraled, Judith. "A Necessary Allegory", *Canadian Forum.* October 1985, 30.

Fleenor, Julian E. "Introduction", in her *The Female Gothic* Montreal: Eden Press, 1983, 16.

Freibert, Lucy M. "Control and Creativity: The Politics of Risk in Margaret Atwood's The Handmaid's Tale", *Critical Essay on Margaret Atwood*, ed. Judith McCombs. New York: G.K. Hall & Co., 1988, 280-91.

——. "The Artist as Picaro: The Revelation of Margaret Atwood's Lady Oracle", *Canadian Literature*, 92, Spring 1982, 23-33.

Friedan, Betty. *The Feminine Mystique,* 1963; rpt. Middlesex: Penguin Books, 1983, 16.

Frye, Northrop. "Conclusion", *Literary History of Canada: Canadian Literature in English*, 2nd ed. Carl F. Klink, et al. Toronto: University of Toronto Press, 1976, 321.

Gilbert, Sandra M. and Susan Gubar. "The Burden of the Future", *No Man's Land, The Place of the Women Writer in the Twentieth Century,* Vol. 3, London, New Haven: Yale University Press, 1994, 342-48.

Givner, Jessie. "Names, Faces and Signatures in Margaret Atwood's Cat's Eye and The Handmaid's Tale", *Canadian Literature,* 133, Summer 1992, 56-75.

Goldblatt, Patricia. "Reconstructing Margaret Atwood's Protagonist", *World Literature Today*, Spring 1999, 275-82.

Hansen, Elaine Tuttle. "Fiction and (Post) Feminism in Atwood's Bodily Harm", *Novel,* 19.1, Fall 1985, 5-21.

Hendenstrom, Joanne. "Puzzled Patriarchs and Free Women: Patterns in the Canadian Novel", *Atlantis*, 4, No. 1, 1970, 2-9.

Hite, Molly. "Other Side, Other Woman: Lady Oracle", *The Other Side of the Story Structure and Strategies of Contemporary Feminist Narrative*. London: Cornell University Press, 1989, 127-67.

——. "Optics and Autobiography in Margaret Atwood's Cat's Eye," *Twentieth Century Literature,* 137, Summer 1993, 12.

Hogan, Patrick C. "Identity and Imperialism in Margaret Atwood's Surfacing", *Commonwealth and American Woman's Discourse, Essay in Criticism,* ed. A.L. McLead. New Delhi: Sterling Publisher, 181-90.

Howells, Coral Ann. "Margaret Atwood: Bodily Harm, The Handmaid's Tale", *Private and Fictional Words: Canadian Women Novelists of the 1970s and 1980s.* London: Methuen Co., 1987, 53-70.

——. “Margaret Atwood Canadian Signature: From Surfacing and Survival to Wilderness Tips”, *British Journal of Canadian Studies*, 9.2, 1994, 205-15.

Huggan, Graham. “Margaret Atwood, Inc. or, Some Thoughts on Literary Celebrity”, *The Post Colonial Exotic Marketing and Margins*. New York: Routledge, 2001, 209-27.

Humm, Maggie. “Myth Criticism: Margaret Atwood’s Surfacing”, *Practising Feminist Criticism an Introduction*. Hertfordshire: Prentice Hall, 1995, 23-33.

Hutcheon, Linda. “Atwood and Laurence. Poet and Novelists”, *Studies in Canadian Literature*, 3, No. 2, Summer 1978, 255-63.

——. *The Canadian Postmodern: A Study of Contemporary English-Canadian Fiction*. Don Mills: Oxford University Press, 1988, 138.

Jaidev. “A Study of Margaret Atwood’s Surfacing”, *Lessons for M.Phil English, Correspondence Courses*. Punjabi University, Patiala, 1990, 66.

——. “Women as Metaphor: A Note on Atwood’s Feminism”, *The Indian Journal of English Studies*, 25, 1995, 111-17.

Jain, Jasbir. “Writing Women”, *Across Cultures*. New Delhi: Rawat Publishers, 2002, 60-67.

James, Jancy. “Canadian Paradigms of Postmodern Feminism”, *Postmodernism and Feminism: Canadian Context*, ed. Shirin Kudchedkar. New Delhi: Pencraft International, 1995, 99-111.

John, Thieme. “A Female Houdini: Popular Culture in Margaret Atwood’s Lady Oracle”, *Kunapipi*, xiv, 1, 1992, 78.

Jones, Dorothy. “Waiting for the Rescue: A Discussion of Margaret Atwood’s Bodily Harm”, *Kunapipi*, 6.3, 1984, 86-100.

Joyce, Nelson. “Speaking the Unspeakable”, *Canadian Forum*, March 1990.

Klarer, Mario. “Orality and Literature as Gender-Supporting Structures in Margaret Atwood’s The Handmaid’s Tale”,

Mosaic Spl. Media Matters: Technologies of Literary Production, 28.4, 1995, 129-42.

Lal, Malashri. "Inheriting Nature: Eco-feminism in Canadian Literature", *Postmodernism and Feminism: Canadian Contexts*, ed. Shirin Kudchedkar. New Delhi: Pencraft International, 1995, 318.

——. "Canadian Gynocritics: Contexts of Meaning in Margaret Atwood's Surfacing", *Perspectives on Women: Canada and India*, ed. Aparna Basu. New Delhi: Allied Publishers, 1995, 186.

Laurence, Margaret. Review of Surfacing, *Quarry*, 22, Spring 1973.

Le Anne, Schreiber. "Motley with Method", *Time*, 108 (11 October 1976), 54.

Litvack, Leon. "Canadian Writing in English and Multiculturalism English Post Coloniality", *Literature from Around the World*, eds. by Radhika Mohrram and Gita Rajan. London: Greenwood Press, 1996, 119-31.

Lyons, Bonnie. "Neither Victims Nor Excutioners in Margaret Atwood's Fiction", *World Literature Written in English*, 17, No. 1, April 1970, 181-87.

MacLulich, T.D. "Atwood's Adult Fairy Tale: Levi Straus Bettelcheim and The Edible Woman", *Essays on Canadian Writing*, 1978, 11-29.

Macridis, Roy C. Contemporary Political Ideologies. *Glen View*. London: Scott, Foreman and Company, 1989, 283.

Malak, Amin. "Margaret Atwood's The Handmaid's Tale and The Dystopian Tradition", *Canadian Literature*, 112, Spring 1987, 13.

Mansbridge, Francis. "Search for Self, In the Novels of Margaret Atwood", *Journal of Canadian Fiction*, 22, 1978, 106-17.

Marta, Cominero-Santangel. "Moving Beyond The Black White Spaces: Atwood's Gilead, Postmodernism, and Strategic Resisance", *Studies in Canadian Literature,* 19.1, 1994, 27.

Millet, Kate. "Prostitution: A Quartet for Female Voices", *Woman in Sexist Society: Studies in Power and*

Powerlessness, eds. Vivian Gornick & Barbara K. Moran. New York & London: Basic Books, 1971, 21-23.

——. "Sexual Politics: A Manifesto for Revolution", *Radical Feminism,* eds. Anne Koedt, et al. New York: The New York Times Book Co., 1973, 365-67.

Mills, Sora, Lynne Pearce, Sue, Sapaull & Elaine Millard. "Gyno Criticism", *Feminist Readings/Feminists Reading*. Harvester Wheatsheaf, 109-20.

Monkman, Leslie. "Canada", *The Commonwealth Novel* Since 1960, ed. Bruce King. Hampshire: The Macmillan Press, 33-37.

Mort, Mary-Ellen. Review of Bodily Harm, *Library Journal,* 107, No. 4, 15 Feburary 1982, 471.

Nichlin, Linda. "Why Are There No Great Women Artists", *Women in Sexist Society*, eds. Vivian Gornic and K. Moron. New York, London: Basic Books, 1971, 344-66.

Ozick, Cynthia. "Women and Creativity: The Demise of the Dancing Dog", *Woman in Sexist Society*, eds. Vivian Gornick and K. Moran. New York, London: Basic Books, 1971, 307-22.

Padmanabhan, Manjula. "Nightmares in the Sun", *Biblio A Review of Books*, Vol. V, No. 7 and 8, 2000. II.

Parker, Emma. "You Are What You Eat: The Politics of Eating in the Novels of Margaret Atwood", *Twentieth Century Literature*, 41.3, Fall 1995, 349-68.

Parsons, Ann. "The Self-Inventing Self: Women Who Lie and Pose in the Fiction of Margaret Atwood", *Gender Studies: New Directions in Feminist Criticism,* ed. Judith Spector. Ohio: Bowling Green State U. Popular P., 1986, 107-08.

Pateman, Carole. *The Sexual Contract*. Stanford: Standford University Press, 1988, 148.

Patton, Marilyn. "Lady Oracle: The Politics of the Body", *Ariel,* 22.4, Oct. 1991, 41-42.

Pinard, Mary. "A Cautionary Tale", *New Directions for Women,* Vol. 15, No. 3, May-June 1986, 15.

Pressman, Barbara M. *Family Violence, Origins and Treatment.* Guelph: Children's and Society of Guelph, 1984.

Punter, Davi. "Violent Geographics", *Postcolonial Imaginings Fictions of a New World Order.* Edinburgh University Press, 2000, 29-32.

Ramamurti, K.S. "The Canadian Women Novelists in a Multicultural Contex", *Commonwealth Literature: Themes and Techniques,* eds. P.K. Rajan, et al. Delhi: Ajanta, 1993, 186.

Ramaswamy, S. "Women's Writing in the 1970s in Canada", *Commentaries on Commonwealth Poetry and Drama.* New Delhi: Prestige Books, 1994, 13-24.

Reddy, K. Venkata. "Novelists of the Interior Landscape: Margaret Atwood and Margaret Laurence", *Critical Studies in Commonwealth Literature.* New Delhi: Prestige Publication, 1994, 25-37.

Robinson, Sally. "'The Anti-Logos Weapon': Multiplicity in Women's Texts", *Contemporary Literature,* 29.1, Spring 1988, 105-24.

Rosengarten, Herbert. "Urbane Comedy", *Canadian Literature.* Spring 1977, 84.

Rosowski, Susan J. "Margaret Atwood's Lady Oracle: Fantasy and the Modern Gothic Novel", *Critical Essays on Margaret Atwood,* ed. Judith McCombs. Boston: G.K. Hall, 1988, 197-208.

Rubenstein, Roberta. "Nature and Nurture in Dystopia: The Handmaid's Tale", *Margaret Atwood: Vision and Forms,* eds. Kathryn Vanspankeren and Jan Garden Castro. Carbondaleand Edwardsville: Southern Illinois University Press, 1988, 101.

Sage, Lora. "Sisterly Sentiments", *The Times Literary Supplement,* No. 5087, Sept. 2000, 24.

Salat, M.F. "Canadian Nationalism and Feminist Ideology: Margaret Atwood", *The Canadian Novel: A Search for Identity.* New Delhi: B.R. Publishing, 50-60.

Schreiber, Le Anne. "Motley with Method", *Time,* 108, 11 October 1976, 54.

Sharpe, Martha. "Margaret Atwood and Julia Krishteva: Space Time, the Dissident Woman Artist, and the Pursuit of Female Solidarity in Cat's Eye", *Essays on Canadian Writing,* 50, Fall 1993, 174-89.

Showalter, Elaine. ed. *The New Feminist Criticism: Essays on Women, Literature and Theory.* New York: Pantheon, 1985, 5.

Sicff, Roberta-Zamaro. "The Re/membering of the Female Power in Lady Oracle", *Canadian Literature*, 112, Spring 1987, 32-38.

Singh, Sunaina. "Margaret Atwood's Surfacing", *Indian Journal of American Studies*, Vol. 13, No. 2, July 1983, 189.

Singh, Sushila. "Joyce Carol Oates and Margaret Atwood: Two Faces of the New World Feminism", in *Punjab University Research Bulletin*, Vol. 18, No. 1, 1987, 82-93.

Snitow, "The Front Line: Notes on Sex in Novels by Women", *Women, Sex and Sexuality*, eds. Catherine R. Stimpson and Ethel Spector Peison. Chicago: University of Chicago, 1980, 174.

Stewart, Grace A. *New Mythos: The Novels of the Artist As Heroine 1877-1977.* Montreal, Canada: Eden Press, Women's Publication, 1981, 156.

Stimpson, Catharine R. "*Feminism and Feminist Criticism: Where the Meaning are.* New York: Routledge, 1988, 166-79.

Suallivan, Rosemary. "Margaret Atwood", *The Oxford Companion to Canadian Literature*, ed. William Toye. Toronto: Oxford University Press, 1983, 31.

Thomas, Audrey. "Topic of Cancer", *Books in Canada.* Oct. 1981, 9-12.

Valerie, Mine. "Atwood in Metamorphosis: An Authentic Fairy Tale" in Myrna Kastash, et al. *Her Own Woman: Profiles of Ten Canadian Women.* Toronto: MacMillan of Canada, 1975, 16.

Vevaina, Coomi S. "I tend to see symbols", *Times of India, Sunday Review Section*, 20, March 1988, 8.

——. "Wastelanders in This New Gilead: An Analysis of Margaret Atwood's The Handmaid's Tale", *Ambivalence Studies in Canadian Literature*, eds. O.M.P. Juneja and Chandra Mohan. New Delhi: Allied Publishers Ltd., 1990, 224.

Vincent, Sybil Korff. "The Mirror and The Cameo: Margaret Atwood's Comic/Gothic Novel, Lady Oracle", in *The Female Gothic,* Juliann E. Fleenor. Montreal: Eden Press, 1983, 153.

Wagner, Linda W. Martin. "Epigraphs to Atwood's The Handmaid's Tale", *Notes on Contemporary Literature*, 17.2, March 1987, 4.

Wainwright, J.A. Rev. "Bodily Harm", *Dalhousie Review*, 61, Autumn 1981, 58.

Walker, Nancy A. *Feminist Alternatives: Irony and Fantasy in the Contemporary Novel by Women.* Jackson: University Press of Mississippi, 1990, 79.

Warren. "The Power and the Promise of Ecological Feminism", *Environmental Ethics*, 235.

Waugh, Patricia. "Margaret Atwood", *Feminine Fictions, Revisiting the Post Modern.* London: Routledge, 1989, 181.

Weaver, Richard M. *A Rhetoric and Handbook.* New York: Holt Rinehert and Winston, 1967, 80.

Weitzman, Lenore J. "Sex Role Socialization", *Women A Feminist Perspective,* ed. J. Freeman. California: Mayfield Publishing Co., 1975, 106-07.

White, Roberta. "Margaret Atwood: Reflections in a Convex Mirror", *Canadian Women: Writing Fiction,* ed. Mickey Pearlman. Jackson: University Press of Mississippi, 1993, 53.

Wilson, Sharon R. "Turning Life into Popular Art: Bodily Harm's Life Tourist", *Studies in Canadian Literature,* 1985, 137.

Wimsatt, Margaret. "Surfacing", *Commonwealth,* 7 Sept. 1973, 483.

Woodcock, George. "Margaret Atwood", *The Literary Half Yearly*, 13.2, July 1972, 237.

——. "Margaret Atwood: Poet as Novelist", *The World of Canadian Writing: Critiques and Reflections,* Vancouver: Douglas and Intyre; Seattle: University of Washington Press, 1980, 153.

Woodcock, George. "Recent Canadian Novels (1) Major Publishers", *Queen's Quarterly*, 89, No. 4, Winter 1982, 748, 34.

Yalom, Marilyn. *Maternity, Mortality and the Literature of Madness*. London: The Pennsylvania State University Press, 1985, 71-78.

ELECTRONIC MEDIA

Online Articles

Agnew, Eadaoin. *Colonialism in Margaret Atwood's Surfacing*, www.qub.ac.uk/en/imperial/canada/surfacing.htm-24k-5oct.

Carley, Dave. *The Edible Atwood, from Page to Stage*. www.cariboo.bc.ca/atwood/edible.htm.

Davidson, Arnold E. Seeing in the Dark: Margaret Atwood's Cat's Eye, *Canadian Fiction Studies 35,* www.utpjournals.com

Deery, June. Science for Feminist: Margaret Atwood's Body of Knowledge, *Twentieth Century Literature,* Winter 1997, www.findarticles.com/P/articles/mi-mo403/is_n4_V43/ai_20614548-30k

Foster, Malcolm and Margaret Atwood. *Margaret Atwood's The Handmaid's Tale*, http://print.google.co.in

Gerson, Carole, Margaret Atwood and Quebec: A Footnote on Surfacing, *Studies in Canadian Literature,* Vol. II, 1976, <file://A:\Studies in Canadian Literature.htm.

Growe, Aaron. *To the Lighthouse and LadyOracle-Gender: Society's Restraint*, 28 June 2004, <file://C:\Documents% 20and%20 settings\internet\Desktop\atwood1.htm.

Justin. *Margaret Atwood, The Treatment of the Female Protagonist in The Handmaid's Tale and Bodily Harm,* www.english.literature.org/essays/margaret atwood.html.

Michael, Magali Cornier. *Feminism and the Postmodern Impulse: Post-world War II Fiction*, http://print.google.co.in

Moore, Lorrie. *Every Wife's Nightmare,* www.nytimes.com/books/98/09/20/specials/moore-atwood.html-19k

Sanchez, Clarissa. *Identity and Margaret Atwood's Lady Oracle* www.findarticles.com/P/articles/mi-mo403/is_n4_V43/ai_20614548-30k

Wilson, Jenna. *Ecofeminism in Margaret Atwood's Surfacing,* athena.english.vt.edu/exlibris/essays99/wilson.htm-22k

Websites

www.amazon.com

www.writers.com

www.feminist.org

www.Lit.Encyc.com

www.geometry.net/index.html

www.wcb.net/owtoad/toc.html

www.randomhouse.com/anchor/

www.webauthors/atwood 1261-av-html

www.randomhouse.com/boldtype/0597/atwood

www.ala.org/bookist/v96/ault/je1/02atwood.html.

www.hallworldliterature.com/world literature/648.shtml

www.wsu.edu:8000/~brains/science_fiction/handmaid.html

www.readinggroupguides.com/guides/edible_woman.asp